Discourse in Psychoanalysis and
Literature

18'

Edited by Shlomith Rimmon-Kenan

Discourse
in
Psychoanalysis
and
Literature

METHUEN   LONDON & NEW YORK

First published in 1987 by
Methuen & Co. Ltd
11 New Fetter Lane, London EC4P 4EE

Published in the USA by
Methuen & Co.
in association with Methuen, Inc.
29 West 35th Street, New York NY 10001

Typeset in Monophoto Garamond by
Vision Typesetting, Manchester
Printed in Great Britain by
Richard Clay Ltd, Bungay, Suffolk

British Library Cataloguing in Publication Data

Discourse in psychoanalysis and literature.
1. Psychoanalysis and literature
I. Rimmon-Kenan, Shlomith
801'.92   PN56.P92

ISBN 0-416-00462-8
ISBN 0-416-00452-0 Pbk

Library of Congress Cataloging in Publication Data

Discourse in psychoanalysis and literature.
Bibliography: p.
Includes index.
1. Psychoanalysis and literature.
2. Discourse analysis.
I. Rimmon-Kenan, Shlomith.
PN56.P92D57   1987   801'.92   86-33286

ISBN 0-4160-0462-8
ISBN 0-4160-0452-0 (pbk.)

Contents

Acknowledgements

This volume presents the fruits of a collective research project carried out by the Centre for Literary Studies of the Hebrew University of Jerusalem during the academic year 1984/5. I wish to acknowledge very gratefully the constant encouragement and help the Centre has received from Dan Patinkin, President of the Hebrew University; Amnon Pazi, rector; Avraham Harman, chancellor; Bernard Cherrick, vice-president; Michael Ottolenghi, vice-president; Charlotte Goldfarb of the Research and Development Authority of the University; and Eliyahu Honig of the Public Relations Department. For facilitating our dialogue with scholars abroad, the Centre is deeply indebted to Ian Seaton of the British Council, Jacques Teynier of the French Embassy, Frans Potuyt of the Dutch Embassy, as well as to the Royal Dutch Academy, and Daniel Krauskopf of the US–Israel Educational Foundation.

Many scholars have contributed to the interest and success of the project, in particular Jacob Arlow, Rami Bar-Giora, Shuli Barzilai, Sanford Budick, Emmanuel Berman, H.M. Daleski, Yaël Feldman, Ruth Ginsburg, André Green, Galit Hasan-Rokem, Alvin Kibel, Itamar Levi, Ruth Nevo, Pinchas Noy, Avigdor Posèq, Freddie Rokem, Moshe Ron, Mordechai Rottenberg, Shimon Sandbank, Ora Segal, Gershon Shaked, Ruth Stein, A.B. Yehoshua and Silvio Yeschua. I am grateful to the Institute for Advanced Studies of the Hebrew University of Jerusalem both for giving me free time for research during the academic year 1985/6 and for providing efficient clerical assistance during my work on this book. Special thanks are due to the Centre's excellent research assistants, Ruth Fine, Doron Narkiss and Eva Vilarrubí, as well as to Dalia Diengott of the Bloomfield Library for the Humanities and Social Sciences, Mount Scopus, Jerusalem, for invaluable help with various technical aspects of the volume.

Finally, I wish to express my deep appreciation to Mr Sam Krupnick of St Louis, Missouri, and Mr Max Zimmer of Los Angeles, California, whose generous gifts to the Centre for Literary Studies greatly facilitated the completion and publication of this book.

The editor and publishers wish to thank the following for permission to reproduce copyright material which appears on the pages below. Although every effort has been made to trace copyright holders, they apologise in advance for any unintentional omission or neglect and will be pleased to insert the appropriate acknowledgement in any subsequent edition of this book:

The editors of *Critical Inquiry* for 'The idea of a psychoanalytic literary criticism' by Peter Brooks on pp. 1–18; The Hogarth Press and W.W. Norton & Co. for the extract from *Totem and Taboo* by Sigmund Freud on pp. 82–3; Martin Secker & Warburg Ltd. and Alfred A. Knopf, Inc. for the extract from *Joseph and his Brothers* on pp. 83–5; Teyler's Museum, Haarlem, The Netherlands, for the Rembrandt etching *Joseph and Potiphar's Wife* on p. 88; Danielle Keunen for the drawings on p. 89; and Suhrkamp Verlag for the extract from *The Seven Deadly Sins of the Petit-Bourgeois* on p. 95.

Notes on the contributors

MIEKE BAL is professor of Comparative Literature and holder of the Susan B. Anthony Chair in Women's Studies at the University of Rochester, USA. Of her six books, published variously in French or Dutch, probably the best known is *Narratologie* (1977). Several of her articles have been published in English in *Poetics Today*. She is currently completing a book on the theory of the subject, focusing on women in the Old Testament.

PETER BROOKS is Tripp Professor of French and Comparative Literature at Yale University. Author of *The Novel of Worldliness* (1969), *The Melodramatic Imagination* (1976) and the recently published *Reading for the Plot* (1984), as well as numerous articles in literary theory and psychoanalytic criticism.

CHRISTINE BROOKE-ROSE is a novelist and professor of Anglo-American Studies at the University of Paris VIII. Her latest novel is *Amalgamemnon*. Among her theoretical works are *A Grammar of Metaphor* (1965) and *A Rhetoric of the Unreal: Studies in Narrative and Structure, Especially of the Fantastic* (1981).

CYNTHIA CHASE is professor of English Literature at Cornell University. She has published many articles on literary theory and psychoanalytic criticism and is currently completing a book *Decomposing Figures: Rhetorical Readings in the Romantic Tradition*.

RIVKA EIFERMANN is president of the Israel Psychoanalytic Society, a practising psychoanalyst and senior lecturer in the Department of Psychology at the Hebrew University of Jerusalem. Her main publications are in the fields of psycholinguistics, thought processes and children's games. In recent years she has taken an interest in the process of psychoanalytic interpretation and the status of self-analysis as a method of investigation.

JULIA KRISTEVA is a psychoanalyst and professor of Linguistics at the University of Paris VII. Among her many books are *Séméiotike: recherches pour une sémanalyse* (1969), *Le Texte du roman* (1970), *La Révolution du langage poétique* (1974), *Pouvoirs de l'horreur: essai sur l'abjection* (1980), and most recently *Histoires d'amour* (1983).

SHLOMITH RIMMON-KENAN is associate professor of English and Comparative Literature at the Hebrew University of Jerusalem. She has published *The Concept of Ambiguity: The Example of James* (1977), *Narrative Fiction: Contemporary Poetics* (1983) and many articles combining theoretical considerations with a study of specific works of literature.

BENNETT SIMON is clinical associate professor in the Department of Psychiatry of Harvard Medical School (Beth Israel Hospital). He is a member of the Boston Psychoanalytic Society and Institute and a training and supervisor analyst there. He has published many articles on various psychoanalytic issues.

DONALD SPENCE is professor of Psychiatry at Rutgers Medical School and a practising psychoanalyst. Author of *Narrative Truth and Historical Truth* (1982) and many articles on various issues in psychoanalysis.

SUSAN RUBIN SULEIMAN is professor of Romance Languages and Literatures at Harvard University. She is author of *Authoritarian Fictions: The Ideological Novel as a Literary Genre* (1983), and co-editor of *The Reader in the Text: Essays on Audience and Interpretation* (1980). She is currently working on a study of French avant-garde writing from the Surrealists to the 'new French feminists'.

ELIZABETH WRIGHT is lecturer and fellow in German, Girton College, Cambridge. She is the author of *E. T. A. Hoffman and the Rhetoric of Terror* (1978) and *Psychoanalytic Criticism* (1984), as well as various articles combining modern literary theory and critical practice.

Introduction

Let's face it, the conjunction between literature and psychoanalysis has become highly popular these days. If in the near past, New Critics, Formalists and Structuralists all tended to avoid psychoanalysis because it seemed to them to lead the study of literature outside the domain of the specifically literary, today there is a renewed interest in psychoanalysis (not least on the part of New Critics, Formalists and Structuralists) in an attempt to go beyond formalism without abandoning the formal aspects of literature. Similarly, there is a renewed interest in literature in various psychoanalytic quarters, inspired at least partly by a perception of the relevance of 'literary' concepts like 'narrativity', 'fictionality' and 'rhetoric' (to mention only a few) to the understanding of the psychoanalytic process. An ever-increasing number of interdisciplinary studies on the part of both psychoanalysts and literary theoreticians have shown the richness of the dialogue and its beneficial potential for both fields. To be sure, the *rapprochement* is still riddled with theoretical and methodological problems (see Bal 1984), but these appear to have become a source of exciting intellectual inquiries rather than a paralysing threat to the legitimacy of the enterprise.

   Given this situation, what seems to be called for today is not a defence of the attempt to mediate between these discourses, but rather an explanation of the need for yet another collection of articles in this already popular (some would say 'overpopular') interdisciplinary junction. This is the challenge I shall try to meet in the following pages, outlining what I see as the contribution of this volume and situating it within ongoing discussions in the field.

The organizing principle of my opening remarks is conveniently provided by the book's title, 'discourse' being the object of study, and 'psychoanalysis' and 'literature' being shorthand terms for the areas with which the study is concerned.

The choice of 'discourse' does not only shift the emphasis away from the personality of the artist, the creative process or the psyche of the fictional characters. It also stresses the rhetorical structures or textual strategies employed, as well as the communication situation and the investment of the structures with desire, power and other aspects of subjectivity. While the emphasis on rhetorical structures and textual strategies distinguishes this volume from traditional encounters between psychoanalysis and literature and aligns it with structuralist and post-structuralist oriented studies, the claim that the structures in question are not merely linguistic, semiotic or narratological – although they *are* all these – goes beyond most contemporary contributions in restoring the human dimension which was missing in many structuralist and post-structuralist studies. However, the human dimension returns not 'in the raw', as in traditional approaches, but through the traces it leaves in the text, as activated by its reading.

The two other terms in the book's title – 'psychoanalysis' and 'literature' – are used as shorthand for four (not two) discourses. Included under 'psychoanalysis' are both the discourse of the participants in the psychoanalytic sessions and the scholarly discourse of psychoanalysts about their discipline. Similarly, 'literature' is meant to encompass both literary discourse and critical (or theoretical) writings about literature. In traditional terms, one might say that 'psychoanalysis' and 'literature' are meant to designate both object-language and metalanguage in each field. However, I shall refrain from using this distinction because it is one of the received notions which are rendered problematic by the discovery that all discourse is inhabited by the unconscious.

If the essays in this volume tend to put object-language and metalanguage in both fields on an equal footing (although they do not, as a rule, discuss this issue explicitly), how do they view the relations between the two fields? This is the question that Felman had already posed in 1977 by unmasking 'the apparently neutral connective word, the misleadingly innocent, colorless, meaningless conjunction: *and*, in the title "Literature and Psychoanalysis"' (Felman 1977, p. 5). Felman, it will be remembered, deplored the use of the 'and' to conceal a master–slave relationship where 'literature is considered as a body of *language* – to be *interpreted*' and psychoanalysis 'as a body of knowledge, whose competence is called upon *to interpret*' (p. 5, original emphases). In the ten years since Felman's call for 'democratic' relations between the two fields, we have witnessed some real dialogues, but also an interesting reversal of the positions of master and slave – so much so that in 1987 Brooks feels the need to declare himself 'happy to be exonerated from the charge of imperialism in the reverse' (in this volume). Where does this book stand in relation to the question of privilege? Collectively (editorially), it calls for an encounter of equals between two bodies of language and two modes of knowledge (Felman 1977, p. 6). Individually, however, the contributors differ in their attitude to hierarchy, the difference between them not corresponding to the division between psychoanalysts and literary theoreticians. While Suleiman, Bal, and Rimmon-Kenan explicitly or implicitly treat the two fields as equals, several participants tend to confer the force of authority on one or the other. To give only a few examples: Brooke-Rose recommends a view of psychoanalysis as literature, whereas Brooks wishes to grant at least a temporary privilege to psychoanalysis in literary study. Similarly, Spence and Chase use literary notions in a discussion of psychic phenomena, whereas Eifermann employs psychoanalytic concepts in the analysis of both self and text.

Nor is this the only area of divergence among the contributors. Indeed, one of the interesting features of the volume seems to me the variety of approaches brought to bear upon the unifying concern with discourse. With an awareness of the reductiveness of all labels, let me risk an identification of the main psychoanalytic approaches as Freudian (Eifermann), 'narrativist' (Spence) and modified Lacanian (Suleiman). Within literary theory, Bal combines narratological methods with feminist concerns, as Suleiman joins together Lacanian psychoanalysis and feminism; Chase's view is basically deconstructionist (or 'rhetorical', in de Man's sense) and Wright's political-'Marxist'. To turn these approaches into the organizing principle of the book would, I felt, be reductive. Consequently, I chose to emphasize the multiplicity of perspectives on the various issues by letting concepts, not schools, govern the sequence. I can only hope that the interplay of approaches around central conceptual categories (e.g. 'narration', 'rhetorical figures') will prove interesting rather than merely confusing.

In order to render concrete the variety of approaches, the central conceptual categories, and the differing emphases upon one or the other of the main facets of discourse (i.e. the structures themselves or their investment with subjectivity), I propose to conclude by offering a brief description of the eleven essays as well as an explanation of the logic underlying their sequence.

The first two essays offer general discussions of the conjunction between literature and psychoanalysis. Criticizing traditional psychoanalytic approaches to literature as well as recent rhetorical and deconstructive approaches, Brooks advocates a focusing on 'the erotics of form', 'the dramas of desire played out in tropes'. He develops this idea by offering a phantasy model of the literary text, within which the concept of 'transference' is used to describe both the dynamics of plot and the interaction between narrator and narratee. Whereas Brooks suggests what should be *done*, Brooke-Rose concentrates mainly on what should be avoided. She warns against dogmatic tendencies in the discourses of religion, philosophy, literary criticism and psychoanalysis – a dogmatism which takes the form of copula sentences where pseudo-equations pretend to the status of truth – and analyses such a tendency in the psychoanalytically inspired criticism of Harold Bloom.

The three papers that follow develop the idea of the subjective inscribed in the textual, each dealing with a different aspect of the interaction in discourse between subject-matter and human subject. Through a retrospective examination of a paper she wrote on denial in Grimm's *Little Red Riding Hood*, her preliminary notes and comments when working on that paper, and her own related self-analysis, Eifermann shows both how unconscious personal concerns can influence textual analysis and how textual analysis is capable of rendering aspects of the inner life accessible from new angles and amenable to a new working through.

The centrality of the subjective for the interpretation of texts is argued for by Bal in relation to myth. In opposition to the traditional and structuralist conception of myth as objective, transhistorical, universal content, Bal advocates a view of it as a screen onto which different readers and different historical periods project transference-like interpretations. Laplanche and Pontalis, Freud, Mann, Genesis 39 and a Rembrandt etching are discussed as illustrations of this contention.

The place of the subject and the role of transference in discourse are treated by Wright within a political context. She examines the phenomenon of 'transference to the instituted authority' in the training of analysts, in literature, and in the theatre, arguing that Brecht's plays endeavour precisely to break this kind of trans-ference without knowingly availing themselves of psychoanalytic theory.

The next block of essays narrows the focus down to the phenomenon of narration (and its more formal version-writing). Kristeva explores the basic problem of mediating between the pre-language and pre-sign status of moods (such as melancholy) and their expression in words. She also argues – giving examples from Nerval and Dostoevsky – that writing may be a way of overcom-ing both the melancholy and the congenital deficiency (rather than aggression against a lost object) which underlies it.

Suleiman discusses the involvement of three male narrators with the mad women whose stories they narrate, suggesting that a full involvement is characteristic of 'feminine writing' and may contribute to psychoanalysis by substituting the discourse of mutual entanglement (as in Duras' *Lol V. Stein*) for the discourse of mastery (such as Freud attempted in reporting the Dora case).

The relations between the act of narration and the story narrated are also the subject of Simon's examination of the way in which plays that involve the killing of children also betray an anxiety about the prospects of story-telling, the narration of infanticide thus becoming the suicide of narration.

Analogies between narration and story are taken by Rimmon-Kenan as a sign of the entanglement – through a compulsion-like repetition – of the narrator with the story he would rather not tell. Whereas Kristeva emphasizes the triumphant potential of writing, Rimmon-Kenan shows that sometimes, as in Grass's *Cat and Mouse*, it can remain entrapped within the events it both tells and conceals.

The two last papers have a double effect: on the one hand they narrow the discussion even further to the issue of rhetorical figures, but on the other hand they pose again the whole question of the rhetorical status of psychoanalysis, thereby joining the level of generality of the first two papers. Thus Spence borrows the narratological (and before that, mathematical) concept of recur-sion to analyse the relations between the latent and the manifest dream, the transformation of an unconscious phantasy or early memory into a variety of behaviour patterns, the phenomenon of transference and the process of self-analysis. Then, in a gesture of broadening, he considers the shift from 'the Freudian metaphor' to a 'post-Freudian metaphor' and its implications for psychoanalysis as well as for man's understanding of his place in the world. Similarly, Chase considers transference as a trope, showing its proximity to rhetorical figures with discrepant intentional structures, such as metaphor, metonymy and anthropomorphism, and through this analysis she poses afresh the whole question of the relations between psychoanalytic and rhetorical theory.

It is hard to say enough about the various contributions without saying too much, and I feel the time has come to stop summarizing and let the essays speak for themselves.

Just one technical remark: most of the contributors quote Freud from *The Standard Edition*, but some use other sources. Knowing that scholars sometimes disagree about the quality of Strachey's translation, I have decided to treat quotations from other editions as possible signs of disagreement, and for this reason uniformity has been sacrificed.

Shlomith Rimmon-Kenan

References

Bal, Mieke (1984) 'Introduction', *Poetics: Psychopoetics*, 13, 279–98.

Felman, Shoshana (1977) 'To open the question', *Yale French Studies: Literature and Psychoanalysis. The Question of Reading: Otherwise*, 55/6, 5–10.

I

The idea of a psychoanalytic literary criticism*

PETER BROOKS

Psychoanalytic literary criticism has always been something of an embarrassment. One resists labelling as a 'psychoanalytic critic' because the kind of criticism evoked by the term mostly deserves the bad name it has largely made for itself. Thus I have been worrying about the status of some of my own uses of psychoanalysis in the study of narrative, in my attempt to find dynamic models that might move us beyond the static formalism of structuralist and semiotic narratology. In general, I think we need to worry about the legitimacy and force that psychoanalysis may claim when imported into the study of literary texts. If versions of psychoanalytic criticism have been with us at least since 1908, when Freud published his essay on 'Creative writers and daydreaming' (1953a), and if the enterprise has recently been renewed in subtle ways by post-structuralist versions of reading, a malaise persists, a sense that whatever the promises of their union, literature and psychoanalysis remain mismatched bedfellows – or should I say playmates.

The first problem, and the most basic, may be that psychoanalysis in literary study has over and over again mistaken the *object* of analysis, with the result that whatever insights it has produced tell us precious little about the structure and rhetoric of literary texts.

*The editor and publishers wish to thank the editors of *Critical Inquiry* for permission to reproduce this essay which originally appeared in vol. 13, No. 2 (1986), pp. 334–48.

Traditional psychoanalytic criticism tends to fall into three general categories, depending on the object of analysis: the author, the reader or the fictive persons of the text. The first of these constituted the classical locus of psychoanalytic interest. It is now apparently the most discredited, though also perhaps the most difficult to extirpate, since if the disappearance of the author has been repeatedly announced, authorial mutants ceaselessly reappear, as for instance in Harold Bloom's psychomachia of literary history. Like the author, the fictive character has been deconstructed into an effect of textual codes, a kind of thematic mirage, and the psychoanalytic study of the putative unconscious of characters in fiction has also fallen into disrepute. Here again, however, the impulse resurfaces, for instance in some of the moves of a feminist criticism that needs to show how the represented female psyche (particularly, of course, as created by women authors) refuses and problematizes the dominant concepts of male psychological doctrine. Feminist criticism has in fact largely contributed to a new variant of the psychoanalytic study of fictive characters, a variant one might label the 'situational-thematic' – studies of Oedipal triangles in fiction, their permutations and evolution, of the roles of mothers and daughters, of situations of nurture and bonding, and so forth. It is work often full of interest, but none the less methodologically disquieting in its use of Freudian analytic tools in a wholly thematic way, as if the identification and labelling of human relations in a psychoanalytic vocabulary were the task of criticism. The third traditional field of psychoanalytic literary study, the reader, continues to flourish in ever-renewed versions, since the role of the reader in the creation of textual meaning is very much on our minds at present, and since the psychoanalytic study of readers' responses willingly brackets the impossible notion of author in favour of the acceptable and also verifiable notion of reader. The psychoanalytic study of the reader may concern real readers (as in Holland 1975) or the reader as psychological everyman (as in Lesser 1957). But like the other traditional psychoanalytic approaches, it displaces the object of analysis from the text to some person, some other psychodynamic structure, a displacement I wish to avoid since – as I hope to make clear as I go along – I think psychoanalytical criticism can and should be textual and rhetorical.

If the displacement of the object of analysis has been a major failing of psychoanalytic literary criticism, it has erred also in its inability to rid itself of the underlying conviction that it is inherently explanatory. The problem with 'literature and psychoanalysis', as Shoshana Felman has pointed out more effectively than any other critic, lies in that 'and' (Felman 1977, pp. 5–10). The conjunction has almost always masked a relation of privilege of one term to another, a use of psychoanalysis as a conceptual system in terms of which to analyse and explain literature, rather than an encounter and confrontation of the two. The reference to psychoanalysis has traditionally been used to close rather than open the argument, and the text. This is not surprising, since the recourse to psychoanalysis usually claims as its very *raison d'être* the capacity to explain and justify in the terms of a system and a discourse more penetrating and productive of insight than literary-critical psychology as routinely practised, which of course harbours its own, largely unanalysed, assumptions. As Simon O. Lesser states the case, 'no "common-sense" psychology yet employed in criticism has been helpful' (Lesser 1957, p. 297), whereas psychoanalysis provides a way to explore 'the deepest levels of meaning of the greatest fiction' (p. 15).

Why should we reject such a claim? Even if psychoanalysis is far from being a 'science' with the formal power of linguistics, for instance, surely certain of its hypotheses are so well established and so universally illustrated that we can use them with as much impunity as such linguistic concepts as 'shifters' or 'the double articulation'. Yet the recourse to linguistic and to psychoanalytic concepts implies a false symmetry: linguistics may be universalistic, but its tools and concepts are 'cool' and their overextension easily recognized as trivial, whereas psychoanalysis is imperialistic, almost of necessity. Freud works from the premise that all that appears is a sign, that all signs are subject to interpretation and that they speak of messages that ultimately tell stories that contain the same *dramatis personae* and the same narrative functions for all of us. It is no wonder that Freud called himself a 'conquistador': he extends remarkably the empire of signs and their significant decipherment, encompassing all of human behaviour and symbolic action. Thus any 'psychoanalytic explanation' in another discipline always runs the risk of appearing to claim the last word, the final hermeneutic power. If there is one thing that post-structuralist criticism has most usefully taught us, it is the suspicion and refusal of this last word in the interpretive process and history, the refusal of any privileged position in analysis.

But if we refuse to grant psychoanalysis any position of privilege in criticism, if we refuse to consider it to be explanatory, what do we have left? What is the status of a de-authorized psychoanalytic discourse within literary-critical discourse, and what is its object? If we don't accord explanatory force to psychoanalysis, what is the point of using it at all? Why do we continue to read so many critical essays laced with the conceptual vocabulary of psychoanalysis? What is *at stake* in the current uses of psychoanalysis?

I want to begin this inquiry with the flat-footed (and un-fashionable) assertion that I believe that the persistence, against all the odds, of psychoanalytic perspectives in literary study must ultimately derive from our conviction that the materials on which they exercise their powers of analysis are in some basic sense the same: that the structure of literature *is* in some sense the structure of mind – not a specific mind, but what the translators of *The Standard Edition* call 'the mental apparatus', which is more accurately the dynamic organization of the psyche, a process of structuration. We continue to dream of a convergence of psycho-analysis and literary criticism because we sense that there ought to be, that there must be, some correspondence between literary and psychic process, that aesthetic structure and form, including literary tropes, must somehow coincide with the psychic structures and operations they both evoke and appeal to. Yet here we encounter the truth of the comment made by Jack Spector that, 'Neither Freud nor his followers . . . have ever shown concretely how specific formal techniques correspond to the processes of the unconscious' (Spector 1973, p. 118).

Part of the attraction of psychoanalytic criticism has always been its promise of a movement *beyond* formalism, to that desired place where literature and life converge and where literary criticism becomes the discourse of something anthropologically important. I very much subscribe to this urge, but I think that it is fair to say that in the case of psychoanalysis, paradoxically we can go beyond formalism only by becoming more formalistic. Geoffrey Hartman wrote a number of years ago – in *Beyond Formalism* in fact – that the trouble with Anglo-American formalism was that it wasn't formalist enough (Hartman 1970, p. 42). One can in general indict Anglo-American 'New Criticism' for being too quick to leap from the level of formal explication to that of moral and psychological interpretation, neglecting the trajectory through linguistics and poetics that needs to stand between. This has certainly been true in traditional psychoanalytic criticism, which has regularly short-circuited the difficult and necessary issues in poetics. The more recent – rhetorical and deconstructive – kind understands the formalist imperative, but I fear that it may too often remain content with formal operations, simply bracketing the human realm from which psychoanalysis derives. Given its project and its strategies, such rhetorical/deconstructive criticism usually stays within the linguistic realm. It is not willing to make the crossover between rhetoric and reference and that interests me – and ought to be the *raison d'être* for the recourse to psychoanalysis in the first place.

One way to try to move out from the impasse I discern – or have perhaps myself constructed – might be through a return to what Freud has to say about literary form, most notoriously in the brief 1908 essay, 'Creative writers and daydreaming' (1953a). We would probably all agree that Freud speaks most pertinently to literary critics when he is not explicitly addressing art: the most impressive essays in psychoanalytical criticism have drawn more on *The Interpretation of Dreams*, the metapsychological essays and *Beyond the Pleasure Principle*, for example, than on *Delusion and Dream*, *The Moses of Michelangelo* or the essays on Leonardo and Dostoevsky. 'Creative writers and daydreaming' in fact gives an excessively simplistic view of art, of the kind that allows Ernst Kris to describe artistic activity as regression in the service of the ego (Kris 1952). Yet the essay may be suggestive in other ways.

Freud sets out to look for some common human activity that is 'akin to creative writing', and finds it in daydreaming or the creation of phantasies. Freud then stresses the active, temporal structure of phantasy, which:

> hovers, as it were, between three times – the three moments of time which our ideation involves. Mental work is linked to some current impression, some provoking occasion in the present which has been able to arouse one of the subject's major wishes. From there it harks back to the memory of an earlier experience (usually an infantile one) in which this wish was fulfilled; and it now creates a situation relating to the future which represents a fulfilment of the wish. What it thus creates is a day-dream or phantasy, which carries about it traces of its origin from the occasion which provoked it and from the memory. Thus past, present and future are strung together, as it were, on the thread of the wish that runs through them.
>
> (Freud 1953a, pp. 147–8)

Freud will promptly commit the error of making the past evoked in the construction of phantasy that of the author, in order to study 'the connections that exist between the life of the writer and his works' (p. 151) – an error in which most critics have followed his lead. For instance, it is this phantasy model, reworked in terms of Winnicott and object-relations psychoanalysis, that essentially shapes the thesis of one of the most interesting recent studies in literature and psychoanalysis, L. Meredith Skura's *The Literary Use of the Psychoanalytic Process* (1981); Skura, too, ultimately makes the past referred to in phantasy a personal past, that of author or reader, or both. Yet the phantasy model could instead be suggestive for talking about the relations of textual past, present and projected future, in the plot of a novel, for example, or in the rhyme scheme of a sonnet, or simply in the play of verb tenses in any text. I would want to extrapolate from this passage an understanding of how phantasy provides a dynamic model of intratextual temporal relations, and their organization according to the plot of wish, or desire. We might thus gain a certain understanding of the interplay of *form* and *desire*.

Freud is again of great interest in the final paragraph of the essay – one could make a fruitful study of Freud's final paragraphs, which so often produce a flood of new insights that can't quite be dealt with – where he asks how the writer creates pleasure through the communication of his phantasies, whereas those of most people would repel or bore us. Herein lies the poet's 'innermost secret', his 'essential *ars poetica*' (Freud 1953a, p. 153). Freud sees two components of the artistic achievement here:

> The writer softens the character of his egoistic day-dreams by altering and disguising it, and he bribes us by the purely formal – that is, aesthetic – yield of pleasure which he offers us in the presentation of his phantasies. We give the name of an *incentive bonus*, or a *fore-pleasure*, to a yield of pleasure such as this, which is offered to us so as to make possible the release of still greater pleasure arising from deeper psychical sources. In my opinion all the aesthetic pleasure which a creative writer affords us has the character of a fore-pleasure of this kind
>
> (Freud 1953a, p. 153)

I am deliberately leaving aside the end of this paragraph, where Freud suggests that the writer in this manner enables us 'thenceforward to enjoy our own daydreams without self-reproach or shame', since this hypothesis brings us back to the *person* of the reader, whereas I wish to remain on the plane of form associated with 'forepleasure'.

The equation of the effects of literary form with forepleasure in this well known passage is perhaps less trivial than it at first appears. If *Lust* and *Unlust* don't take us very far in the analysis of literary texture, *Vorlust* – forepleasure – tropes on pleasure and thus seems more promising. Forepleasure is indeed a curious concept, suggesting a whole rhetoric of advance towards and retreat from the goal or the end, a formal zone of play (I take it that forepleasure somehow implicates foreplay) that is both harnessed to the end and yet autonomous and capable of deviations and recursive movements. When we begin to unpack the components of forepleasure we may find a whole erotics of form, which is perhaps what we most need if we are to make formalism serve an understanding of the human functions of literature. Forepleasure would include the notion of both delay and advance in the textual dynamic, the creation of that 'dilatory space' which Roland Barthes, in *S/Z*, claimed to be the essence of the textual middle, through which we seek to advance toward the discharge of the end, yet all the while perversely delaying, returning backwards in order to put off the promised end, and perhaps to assure its greater significance (Barthes 1970, p. 82).

Forepleasure implies the possibility of fetishism, the interesting threat of being waylaid by some element along the way to the 'proper' end, taking some displaced substitute or simulacrum for the thing itself, a mystification in which most literature deals, sometimes eventually to expose the displacement or substitution as a form of false consciousness, sometimes to expose the end itself as the false lure. It includes as well the possibilities of exhibitionism and voyeurism, which surely are central to literary texts and their reading. In the notion of forepleasure there lurks in fact all manner of perversity and ultimately the possibility of the polymorphous perverse, the possibility of a text that would delay, displace and deviate terminal discharge to an extent that it became non-existent – as, perhaps, in the textual practice of the 'writable text' (*texte scriptible*) prized by Barthes (1970), in Beckett, for instance, or Phillippe Sollers. But we find as good an illustration of effective perversity in the text of Henry James and in the principle (well known to the New Critics) that the best poems accommodate a maximum of ironic texture within their frail structures, a postponement and ambiguation of overt statement. In fact, the work of textuality may ensure that all literature is, by its very nature, essentially perverse.

What is most important to me is the sense that the notion of forepleasure as it is advanced by Freud implies the possibility of a formalist aesthetic – one that can be extended to the properly rhetorical field – that speaks to the erotic, which is to say the dynamic, dimensions of form: form as something that is not inert but part of a process that unfolds and develops as texts are activated through the reading process. A neo-formalist psycho-analytic criticism could do worse than attach itself to studying the various forms of the 'fore' in forepleasure, developing a tropology of the perversities through which we turn back, turn around, the simple consumption of texts, making their reading a worthy object of analysis. Such a study would be, as Freud suggests, about 'bribing', or perhaps about *teasing* in all its forms, from puns to metaphors, perhaps ultimately – given the basic temporal structure of phantasy and of the literary text – what we might call 'clock-teasing', which is perhaps the way we create the illusion of creating a space of meaning within the process of ongoing temporality.

A more formalist psychoanalytic criticism, then, would be attuned to form as our situation, our siting, within the symbolic order, the order within which we constitute meaning and ourselves as endowed with meaning. This kind of psychoanalytic criticism would, of course, pay the greatest attention to the rhetorical aspect of psychic operations as presented by psychoan-alysis and would call upon the rhetorical and semiotic reinterpre-tation of Freud advanced by Emile Benveniste, Jacques Lacan and others. Yet it might be objected that this more obviously rhetorical version does not automatically solve the problem of how to use the crossover between psychic operations and tropes. The status of the 'and' linking psychoanalysis and literary text may still remain at issue: what does one want to *claim* in showing that the structure of a metaphor in Victor Hugo is equivalent to the structure of a symptom? What is alleged to be the place and the force of the occulted name of the father that may be written in metaphor as symptom, symptom as metaphor?[1] Is there, more subtly now, a claim of explanation advanced in the crossover? Or is an ingenious piece of intertextuality all that takes place?

I think it is something that lies between these two alternatives.

My views on this question have been clarified by an acute and challenging review by Terence Cave of my book *Reading for the Plot* (Cave 1985). Cave asks what he calls 'the embarrassing question . . . what is the Freudian model worth?' (p. 14). In his discussion of a possible answer to this question, Cave notes that:

> Brooks's argument for a Freudian poetics doesn't appear to depend on an imperialist move which would simply annex a would-be science of the psyche and release it from its claim to tell the truth. He talks repeatedly as if the value of the Freudian model is precisely that it does, in some sense, give access to the way human desires really operate.
>
> (p. 14)

I think this is accurate, and I am happy to be exonerated from the charge of imperialism in the reverse – the imperialism that would come from the incursion of literary criticism into psychoanalysis in search of mere metaphors, which has sometimes been the case with post structuralist annexations of psychoanalytic concepts. I certainly do want to grant at least a temporary privilege to psychoanalysis in literary study, in that the trajectory through psychoanalysis forces us to confront the human stakes of literary form, while I think that these stakes need to be considered *in* the text, as activated in its reading. As I suggested earlier, I believe that we constitute ourselves as human subjects in part through our fictions and therefore that the study of human fiction-making and psychic process are convergent activities and superimposable forms of analysis. To say precisely in what sense psychoanalysis can lead us to models for literary study that generate new insight, we might best look towards a concept that lies at the very heart of Freudian analytic practice, the concept of the transference, as it is constituted between analysand and analyst. Here we may find the most useful elaboration of the phantasy model of the text. Let me, then, briefly explore the transference in order to indicate one possible way of conceiving the relations of psychoanalysis to literary discourse.

The transference, as I understand it, is a realm of the *as-if*, where affects from the past become invested in the present, notably in the dynamics of the analysand–analyst relation, and the neurosis under treatment becomes a transference-neurosis, a present representation of the past. As Freud puts it in the *Dora* case history, the transference gives us 'new impressions or reprints', and 'revised editions', of old texts (1953 [1905], p. 116). One can call the transference textual because it is a semiotic and fictional medium where the compulsions of unconscious desire, and its scenarios of infantile fulfilment, become symbolically present in the communicative situation of analysis. Within the transference, recall of the past most often takes place as its unconscious repetition, acting it out as if it were present: repetition is a way of remembering, brought into play when recollection in the intellectual sense is blocked by repression and resistance. Repetition is both an obstacle to analysis – since the analysand must eventually be led to renunciation of the attempt to reproduce the past – and the principal dynamic of the cure, since only by way of its symbolic enactment in the present can the history of past desire, its objects and scenarios of fulfilment, be made known, become manifest in the present discourse. The analyst (I paraphrase Freud here) must treat the analysand's words and symbolic acts as an actual force, active in the present, while attempting to translate them back into the terms of the past (1958a [1912], 1958b [1914]). That is, the analyst must work with the analysand to fit his emotional impulses into their proper place in his life history, to restore the links between ideas and events that have fallen away, to reconnect isolated memories and to draw conclusions from interconnections and patterns. The analyst must help the analysand construct a narrative discourse whose syntax and rhetoric are more plausible, more convincing, more adequate to give an account of the story of the past than those that are originally presented, in symptomatic form, by the analysand.

Freud writes in one of his key essays on the transference, 'Remembering, repeating and working-through':

> The transference thus creates an intermediate region [*Zwischen-reich*] between illness and real life through which the transition from the one to the other is made. The new condition has taken over all the features of the illness; but it represents an artificial illness which is at every point accessible to our intervention. It is at the same time a piece of real experience, but one which has been made possible by especially favourable conditions, and it is of a provisional nature.
>
> (Freud 1958b, p. 154)

Freud's description of this intermediate region – this *Zwischenreich* – that is both artificial and a piece of real experience, makes it sound very much like the literary text. He who intervenes in it is the analyst or reader, first of all in the sense that the simple presence of this other brings to the analysand's discourse what Jacques Lacan calls 'the dimension of dialogue' (Lacan 1966b, p. 216).[2] Texts are always implicitly or even explicitly addressed to someone. The 'I' that speaks in a lyric ever postulates a 'thou'. Indeed, as Emile Benveniste has shown, 'I' and 'thou' are linguistically interdependent, both signifiers without signifieds, and with referents that constantly change as each speaker in turn assumes the 'I' in relation to the interlocutor, who from 'I' becomes 'thou' (Benveniste 1966, pp. 258–66). This situation is frequently dramatized in narrative texts, in what we call 'framed tales', which stage the presence of a listener or narratee, whose reactions to what is told are often what is most important in the narrative – as in the case of Balzac's *Sarrasine* (1977 [1831]), which has become a classic point of reference since Roland Barthes in *S/Z* (1970) made it a model for the workings of the 'narrative contract' (pp. 95–6), or as in Mary Shelley's *Frankenstein* (1974 [1818]), where each narratee of the imbedded narratives is supposed to act upon what he has been told. In other cases, the simple presence of the narratee, even when silent, 'dialogizes' the speech of the narrator, as Mikhail Bakhtin has so thoroughly demonstrated in the case of the Dostoevskian monologue (Bakhtin 1973). A good example of dialogized monologue is Albert Camus' *La Chute* (1956), where Jean-Baptiste Clamence's abject confession includes within it the unnamed and silent narratee's responses, eventually with the result of implicating the narratee within a discourse he would no doubt rather not listen to. Even in texts which have no explicit narrator or narratee, where the narrative is apparently 'impersonal', there is necessarily a discourse which solicits a response, be it only by the play of personal pronouns and the conjugation of verbs.

The narratee, the addressee, the 'you' of these texts is always in some measure a surrogate for the reader, who must define his own interpretation and responses in response to the implied judgement, and the discursive implication, of the explicit or implicit textual 'you'. Contemporary 'reader response' criticism has often made excessive claims for the role of the reader – to the point of abolishing the semiotic constraint that the text exercises upon reading – but it has usefully shown us that the reader necessarily collaborates and competes in the creation of textual meaning. To return to Freud's term, we 'intervene' in a text by our very act of reading, in our (counter-)transferential desire to master the text, as also in the desire to be mastered by it. When we are what we call literary critics, our interventions – our efforts to rewrite and retransmit it – may closely resemble the psychoanalyst's, with all the attendant perils of transference and counter-transference.

However self-absorbed and self-referential they may appear, lyric and narrative discourses are always proffered for a purpose, to create an effect: to establish a claim on the listener's attention, an appeal to complicity, perhaps to judgement, and inevitably to interpretation and retransmission. In the transferential situation of reading, as in the psychoanalytic transference, the reader must grasp not only what is said but always what the discourse intends, its implications, how it would work on him. He must, in Lacanian terms, refuse the text's demand in order to listen to its desire. In narrative, for instance, the reader must not only reconstruct and understand story events but also the relation of this story to the narrative discourse that conveys it in a certain manner, that is itself an interpretation which demands further interpretation. As Freud writes in 'Remembering, repeating and working-through', it occurs that the analysand 'does not listen to the precise wording of his obsessional ideas' (Freud 1958b, p. 152). Narrators may be similar to the analysand in this respect, most obviously in modernist and post-modernist narratives (those of Conrad, Gide, Faulkner, Nathalie Sarraute, for instance) but also in many more traditional novels, especially in the eighteenth century (in the work of Diderot and Sterne, for instance) and even at the very origins of the genre, in the *Lazarillo de Tormes*, a novel which both reveals and conceals its story. A certain suspicion inhabits the relation of narrative discourse to its story, and our role as readers calls for a suspicious hearing, a rewriting of the narrative text in a sort of agonistic dialogue with the words we are given to work with. Freud repeatedly describes the relation of analyst and analysand in the transference as one of struggle, struggle for the mastery of resistances and the lifting of repressions, which continually evokes a realm of the daemonic. With reader and text, the struggle must eventually put into question any assumed position of mastery or privilege, which is why we must reread, speak again, retransmit.

The advantage of such a transferential model, it seems to me, is that it illuminates the difficult and productive encounter of the speaker and the listener, the text and the reader, and how their exchange takes place in an 'artificial' space – a symbolic and semiotic medium – that is none the less the place of real

take the form of a simple assent: a Yes from the analysand has little
value, says Freud, 'unless it is followed by indirect confirmations,
unless the patient . . . produces new memories which complete and
extend the construction' (p. 262). As in reading, hypotheses of
construal prove to be strong and valuable when they produce more
text, when they create in the text previously unperceived networks
of relation and significance, finding confirmation in the extension
of the narrative and semantic web. The analytic work, the process
of finding and making meaning, is necessarily a factor of listening
and reading as well as telling. Freud, indeed, goes on to concede
that there are moments when the analyst's construction does not
lead to the analysand's recollection of repressed elements of his
story, but none the less produces in him 'an assured conviction of
the truth of the construction which achieves the same therapeutic
result as a recaptured memory' (p. 256). Parts of the story thus
seem to belong to the interpreter rather than to the person whose
story it is, or was.

'Constructions in analysis' as a whole gives a view of psychoanalytic interpretation and construction that notably resembles
the active role of the reader in making sense of a text, finding
hypotheses of interpretation that open up ever wider and more
forceful semantic patterns, ever attempting to reach the totality of
the supreme because necessary fiction. The reader may not have
written the text, yet it does change and evolve as he works on it — as
he rewrites it, as those readers we call literary critics necessarily do.
And as the reader works on the text, it does 'rephrase' his
perceptions. I think any of us could find confirmation of such a
truly transferential and dialogic relation of text and analysis in our
own experience. And there are of course literary texts that inscribe
and dramatize acts of reading, interpretation and construction: for
instance, Balzac's *Le Lys dans la vallée* (1978 [1836]), where Nathalie
de Manerville reads Félix de Vandenesse's long confession, and
tells him that he has misinterpreted his own desires. Benjamin
Constant's *Adolphe* (1957 [1816]) stages a similar case of retrospective reading that provokes an entire reconstruction of the
story. The epistolary novel of course stages nothing else: Laclos'
Les Liaisons dangereuses (1964 [1782]) is all about different models
and levels of construction in the reading of messages, and the
writing of messages with a view towards their interpretation. The
novels of Conrad and Faulkner are similar to Laclos' masterpiece
in that they offer multiple constructions of events that never are

verifiable, that can be tested only by the force of conviction they produce for listeners and readers.

Interpretation and construction are themselves most often dramas of desire and power, both within literature and in the reading of literary texts. Hence I would claim that the model of the transference is a far more literal model of reading than Cave would allow. I find it significant that towards the end of 'Constructions in analysis' Freud turns to a discussion of delusions, similar to hallucinations, produced in the analysand by the analyst's constructions: delusions that evoke a 'fragment of historical truth' that is out of place in the story. Freud writes at this point, in an astonishing sentence, 'The delusions of patients appear to me to be the equivalents of the constructions which we build up in the course of an analytic treatment – attempts at explanation and cure' (Freud 1964, p. 268). That is, not only does the patient, in any successful analysis, become his own analyst, the analyst also becomes the patient, espouses his delusional system and works towards the construction of fictions that can never be verified other than by the force of the conviction that they convey. And this seems to me a fair representation of good criticism, which involves a willingness, a desire, to enter into the delusional systems of texts, to espouse their hallucinated vision, in an attempt to master and be mastered by their power of conviction.

One final point needs to be made, again in reference to Cave, a resourceful critic whom one can never finally lay to rest. It can be argued – and I have myself argued – that much of Freud's understanding of interpretation and the construction of meaning is grounded in literature, in those 'poets and philosophers' he was the first to acknowledge as his precursors. 'In which case', writes Cave, psychoanalysis 'can't itself provide a grounding, since it is part of the system it attempts to master'. Cave continues, 'Its advantage (though a precious one) would only be that, in its doubling of narrative and analysis, story and plot, it provides a poetics appropriate to the history of modern fiction' (Cave 1985, p. 14). Cave here reverses the more traditional charge that psychoanalysis imperialistically claims to explain literature, to make the more subtle (and contemporary) charge that psychoanalysis may be nothing *but* literature, and the relations of the two nothing more than a play of intertextuality, or even a tautology.

I am unwilling to concede so much. One can resist the notion that psychoanalysis 'explains' literature and yet insist that the kind of intertextual relation it holds to literature is quite different from the intertextuality that obtains between two poems or novels, and that it illuminates in quite other ways. For the psychoanalytic intertext obliges the critic to make a transit through a systematic discourse elaborated to describe the dynamics of psychic process. The similarities and differences, in object and in intention, of this discourse from literary analysis creates a tension which is product- ive of perspective, of stereoptical effect. Psychoanalysis is not an arbitrarily chosen intertext for literary analysis but rather a particularly insistent and demanding intertext, in that mapping across the boundaries from one territory to the other both confirms and complicates our understanding of how mind re- formulates the real, how it constructs the necessary fictions by which we dream, desire, interpret, indeed by which we constitute ourselves as human subjects. The detour through psychoanalysis forces the critic to respond to the erotics of form, that is to an engagement with the psychic investments of rhetoric, the dramas of desire played out in tropes. Psychoanalysis matters to us as literary critics because it stands as a constant reminder that the attention to form, properly conceived, is not a sterile formalism but rather one more attempt to draw the symbolic and fictional map of our place in existence.

Notes

1 I allude here to an example used by Lacan (1966a, pp. 506ff).
2 I note that Schwartz (1978, pp. 1–17) argues, briefly but evocatively, the relevance of the transference to literary interpretation.
3 On this point, I am indebted to an exposition of the transference according to Lacan presented by Jacques-Alain Miller at the Con- ference, 'Lacan's legacy', held at the University of Massachusetts, Amherst, 14–16 June 1985.

References

Balzac, Honoré de (1977) [1831] *Sarrasine*, in *La Comédie humaine*, Paris, Pléiade, vol. 6, pp. 1043–76.
—(1978) [1836] *Le Lys dans la vallée*, in *La Comédie humaine*, Paris, Pléiade, vol. 9, pp. 969–1229.
Bakhtin, Mikhail (1973) *Problems of Dostoevsky's Poetics*, Ann Arbor, Mich., Ardis.
Barthes, Roland (1970) *S/Z*, Paris, Seuil.

Benveniste, Emile (1966) 'De la subjectivité dans le langage', in *Problèmes de linguistique générale*, Paris, Gallimard, pp. 258–66.

Camus, Albert (1956) *La Chute*, Paris, Gallimard.

Constant, Benjamin (1957) [1816] *Adolphe (suivi de Cécile)*, Paris, Livre de Poche.

Cave, Terence (1985) 'The prime and precious thing', *Times Literary Supplement*, London, January 4, 14.

Felman, Shoshana (1977) 'To open the question', *Yale French Studies: Literature and Psychoanalysis. The Question of Reading: Otherwise*, 55/6, 5–10.

Freud, Sigmund (1953a) [1908] 'Creative writers and daydreaming', in *The Standard Edition of the Complete Psychological Works*, London, Hogarth Press, vol. 9, pp. 141–54.

—(1953b) [1905] 'Fragment of an analysis of a case of hysteria', in *The Standard Edition of the Complete Psychological Works*, London, Hogarth Press, vol. 7, pp. 1–123.

—(1958a) [1912] 'The dynamics of transference', in *The Standard Edition of the Complete Psychological Works*, London, Hogarth Press, vol. 12, pp. 97–108.

—(1958b) [1914] 'Remembering, repeating and working-through', in *The Standard Edition of the Complete Psychological Works*, London, Hogarth Press, vol. 12, pp. 145–56.

—(1964) [1937] 'Constructions in analysis', in *The Standard Edition of the Complete Psychological Works*, London, Hogarth Press, vol. 23, pp. 255–70.

Hartman, Geoffrey (1970) *Beyond Formalism*, New Haven, Conn., Yale University Press.

Holland, Norman (1975) *Five Readers Reading*, New Haven, Conn., Yale University Press.

Kris, Ernst (1952) *Psychoanalytic Exploration in Art*, New York, International Universities Press.

Lacan, Jacques (1966a) 'L'Instance de la lettre dans l'inconscient ou la raison depuis Freud', in *Ecrits*, Paris, Seuil, pp. 493–528.

—(1966b) 'Intervention sur le transfert', in *Ecrits*, Paris, Seuil, pp. 215–26.

Laclos, Choderlos de (1964) [1782] *Les Liaisons dangereuses*, Paris, Garnier-Flammarion.

Lesser, Simon O. (1957) *Fiction and the Unconscious*, Chicago, University of Chicago Press.

Schwartz, Murray (1978) 'Critic, define thyself', in Hartman, Geoffrey (ed.) *Psychoanalysis and the Question of the Text*, Baltimore, Johns Hopkins University Press.

Shelley, Mary (1974) *Frankenstein*, Indianapolis, Bobbs-Merrill.

Skura, Meredith (1981) *The Literary Use of the Psychoanalytic Process*, New Haven, Conn., Yale University Press.

Spector, Jack (1973) *The Aesthetics of Freud*, New York, Praeger.

2

Id is, is Id?

CHRISTINE BROOKE-ROSE

The Concise Cambridge History of English Literature (1942), which I read assiduously long before going up to Oxford and being taught not to rely on such summaries but to read the texts, contained a paragraph that made a great impression on me:

> As the physicians had explained temperament to be dependent on the predominance of one of the four 'humours' or moistures – phlegm, blood, choler and melancholy – it became fashionable to dignify any eccentricity or pose with the name of 'humour', and to deem the most miserable affectations worthy of literary comment. Hence arose a literature of 'humours', and 'humour' became as tiresome a word in that age as 'complex' is in this.
> (Sampson 1942, pp. 219–20)

In those unformed days it never occurred to me to question whose view this was or how the tiresomeness of a word 'in that age' could be gauged, and I similarly accepted that 'complex' had become tiresome 'in this'. And, in fact, the humours were also called complexions.

My point in recounting this is that I also remember wondering as corollary whether the explanations of modern psychology would seem as quaint and unscientific in a century or so as the humours do today. In other words, that facile and perhaps dismissive comparison had one important effect: it instilled into me a solid dose of healthy scepticism about all scenarios, however useful, that purport to explain human behaviour and, by the same token, their extremely curious by-products.

19

Over forty years later, that healthy scepticism is still there, and I even ask myself practically the same question, though it now concerns the knotty problem of hermeneutics in general. For although criticism of any school continues to make assertive statements ('what the poet is saying is', 'the text tells us that', 'the reader infers that'), we nevertheless keep declaring that we have lost our innocence at last and no longer believe in truth as something out there, to be discovered and merely stated, independent of our many systems of perception, including of course language. Even history is now considered to be a product of our tropes (White 1978).

And a trope is a lie based on the verb 'to be', even if the verb 'to be' is not actually used to express it: love is a *fire* → love . . . *that fire, such a fire*; O love . . . *O fire!*; the *fire* of love, the *fire* in my heart; *fiery* love; love *burns* me, and so on. And although the most banal metaphors (like the above) seem gratuitous with a grammatical link as dogmatic as the copula, the copula allows the most outrageous metaphors ('She is *all States*, and *all Princes*, I'; 'And her who is *dry corke*'; see Brooke-Rose 1958, pp. 105ff). This, however, is a matter of style: whichever grammatical link is used, the equation A is B underlies the metaphor (or other trope).

Plato exiled the poet from his Republic because (1) he tells lies and (2) he tells beautiful lies that corrupt: the referential function (1) and the conative function (2) already problematic. What Plato meant by truth, however, was itself a beautiful scenario. He merely happened to believe it *as* the truth – and the 'happened' is a neutral way of saying that belief is always based on desire.

There, I have used the copula dogmatically myself. We all do. We can't do otherwise, unless we become mathematicians and use equations, which are in a way like copulas, but carefully, complexly demonstrated. And even there another demonstration might upset and has in the past upset the whole paradigm. Scientists cheerfully admit this and have to work within current paradigms, or nothing would be done at all and whole societies would grind to a halt on philosophic doubt. Indeed, when one reads modern deconstructions of twenty-five centuries of 'the metaphysics of presence', one sometimes wonders whether philosophers have done anything for civilization except *suivre leur idée, et comme elle était fixe, ils piétinaient*. It is however perhaps a moot point which of them have done more harm, those who have argued about Truth and Being, or those who have helped to produce our present splendid and fearful civilization.

The eternal divisions start early: the poet who knows less about charioteering and potions and beds than a charioteer or a doctor or a carpenter, and even less about 'truth', that 'real' (ideal) bed, model for the carpenter's bed. For Plato the poet fails on two versions of the referential function: he cannot have the technical knowledge of chariots, potions and beds as we know them in the world (poetry versus science); and he does not have access to the 'true', the 'real' (ideal) models of these things, since no man has, except apparently Plato, who postulates their existence and even produces scenarios of superior souls (philosophers) who in their transmigration 'remember' more of this inaccessible truth than others do (poetry versus philosophy, or in later, medieval versions, poetry versus theology).

These divisions, as we know, have pursued us through the ages, in various versions of a two-truths theory, poetry in fact rejoining religion as against science in the nineteenth century: one truth for religion and one for science, or in I.A. Richards's psychologizing type of criticism earlier this century, one truth (language) for poetry and one truth (language) for science.

Meanwhile, there slowly arose that shadowy area of the ersatz or 'human' sciences; ersatz because they cannot observe even the elementary rules of science such as, for instance, the exact reproducibility of an experiment in identical conditions. Thus they can have it both ways: their systems allow them to speculate about relationships and structures as scientific systems do, but they can state these speculations as dogmatically and without empirical proof as poetry and metaphysics always have: in the name of the principle of non-contradiction, which produces the principle of identity A is A, you could also state that A is B or Z.

In a passage quoted by Derrida, Nietzsche questions even our right to say '"the stone is hard"', as if "hard" were known to us otherwise than through a subjective excitation' (Nietzsche, quoted in Derrida 1972a, p. 213). Derrida notes:

l'illusion diagnostiquée porte sur la valeur du 'est' qui a pour fonction de transformer 'une excitation subjective' en jugement objectif, en prétension à la vérité. Fonction grammaticale? Fonction lexicologique? C'est une question qui se déterminera plus loin.

the diagnosed illusion rests on the value of the 'is' whose function is to transform 'a subjective excitation' into objectified judgement and claim to truth. Grammatical function? Lexicological function? This question will be dealt with below.

(p. 213; my translation)

However, 'plus loin' turns out to be, a little disappointingly, a harping on Benveniste's apparent unawareness that others had criticized Aristotle's categories before him; and on the non-coincidence of the copula's functions with different forms of the verb 'to be' in various languages. It could be argued that Nietzsche's example is badly chosen since science can, in fact, define hardness in molecular and other terms, whereas philosophy can't.

Paul de Man, that other great deconstructor of our time, has also paid much attention to Nietzsche on this point: in Section 516 of *Der Wille zur Macht* Nietzsche says:

> suppose there were no self-identical A, such as is presupposed [*vorausgesetzt*] by every proposition of logic (and of mathematics), and the A were already mere *appearance*, then logic would have a merely *apparent world* as its precondition [*Voraussetzung*]. . . . The A of logic is, like the atom, a reconstruction [*Nachkonstruktion*] of the 'thing'. . . . In fact, *logic (like geometry and arithmetic) applies only to fictitious truths [fingierte Wahrheiten] that we have created.* Logic is the attempt to *understand the actual world by means of a scheme of being posited [gesetzt] by ourselves, more correctly to make it easier to formalize and to compute [berechnen].*

(Nietzsche 1968, p. 279; quoted in de Man 1979,
pp. 120–1; de Man's emphases)

Later de Man comments:

> The unwarranted substitution of knowledge for mere sensation becomes paradigmatic for a wide set of abberations all linked to the positional power of language in general, and allowing for the radical possibility that all being, as ground for entities, may be linguistically 'gesetzt', a correlative of speech-acts.

(de Man 1979, p. 123)

We cannot assert that logical axioms are adequate to reality without having previous knowledge of entities, says Nietzsche, who adds, 'which is certainly not the case'. De Man points out that while this last sentence has not been proved explicitly, neither can we prove it is not so. Nietzsche is drawing our attention to the possibility of unwarranted substitution (e.g. of identity for signification) and hence puts into question the postulate of logical adequacy. Indeed:

> Nietzsche seems to go further than this and concludes: '[The law of contradiction] *therefore* [de Man's emphasis] contains no *criterion of truth* [Nietzsche's emphasis] but an *imperative* concerning that which should count as true.' The conclusion seems irrevocable. As is stated at the beginning of the passage (in the form of a thesis), the inability to contradict – to state at the same time that A is and is not A – is not a necessity but an inadequacy, 'ein Nicht-vermögen'. Something one has failed to do can become feasable again only in the mode of compulsion; the performative correlate of 'I cannot' is 'I [or you] must.'
>
> (p. 124)

And de Man goes on to ask:

> Can we consequently free ourselves once and forever from the constraints of identity by asserting and denying the same proposition at the same time? Is language an act, a 'sollen' or a 'tun', and now that we know that there is no longer such an illusion as that of knowledge but only feigned truths, can we replace knowledge by performance? The text seems to assert this without question. ... But in so doing it does not do what it claims to be entitled to do. The text does not simultaneously affirm and deny identity but it denies affirmation.
>
> (p. 124)

But de Man had begun his essay by noting that 'value-seductions are tolerated (even admired) in so-called literary texts in a manner that would not pass muster in "philosophical" writings', and that one of the first difficulties of Nietzsche's texts is their patent literariness, although they make 'claims usually associated with philosophy rather than with literature. Nietzsche's work raises the perennial question of the distinction between philosophy and literature by way of a deconstruction of the value of values' (p. 119), of which the most fundamental is the principle of non-contradiction, ground of the identity principle. And de Man confronts the passage about 'tun ist alles', in *Genealogy of Morals* ('there is no "being" behind "doing" ... the "doer" is merely a fiction added to the deed – the deed is everything', Nietzsche 1922, vol. 15, p. 295) with another, from Section 477 of *The Will to Power*:

> The Spirit [*Geist*, better translated as 'Mind'], *something that thinks*
> . . . here we *first* imagine an act that does not exist, 'thinking', and
> *second* we imagine as substratum of this act a subject in which every
> act of thought and nothing else originates: this means that *the deed
> as well as the doer are fictions* [*sowohl das Tun, als der Täter sind fingiert*].
> (Nietzsche 1968, p. 264)

> The parallel that concerns us is the symmetry between this
> fictitious doing [*fingiertes Tun*] and the fictitious truths [*fingierte
> Wahrheiten* in authorized edition, not *Wesenheiten* or 'entities', as
> in earlier editions] that appear in the previously discussed
> passage on the principle of identity ['logic . . . applies only to
> fictitious truths']: here, in Section 516, truth is opposed to action
> as fiction is opposed to reality. In the later passage (Section 477)
> this conception of action as a 'reality' opposed to the illusion of
> knowledge, is, in its turn, undermined. Performative language
> is no less ambivalent in its referential function than the language
> of constatation.
> (de Man 1979, p. 127)

Hence, presumably, the now 'literary' language of philosophers
like Nietzsche (or Derrida), and of 'human' scientists like Freud.
Perhaps, after all, as poets have always 'known', the formula of the
identity principle A is A is just as fictitious as the tropic formula A
is B. And since 'love burns' says the same as 'love is a fire' but in a
different way, any action can be attributed to any entity, both being
fictions anyway. Thus may we assert any dogma, any lie, any
scenario.

It is in fact amazing how we continue to assert personal opinions
as equations. Even those who have done most to deconstruct
illusions of language use the copula liberally. 'L'indécidabilité est
une "preuve" d'écriture', says Barthes at a critical moment of *S/Z*
(1970, p. 170), though clearly many must disagree, and Derrida's
readings move splendidly from metaphor to metaphor.

What is a dogma? A dogma is a scenario elaborated from one
premise to be taken on trust, whether that trust be epistemological
or ideological (and some would equate the two). This is the second
of my dogmatic statements based on the verb 'to be'.

To avoid overt politics let's take a harmless Roman Catholic dogma – relatively recent as dogma (1950), though older as apocryphal tradition – that of the Assumption of the Blessed Virgin Mary (BVM), which functions on pure logic, given the initial assumption (with small 'a'): Christ is the Son of God. Elaboration: therefore He is free of Original Sin (another dogma) and therefore He is born through a body also free of Original Sin (the Immaculate Conception of the BVM, another dogma, not proclaimed as such till 1854, and often confused with the Virgin Birth). That's for the Immaculate Birth. But the process is extended to the Immaculate Death. Christ's body could not rot in the earth, hence the Ascension; and later, quite logically, the same applies to the BVM, hence the Assumption – without evangelical evidence, but theologically and structurally satisfying.

All ideology works this way, though not always so transparently – hence the impossibility of arguing (as opposed to discussing) any ideological point without dislodging the one article of faith on which it is erected. This we cannot do, and have learnt or are still learning not to do, out of respect for others' articles of faith, if tenaciously held. Nevertheless, there are sufficient millions of people throughout the world who still kill each other or plan to conquer each other for such articles of faith – at least on the surface, the real drive being power (this is my third dogmatic statement based on the verb 'to be'). Thus a tentative answer to the earlier moot point about who has done most harm (see p. 20), would be that ideologies relying on the metaphysics of presence will not hesitate to use the means science has put at their disposal to destroy each other.

The non-scientific 'human' sciences, that were supposed to cure us all of our libidinal acquisitive and aggressive instincts, seem to function in the same way, by creating dogmatic scenarios, *Nachkonstruktione*, from symptomatic events, of other events that have occurred only once and are supposed to recur as symptoms but not in exactly reproducible conditions; these scenarios have become the paradigm of the systems. The most familiar are the Freudian scenarios which we have all studied, accepted in fascination, rejected and mocked, analysed or been analysed through. Religion having failed, the family romance was better than no romance at all. But the most curious aspect of these scenarios was the detailed topology of the psychic system that 'writes' the romance. With the verb 'to be' and other assertive forms:

The ego is not sharply separated from the id; its lower portion merges into it.

But the repressed merges into the id as well, and is merely part of it. The repressed is only cut off sharply from the ego by the resistance of repression; it can communicate with the ego through the id.

(Freud 1961a [1923], p. 14; see also diagram)

So Descartes placed the soul in the pineal gland. Examples abound throughout Freud's work. Freud is, however, always careful to point out that he is only trying to 'represent pictorially' (p. 14), or that 'what follows is speculation' (1955b [1920], p. 24, on the neurological position of 'the System Pept-Cs' [Perception-Consciousness]), or in his incredible search for a mechanical analogy to the psychic memory, from the 'Project for a scientific psychology' (1966 [1885]), through the *Traumdeutung* (1955 [1900]) to the 'Note on the "Mystic writing pad"' (1961b [1925]), as traced by Derrida (1967), an analogy that has to represent the permanence of both the trace and of the virginity of the substance that receives the trace.

'The machine doesn't function by itself', says Derrida (my translation); 'it is a mechanism without its own energy. The machine is dead, it is death' (Derrida 1967, p. 335). It would be interesting to know how Freud would have used, rather than his waxen *Wunderblock*, the analogy of the computer, with its Read-Only Memory (ROM), called in French 'mémoire morte' – or Derrida for that matter, with his verb 'to be': it is death. 'But what should function by itself is the psychic, and not its imitation or its mechanical representation. Representation is death' (p. 335). And Derrida goes on to show that Freud's concept of writing is essentially Platonic, opposing hypomnesic writing to writing 'in the psyche', itself woven of a truth present out of time (p. 336). And later:

Ainsi s'annoncent peut-être, dans la trouée freudienne, l'au-delà et l'en-deçà de la clôture qu'on peut appeler 'platonicienne'. Dans ce moment de l'histoire du monde, tel qu'il s' 'indique' sous le nom de Freud, à travers une incroyable mythologie (neurologique ou métapsychologique: car nous n'avons jamais songé à prendre au sérieux, sauf en la question qui désorganise et inquiète sa littéralité, la fable métapsychologique. Au regard des histoires neurologiques que nous raconte l'*Esquisse* [*Project*], son avantage peut-être est mince) un rapport à soi de la scène historico-transcendante de l'écriture s'est dit sans se dire, pensé sans s' être pensé: écrit et à la fois effacé, métaphorisé; désigné lui-même en indiquant des rapports intra-mondains, *représenté*.

Cela se reconnait peut-être . . . à ce signe que Freud . . . nous a aussi fait la scène de l'écriture. Comme tous ceux qui écrivent.

(pp. 337–8)

Here in the Freudian thrust, we can perhaps discern both sides of what could be called the 'platonic' closure. In the moment of world history that appears under the name of Freud, and by means of an incredible mythology (neurological or meta-psychological: for the metapsychological fable could never be taken seriously, except in the sense that disorganises and disturbs its literality. Its advantage, as regards the neurological stories told in the *Project*, is slim), a relation of the historico-transcendental writing-scene to the self has been said without being said, thought without being thought: written and at the same time effaced, metaphorised; self-designated through indi-cations of intra-worldly links, *represented* [Derrida's emphasis]. This can perhaps be recognised . . . by the fact that Freud . . . also made us a writing-scene. As do all those who write. (my translation)

Elsewhere, however, Derrida attributes more consciousness to Freud's use of metaphor. Freud, Bergson and Lenin, he says in 'La mythologie blanche', who were all attentive to the metaphoric activity in theoretical or philosophical discourse, 'ont proposé ou pratiqué la multiplication de métaphores antagonistes afin de mieux en neutraliser ou contrôler l'effet' ('have proposed or practised the multiplication of antagonistic metaphors in order the better to neutralise or control their effect' (my translation) (Derrida 1972b, p. 255).

The effect, nevertheless, of Freud's scenarios on many of his disciples has been a certain literalness, and the creation of a new theology, which works on exactly the same principle of faith as do theology and political ideology, except that the unconscious has replaced eternal and dogmatic truth: any individual refusal must come from repression of a truth that is there unrecognized, and this will be analysed as resistance, just as it will be prayed for as a faltering of faith, or 'amicably' discussed (with luck) as revisionism or other ideological heresy.

Scenarios are for poets, for paranoiacs, for schizophrenics; and for those who want to believe in the scenarios in the first place, for people of faith, for sectarians and ideologists of all kinds. Poets, paranoiacs and schizophrenics have one great advantage over the ideologists in that they frequently change scenarios: they get tired of the old ones and invent new ones, equally convincing. Freud himself was a poet in this respect, and as poet *and* doctor he gave an explanation of the functioning of the unconscious on the model of human languages, an explanation which was both neurologically and linguistically more satisfying than he perhaps understood or stated in the elaborations of his scenarios.

Similarly, the most poetic and creative literary critics – those one reads for their own texts rather than to learn about the texts they discuss – have produced enchanting scenarios: Barthes on Balzac, Derrida on Rousseau or Plato (or on Lacan on Poe), Felman on Henry James, and many others – they are themselves poets in prose, critics as writers. But are their beautiful statements 'true'? 'The poet nothing affirmeth, and therefore never lieth', said Sidney four centuries ago. All poets are liars but say so – and so on. Dogmatic statements (and this is my fourth conscious one) are turned into tropes.

But is it always so? No, of course not. We all know the outrageous use of these scenarios for flat, pointless, tropeless, unmagical criticism. Perhaps they do no harm because no one takes them seriously? I believe they do harm in the classroom, but that is another problem. Between these and the best, however, lies a curious zone of Freudian critics who *are* taken seriously and who to my mind fall into the very dogmatic pseudo-equation trap I have tried to point up. I shall end by discussing only one of these, Harold Bloom.

In *The Anxiety of Influence*, Bloom proposes 'a theory of poetry by way of a description of poetic influence, or the story of intra-poetic relationships' (Bloom 1973, p. 5). By which, he has to insist in *A Map of Misprision*:

> I continue *not* to mean the passing on of images and ideas from earlier to later poets. Influence, as I conceive it, means that there are *no* texts, but only relationships *between* texts. These relationships depend upon a critical act, a misreading or misprision, that one poet performs upon another, and that does not differ in kind

from the necessary critical acts performed by every strong reader upon every text he encounters.

(Bloom 1975, p. 3)

Through his theory of influence Bloom offers 'instruction in the practical criticism of poetry'.

In Chapter 5 of *Map of Misprision* he says:

> After Nietzsche and Freud, it is not possible to return wholly to a mode of interpretation that seeks to *restore* meanings to texts. Yet even the subtlest of contemporary Nietzschean 'deconstructionists' of texts must *reduce* those texts in a detour or flight from psychology and history. . . . A semiological enigma, however prized, is generally an elaborate evasion of the inevitable discursiveness of a literary text. Latecomer fictions must know themselves to be fictions. . . .
>
> We can prefer Freud as a clearer-away of illusions to his chief competitor, Jung, who offers himself as a restorer of primal meanings but discredits almost all possibility of such restoration; but we will remain uneasy at the Freudian reductiveness. . . . And we have discovered no way as yet to evade the insights of Nietzsche, which are more dangerously far-reaching even than those of Freud, since Freud would not have told us that rational thought *is* only interpretation according to a scheme we cannot throw off. Yet Nietzsche's 'perspectivism', which is all he can offer us as an alternative to Western metaphysics, is a labyrinth more pragmatically illusive than the illusions he would dispel. One need not be religious in any sense or intention . . . still to conclude that meaning, whether of poems or dreams, of any text, is excessively impoverished by a Nietzsche-inspired deconstruction, however scrupulous.

(pp. 85–6)

Thus Bloom's chief objection to deconstruction, whether Freudian or Nietzschean-inspired or both, is its reductiveness ('reduce', 'reductiveness', 'excessively impoverished'). His own system, however, though excessively rich and immensely complicated, seems equally reductive through arbitrary rigidity of categorization (and, of course, the mere act of reading texts through one system only is reductive).

On the one hand, he describes six stages, called misreadings or revisionary ratios, in the latecomer's relationship to his precursor or 'Father' (I summarize from Bloom's own synopsis, 1973, pp. 14–15):

> *Clinamen*: The later poet swerves from the precursor. This is a corrective movement in his own poem.
>
> *Tessera*: He antithetically completes his precursor by retaining the terms but meaning them differently.
>
> *Kenosis*: He seems to humble and empty himself, but in such a way that the precursor is emptied out also.
>
> *Daemonization*: He opens himself to a power in the parent poem that belongs to a range of being beyond that precursor.
>
> *Askesis*: He yields up part of his own endowment to separate himself. Self-purgation, solitude.
>
> *Apophrades*: He opens his poem again to the precursor's work, but the result is as if the later poet had himself written the precursor's most characteristic work.

Each of these revisionary ratios is then arbitrarily equated with a trope – and Bloom adds two to the 'Four Master Tropes' of Burke out of Vico (irony, metonymy, metaphor and synecdoche): hyperbole and metalepsis (here = fusion of times). Obviously, he has to have six. And he justifies it, 'following Nietzsche and de Man in needing two more tropes of representation to go beyond synecdoche in accounting for Romantic representations' (Bloom 1975, p. 94):

> A trope as I define it is . . . more Vichian than Nietzschean, 'poetic monsters and metamorphoses', . . . necessary errors about language, defending ultimately against the deathly dangers of literal meaning, and more immediately against all other tropes that intervene between the literal meaning and the fresh opening to discourse.
>
> (p. 94)

Each revisionary ratio is *also* equated with a psychic defence (against the precursor), and here he *reduces* Anna Freud's ten defences (themselves a mechanical schematization of highly complex interrelated activities) to six – indeed, Bloom gives priority to psychic defences over tropes (a trope is practically a defence); and *also* equated with types of images; and *also* with terms in the 'dialectic of revisionism' or 'tropes of limitation and tropes of representation' (p. 84; see col. 2 in Table 1 below); and each

Biblical	Dialectic	Images	Tropes		Psychic defence	Rat.
			action / desire \			
election	limitation/ substitution	presence/ absence	irony		Reaction-formation	Clinamen ↕
covenant	represent-ation	part/ whole		synecdoche	reversal (turning against Self)	Tessera
rivalry	limitation/ substitution	fullness/ emptiness	metonymy		regression (undoing, isolation)	Kenosis ↕
incarn'n	represent-ation	high/ low		hyperbole/ litotes	repression	Daemon'n
interp'n	limitation/ substitution	inside/ outside	metaphor		sublim'n	Askesis ↕
revision	represent-ation	early/ late		metalepsis	introj'n/ projection	Apophrades

Table 1 Summary of Bloom's 'revisionary ratios'

category has already been pre-equated (in 'The primal scene of instruction', pp. 51ff) with biblical notions of development: election, covenant, rivalry, incarnation, interpretation, revision. Later, Bloom in fact reduced these six inter-equated categories to three with each a dialectical movement, equivalent to three kinds of psychic defence, so that in fact Clinamen and Tessera go together (as do the others) in a contracting away and reopening movement, repeated three times (Bloom 1977). This gives the chart shown as Table 1.

It must be understood that this is not a biographical theory: it is not the poet who *in his life* goes through all these equivalent stages, but a *poem*, and this is clearly a great advantage.

This is obviously a rich system, and pure structuralists would object that it is *too* rich and arbitrary to *be* a system – as Todorov in his structuralist days objected to Frye's categories on the same ground (Todorov 1970). And Bloom's readings are clearly not meant to be reductive as structuralist, and in his view de-constructionist, readings are.

Yet, as often with structuralist readings, the practice either cannot follow the theory (if it *is* rich and interesting), *or* follows it too obediently (if it is reductive or arbitrary). In Bloom we have both. His best readings do enrich us through the diagram's perspective, but often seem to fall away into personal assertions. Conversely, the temptation to invert the critical procedure and refer a passage back to the diagram through its 'images' and tropes, is very strong. Thus any image of presence/absence belongs to *clinamen* (and to irony, and to reaction-formation, etc.); while any image of earliness/lateness belongs to *apophrades* (etc.). The result is sometimes hilarious.

Wordsworth's *Ode*, for instance, 'sets or follows the patterns of our map of misreading' (Bloom 1975, p. 146) – the precursor being Milton's *Lycidas*. Thus 'images of absence dominate only the poem's first stanza' (p. 145):

> From stanzas V through VIII there are a series of images showing different aspects of emptying out of a prior and valuable fullness. These include trailing clouds, shades, journey-ings westwards, fading of a greater into a lesser light, imitation of the lesser by the greater, darkness and, finally, weighing down by frost. As images of reduction, they show subjectivity yielding to a world of things, of meaningless repetition, the 'realistic' world of metonymies.
>
> (p. 146)

And so on to the final stage, where 'The acceptance of belatedness at first seems complete' [quotation: 'What though the radiance. . ./ We will grieve not']. But the final stanza proclaims freshness and earliness:

> The innocent brightness of a new-born Day
> Is lovely yet . . .
>
> (pp. 147–8)

Je veux bien, as the French say to express doubt. But it does seem rather strange (and to me unacceptable) that this 'final' stage, described in such splendid theoretical terms and receiving the greatest focus of Bloom's hermeneutic machine (for he is only interested in 'strong' poets who reach this final stage), should be illustrated by Wordsworth at his flattest and most bathetic (this is my fifth personal and dogmatic statement).

Would the terrible father figure, the precursor, have pre-cursed his son, the belated newcomer, to suffer so and come through all these deep defences but for this?

This model of poetic creation, moreover, 'works' only for what he calls 'strong' poets; it celebrates heroic struggles of will between a poet and his precursors. And (as it happens?) his strong poets are male poets, for although Marianne Moore (once) and Emily

Dickinson (thrice) figure in lists (pp. 6, 162, 163), they are not in fact discussed. Feminist critics have oddly enough shown much interest in Bloom because, according to Culler, 'it makes explicit the sexual connotations of authorship and authority' (Culler 1983, p. 60n) and therefore also the problematic situation of a woman poet in relation to the tradition – interest by omission as it were, as in their various dealings with Freud. As Leitch observes, 'Presumably, one could take a weak poem and pinpoint its stages of failure' (Leitch 1983, p. 135). I thought this was irony, but he goes on:

> And one might be able to characterize schools and periods of literary history by their practice of a dominant ratio. Poets of mid-eighteenth-century sensibility, for example, favour hyperbole-daemonization. To practice such criticism would be to employ a diachronic rhetoric, which Bloom has lately started to do.
>
> (p. 135)

But as Bove has shown, tradition (which for Freud represented what the individual represses), is itself a trope, a defence mechanism, because:

> it is the rhetorical center upon which the entire Bloomian critical structure depends in its *circular* effort to *demonstrate* the absolute necessity and value of *tradition as center*. This is the classical example of the vicious circle: critical language turns back upon itself, against the author's intent, to reveal its own blindness and unexamined rhetoric.
>
> (Bove 1980, p. 19)

And tropes, Bloom says, are 'necessary errors about language'. It would indeed seem, as Bove concludes via other arguments, that Bloom:

> has proven what he set out, in opposition to Nietzsche, Derrida and de Man, to disprove. The anxiety of influence is necessarily a linguistic structure because the unexamined pressure of what Heidegger calls the ontotheological and Derrida the logocentric language of tradition bring him to demonstrate unwittingly, the fact that to some extent, it is language which thinks, reads, and writes.
>
> (p. 22)

My own necessary but absurd 'reduction' of Bloom is unfair,

which is why I quote the comments of others who have examined him in more generous detail than I could here, yet nevertheless end up in this negative way. It is one thing to say that 'after Nietzsche and Freud it is not possible to return wholly to a mode of interpretation that seeks to *restore* meanings to texts.' It is quite another to read tropes via Freud, whose concepts, Derrida (among others) maintains, one should

> use cautiously and in quotations: they all belong without exception to the history of metaphysics, that is to the system of logocentric repression organised to exclude or lower the body of the written trace, to shove it out and down as a didactic and technical metaphor, as servile and excremental matter.
>
> (Derrida 1967, p. 294; my translation)

Derrida adds that Freud is of course not exhausted by this logocentric inheritance:

> witness the precautions and the 'nominalism' with which he manipulates what he calls conceptual conventions and hypotheses. . . . But the historical and theoretical sense of these precautions was never truly thought out by Freud. Hence the need for the immense work of deconstruction.
>
> (p. 294)

If all reading is misreading, as Bloom insists, this presupposes, as many have pointed out, a correct reading. But Culler goes further than this simplistic objection and turns the proposition round to mean that all understanding can be seen as a special case of misunderstanding (Culler 1983, p. 176).

It is always tempting to deconstruct a text and to show that the author has in his practice done the opposite of what he claims. There is a certain post-Freudian glee in showing the unconscious contradictions, and Bloom himself, though against deconstruction, does precisely that to a passage from Nietzsche, by affirming that 'Nietzsche, like Emerson, is one of the great deniers of anxiety-as-influence, just as Johnson and Coleridge are its great affirmers' (Bloom 1973, p. 50). But in Derrida and de Man and the best deconstructors, the intention is generous and the result enriching: for de Man, the greatest insight comes at the moment of greatest blindness.

Nevertheless, I feel that these problems form part of the Freudian and post-Freudian problem of the status of the analyst versus the analysand (who in literature is not there to 'help' the analyst or, in more aggressive terms, to 'defend himself' – which defence would itself be analysed as part of a highly significant pattern, and so on). However subtly we go about it (thus protected by the 'patient's' absence), we fall into the traps of language and notably of the verb 'to be', behind which is desire and dogma and mastery. Our very institutions of learning encourage 'mastery' of the arts. And these traps of language and desire belong to the scenarios of these mythologies of mastery.

One profound difference between psychoanalysis and philosophy, however, is that the former claims to be a science and behaves like a science: (1) it supersedes itself (the scientist, unless he is a historian of science, is not interested in earlier states of knowledge); (2) it acts in the world; but with rather less success than sciences like, say, medicine or even psychiatry, by which I mean that wholly successful repressions (the most dangerous cases) are inaccessible to its methods, as Freud himself admitted (Freud 1957 [1915], p. 153).

Thus it seems to me more dangerous, more 'dating', as the system of 'humours' is dated, to 'use' psychoanalysis in literary criticism, but fascinating and enriching to consider it, at its best, as a literary text, as Nietzsche's texts are literary texts. Perhaps after all we *should* accept the joyful wisdom and ambiguity of Nietzsche's own position: 'Art treats appearance as appearance; its aim is precisely *not* to deceive, it is therefore *true*' (Nietzsche 1922, vol. 6, p. 98), which says exactly what Sidney said four centuries ago. And the artist who accepts illusion and lie for what they are gains a special kind of *Heiterkeit* or serenity that 'differs entirely from the pleasure principle tied to libido and desire' (de Man 1979, p. 114, who, however, goes on to deconstruct even that: 'Philosophy turns out to be an endless reflection on its own destruction at the hands of literature' (p. 115)).

And isn't that, in the end, what we have all secretly wanted for a hundred years since Arnold? Or even for twenty-five centuries, since our exclusion as writers from that written Republic?

References

Barthes, Roland (1970) *S/Z*, Paris, Seuil.
Bove, Paul A. (1980) *Deconstructive Poetics: Heidegger and Modern American Poetry*, New York, Columbia University Press.

36 Discourse in Psychoanalysis and Literature

Bloom, Harold (1973) *The Anxiety of Influence*, Oxford, Oxford University Press.

—(1975) *A Map of Misprision*, Oxford, Oxford University Press.

—(1977) 'Coda: poetic crossing', in *Wallace Stevens: The Poems of Our Climate*, Ithaca, NY, Cornell University Press, pp. 375–406.

Brooke-Rose, Christine (1958) *A Grammar of Metaphor*, London, Secker & Warburg.

Concise Cambridge History of English Literature (1942) Cambridge, Cambridge University Press. By George Sampson. Ch. 4, 'Prose and poetry: Sir Thomas North to Michael Drayton', Section 16, 'London and the development of popular literature', pp. 217–23.

Culler, Jonathan (1983) *On Deconstruction: Theory and Criticism after Structuralism*, London, Routledge & Kegan Paul.

de Man, Paul (1979) *Allegories of Reading*, New Haven, Conn., Yale University Press.

Derrida, Jacques (1967) 'Freud et la scène de l'écriture', in *L'Écriture et la différence*, Paris, Minuit, pp. 293–340.

—(1972a) 'Le Supplément de copule', in *Marges de la philosophie*, Paris, Seuil, pp. 209–46.

—(1972b) 'La mythologie blanche: la métaphore dans le texte philosophique', in *Marges de la philosophie*, Paris, Seuil, pp. 247–324.

Freud, Sigmund (1955a) [1900] *The Interpretation of Dreams*, in *The Standard Edition of the Complete Psychological Works*, London, Hogarth Press, vols 4–5.

—(1955b) [1920] 'Beyond the pleasure principle', in *The Standard Edition of the Complete Psychological Works*, London, Hogarth Press, vol. 18, pp. 3–66.

—(1957) [1915] 'Repression', in *The Standard Edition of the Complete Psychological Works*, London, Hogarth Press, vol. 14, pp. 46–58.

—(1961a) [1923] 'The ego and the id', in *The Standard Edition of the Complete Psychological Works*, London, Hogarth Press, vol. 19, pp. 3–66.

—(1961b) [1925] 'A note upon the "mystic writing pad"', in *The Standard Edition of the Complete Psychological Works*, London, Hogarth Press, vol. 19, pp. 227–34.

—(1966) [1885] 'Project for a scientific psychology', in *The Standard Edition of the Complete Psychological Works*, London, Hogarth Press, vol. 1, pp. 283–94.

Leitch, Vincent B. (1983) *Deconstructive Criticism: An Advanced Introduction*, New York, Columbia University Press.

Nietzsche, Frederick (1922) *Gesammelte Werke*, Munich, Musarion Verlag.

—(1968) *The Will to Power*, W. Kaufmann (ed. and trans.) New York, Random House, Vintage Books.

—(1970) *Werke Kritische Gesamtausgabe*, Giorgio Colli and Mazzino Montinari (eds), Berlin, de Gruyter.

Sampson, George (ed.) (1942) 'Prose and poetry: Sir Thomas North to Michael Drayton', Section 16, 'London and the development of popular literature' in *Concise Cambridge History of English Literature*, pp. 217–23.

Todorov, Tzvetan (1970) *Introduction à la littérature fantastique*, Paris, Seuil.

White, Hayden (1978) *Tropics of Discourse: Essays in Cultural Criticism*, Baltimore, Johns Hopkins University Press.

3

Interactions between textual analysis and related self-analysis

RIVKA R. EIFERMANN

In a paper entitled 'Varieties of denial: The case of a fairy tale' (Eifermann 1987a) written some months ago,[1] I presented a partial textual analysis, in psychoanalytic terms, of the Grimms' tale *Little Red Riding Hood*, as well as of a revised version of that tale. For purposes of the present investigation I re-examined everything I had written that directly related to the tale: (1) my notes and comments upon reading it and also upon reading Bettelheim's (1976) interpretation; (2) a reconstruction of the tale which I had put down from memory, and my comments on that. Through this re-viewing, and the concomitant self-analysis, I became aware of, and could eventually work through – aided by two childhood recollections that emerged as connecting links – some of the unconscious conflicts, motives and defences which were, again unconsciously, emotional driving forces in writing this particular paper. Of course, the textual analysis presented in the paper retains its independent status as interpretative narrative, prototype or paradigm, and its value depends on public judgement. It should also be mentioned that not all aspects of the self-analysis were linked to the underlying motives which I had uncovered. None the less, it was only later in this analysis that I could see that some of the more original ideas in that paper – indeed, those which seemed to expand upon the ways in which *Little Red Riding Hood* had been viewed up to then – had been inspired, unconsciously, by personal preoccupations.

My steps towards working through these preoccupations now made it possible for me to reflect back on the textual analysis and to become aware of ways in which I could improve upon it; now I was able to recognize where, and why, unconscious motives had affected the style, atmosphere and content of my paper in ways that did not accord with my original aim. At the same time, the process of self-analysis which had been evoked in re-examining my own data made aspects of my inner life, internalized objects and unconscious conflicts, accessible to me from new angles and in ways not available before this undertaking. Making use of this accessibility through further self-analysis has taken me a step further in the unending process of gaining expansion, continuity and integration of my self-experience. Thus self-analysis can contribute to textual analysis, as the latter can evoke and enrich the former.

It is to this process of reciprocal enrichment, and to some difficulties that may arise through the interactions, that I shall devote this paper, using illustrations from my work. My purpose here is not to present a piece of personal analysis, with all its numerous, intimate and intricate details. I shall be able to present here only a rough outline, leaving out a great many connecting threads and even whole areas of experience. Indeed, this is all that is needed for my present, illustrative purposes. Of course, for purposes of my own progress and eventual gains, short-cuts in time, range and intensity of emotional experiencing – or in mental efforts and processing and working through – were not possible. I therefore hope that the brief outline of this undertaking presented here will not offer a misleadingly simplistic view of the extremely elaborate and complex processes involved. In any case, and for a variety of reasons – some of them inevitably unconscious – I evidently consider it worth the attempt.

I shall, then, begin with a short piece of textual analysis from my paper on denial. When describing and interpreting Little Red Riding Hood's encounter with 'grandmother' (the wolf) upon entering 'her' cottage and finding 'her' in bed, basing myself on the Grimms' original text of *Rotkäppchen*, this is what I wrote:

According to the Grimms' original tale (1819), when Little Red Riding Hood drew the curtains of her grandmother's bed, she was facing a grandmother who was 'looking very strange': 'Oh, grandmother,' she exclaimed, 'what big ears you have!' And hearing the gentle reply: 'The better to hear you with', she persisted with 'Oh, grandmother, what big eyes you have!' Again, the gentle reply – 'The better to see you with' – only leads to a further anxious enquiry, 'Oh, grandmother, what large hands you have,' which calls forth: 'The better to seize [*packen*] you with.' The child, at this point horrified, insistently and, it seems desperately, still demands reassurance, 'Oh! but, grandmother, what a *terribly* [*entzezlich*] big mouth [*Maul*] you have!' (my italics). [*Maul*, the German word used here for mouth, is only applied with reference to *animals*]. 'The better to devour you with' comes the reply. And, the tale continues, the wolf had scarcely said this, than, with one bound he was out of bed and swallowed up Little Red Riding Hood.

In the large variety of drawings of 'grandmother' in bed which I have examined, it is the wolf that lies there, quite unmistakably. And children who look at these drawings unhesitantly recognize him for what he is. Thus, it is Little Red Riding Hood's *denial* of the 'reality' in front of her (once we combine picture with tale), that drives her to seek help and reassurance from the very source of her terror – and that leads to her (temporary) doom.

In my personal analysis related to this paragraph of my paper, I shall not begin at the beginning except to say that I know my mother told me the tale of *Rotkäppchen* and other of the Grimms' tales, in German, when I was a small child, and that I do not recall any specific occasion on which she related this tale to me. Nor do I specifically recall having heard or read it in the original German, or in any other version or language, since my childhood. I am aware, however, that I must have encountered other versions because some of its contents quite surprised me when I did, eventually, turn back to the original tale.

It was in one of my graduate seminars on dream analysis (Shanon and Eifermann 1984; Eifermann 1985a) that one of my student's dreams, reminiscent of *Little Red Riding Hood*, triggered my conscious interest in the tale. I then read the tale in the original, as well as Bettelheim's (1976) interpretation of it. As I was making some notes on the tale, I sensed increasingly that the child within me was still preoccupied with it – encapsulated and untouched as it had been for many years – and that it retained many of its early unconscious associations and meanings. Nevertheless, since I was analysing the text of the tale (and not myself), these associations remained largely dormant. I was making some notes on Bettelheim's interpretative narrative when it suddenly occurred to me, in a flash, that Little Red Riding Hood's behaviour when confronted with the wolf in her grandmother's bed 'is precisely my *Tümmel* tale!' *Tümmel* is my little girlish way of pronouncing *Kümmel*, the German word for caraway seed, and I was referring to an event from my early childhood, often told by my mother. I did not stop to consider the personal emotional meanings and implications of my discovery at the time or when I applied it in attempting to construct a coherent narrative of Little Red Riding Hood's behaviour.

I had often heard my mother tell my *Tümmel* tale during my childhood, and I sometimes used to ask her to relate it to me, since it always delighted me and filled me with pride: she related it with warmth and joy, implying that I was a sweet little girl. As I retold it to her some years ago, my mother corrected my recollection (of tale, or event – I no longer know) on two points, to which I shall return later. Here is my *Tümmel* tale.

I (aged 3 or 4) had just stepped out of my home on my way to kindergarten. I opened my leather lunch-bag, which was hanging from my neck, and unwrapped the neatly packed sandwich to see what Mummy had prepared for me today. (This curiosity I recall as being in anticipation of pleasure, for my mother's food was attractively prepared and tasty.) As I looked I suddenly saw something on the bread and cried out to my mother, 'Mummy come! Look what's on the bread!' (there was a little insect there). My mother came, looked, and said, 'It's nothing, it's just a caraway seed' (it was caraway seed bread), and turned back. But soon I was screaming, '*Mamy Mamy tom snel, der Tümmel tan laufen!*', 'Mummy, Mummy come quick, the *caraway* can *run.*' The parallel with, 'But *grandmother*, what a horrible *Maul* you have!' (my italics), seemed overwhelming.

Until I began work on *Little Red Riding Hood* my conscious retention of my own '*Tümmel* tale' was that of the warmth and joy my mother had conveyed to me in telling it. It was through indirect (re)view, as adult, on 'another' little girl's behaviour, that I suddenly, and still indirectly, gained new insight into my own. Indeed, perhaps it could only occur while its implications for myself remained unprovoked, for it was Little Red Riding Hood who was paramount in my mind at the time, and I did not stop to pursue my personal discovery. My own tale served merely as a means for gaining new insight into Little Red Riding Hood's behaviour. To me she was extremely obedient to her mother, *had* to see things through her mother's eyes, and that, therefore, since mother had instructed her to go to *grandmother* (and did not mention any wolf), it *had* to be grandmother lying in the bed in her cottage. This was parallel to my perception of the insect as caraway seed. At the time it did not emerge into my consciousness, however, that my perception of my own mother in that context, and my unconscious motives for seeing an insect as *Tümmel*, were at least partly those I had attributed to Little Red Riding Hood in my analysis.

When I had related my recollection of the tale to my mother some years ago she said that it had all occurred at home and that no lunch-bag had been involved. My reconstruction, of having been sent off by my mother, and with food (in a bag), suggests that I connected Little Red Riding Hood's tale with my own quite early in life.

The relevant sequence in my notes, in which the connection emerged as insight, begins as follows: 'To step off the main path from mother to grandmother'; this was my way of referring to Little Red Riding Hood's act of *dis*obedience, when she had walked off the path to pick flowers for her grandmother. It is significant that, in Hebrew, the language in which my notes are written, my expression, *em-hadérech*: 'main path', means 'mother-path'. I had selected the expression without being aware of its implications, which I had in fact made explicit when I continued with: 'The danger lay [not in walking off the path, but] precisely in *returning* to this path of absolute obedience to mother. [Once she was again acting in accord with mother's instructions.] It then *had* to be grandmother who was lying in bed [since it was no one other than grandmother to whom mother had sent her]. Little Red Riding Hood could do no more than wonder about how strange her "grandmother" looked. *This is precisely my* Tümmel *tale!*'

When I went over the notes I had made as I was reading the original tale of *Little Red Riding Hood*, it became evident to me that I had picked up various signs in the text indicating that Little Red Riding Hood, who was 'loved by everyone', was not loved and not adequately cared for by her mother. It was only much later that I had connected my perception of her as having to obey her mother with not being loved, and that to obey was a condition for being loved. But at this juncture, in writing my paper on denial, I was focusing on mother. My anger about her is rather explicit. This is what I say in the original draft of that paper:

It was quite a revelation for me to discover how unprotective mother is in the original Grimms' tale: She is concerned enough about 'ill and weak' grandmother to send her little girl to her, with a piece of cake and a bottle of wine which 'will do her good.' (Mind you, she does not see to her mother herself.) She does tell her little girl to 'set out before it gets too hot,' but other than that, her rather long-drawn instructions reveal more concern about the child's manners than about her well-being. She does not warn Little Red Riding Hood against talking to strangers (as is the case in later versions of the tale, as well as in Perrult's French version), nor of wicked wolves. She just says, '. . . walk nicely and quietly, and do not run off the path, or you may fall and break the bottle, and then your grandmother will get nothing, and when you go into her room, don't forget to say, "Good-morning", and don't peep into every corner before you do it.' Even when alone in the wood the little girl is to behave like a little lady (indeed the wolf observes, '. . . you walk gravely along as if you were going to school'); Mother prohibits running, 'or you may fall and break the bottle' (not, 'hurt yourself'!); And curiosity (or perhaps even suspiciousness), which would have been quite appropriate under the circums-tances encountered by the child upon entering her grandmother's home, are altogether discouraged: 'Don't peep into every corner' before you say 'Good Morning' are mother's instructions. Again, proper manners above all. Yet, had she followed her feelings upon entering the cottage, Little Red Riding Hood may have saved herself from being swallowed by the wolf. 'She was surprised to find the cottage-door standing open, and when she went into the room, she had such a strange feeling that she said to herself, "Oh dear! How uneasy I feel today, and at other times I like being with grandmother so much."' One may indeed conclude that Little Red Riding Hood's need to deny what she saw, to ignore her feelings and to refrain from peeping anywhere or checking anything, may well have been encouraged by her mother's demand for strict obedience.

The inadequacy, indeed irrelevance (or worse) of mother's

instructions are quite striking. They certainly turn out not to be good enough to ensure the child's safe passage through the wood. As the Grimm brothers put it, 'Little Red Riding Hood did not know what a wicked creature he [the wolf] was.'

These observations were coloured by my feelings about mother, my own *Tümmel* tale looming somewhere in my mind. Though reluctantly, I eventually left this paragraph out of my denial paper after it was pointed out to me that it was irrelevant to a discussion of denial, since nowhere in the paper had I even suggested that Little Red Riding Hood's mother was denying.

On re-examination I discovered that the final version of my denial paper still bears the marks of my complaint against mother, though subtly. Almost unaware, I protested too much and too often against any possibility that readers might misinterpret my statements as being directed personally at (against) the mothers whose behaviour I presented in the paper. My major argument was 'that a story comes alive only as an *interactive process* going on between story teller and receiver – *both* of whom have needs, wishes, conflicts, fantasies, and defences that draw them together with the story as their common focus'. Specifically, I argued that 'amongst many other things, often protective and loving, that she does by the act of reading the story, mother also exposes her child (who is a willing partner) to a tale of cruelty and fright'. I thereby aimed to illustrate that, 'for whatever reasons, conscious and unconscious, mothers will at times expose their children to more gruesomeness than the tale, or the child, invites', and that denial could be operative in the exposing mother. (Rami Bar-Giora, 1985, has made similar, independent, observations with regard to lullabies.)

Let me quote just one such illustration from my paper:

> Dvora Omer, an Israeli writer in her own right, has revised and published (1979) a collection of the Grimms' Tales in Hebrew. She introduces her collection with the following words (translated from Hebrew):
> '[This is] a personal and true story of a writer who is also a mother (of three) and an educator (by profession). ... I have tried to remain as true to the original as my motherly conscience would allow. I exclude most cruel descriptions and emphasize positive motives. ... I also emphasize the distance of the world of fairy tales from reality – in the characters, in time and in name

– so as to enable the children to cope more easily with contents that may be frightening.'

In what follows I shall demonstrate that Dvora Omer is not successful in her attempt. While she excludes some of the frightening details and the cruelty from the tale, she introduces and elaborates on other such features, ending up with a story no less gruesome than the original. In Omer's (unsuccessful) attempt one may discern denial of some of her unwanted feelings.

One of these unsuccessful attempts which I describe in the paper is the following:

> The Grimm brothers describe the events after the wolf had swallowed up Little Red Riding Hood as follows: 'When the wolf had appeased his appetite, he lay down again in bed, fell asleep and began to snore very loudly. The huntsman was just passing the house. ...' Thus, the brief scary description is immediately relieved through the happy coincidence of a rescuer appearing on the scene right-away. But Omer chooses, instead, to dwell on the horror and agony of it all:
>
> 'Since his stomach was full, it was no wonder that the wolf felt tired. After the delicious and voluptuous meal, he returned to grandmother's bed and fell into heavy sleep, snoring loud long snores.'
>
> 'And thus, an hour passed, two hours passed. Grandmother and Little Red Riding Hood were caught in the dark, narrow stomach of the wolf. While the wolf lay in the soft and comfortable bed of the old woman, sleeping deeply and snoring loudly. Then a huntsman passed near grandmother's house. ...'
>
> The slow passage of a long agonizing time is thus described in detail, and in quite realistic terms – contrary to our reviser's declared intention 'to emphasize the distance of the world of fairy tales from reality'.

I sum up my analysis of Omer's revisions, by writing:

> Omer finds it difficult, in terms of her conscience as a mother, to expose [her] children to the excessive cruelty and threat which she finds in the original Grimms' tale. In this she denies some other, contrary, aspect of her feelings, which nevertheless finds direct expression in her revision of the tale.

Many readers who have found the analysis of Omer and other mothers in my denial paper convincing, have nevertheless commented that I had been overcautious and unnecessarily apologetic in discussing the implications of my findings. Indeed, I was vaguely aware of this when, again, I said, with regard to Omer:

At the risk of repeating myself, I would like nevertheless to add that this is not a personal analysis of the writer, which I would in any case consider inappropriate. I do not have access to the personal constellation necessary for any statement regarding Omer's general motives, predominant defenses, or indeed any aspects of her as a person. (Italics not in the original)

At the time of my writing the above I could not see that I was overstressing this point, because I was not then aware that the mother(s) I was thereby protecting from being misperceived and misjudged, were strongly connected with my own internalized mother, as perceived in the context of the Grimms' tale. Rather than present them (her) mercilessly, as I had presented Little Red Riding Hood's mother, I turned to overprotecting her (them). Encapsulated and preserved in my own unconscious version of *Little Red Riding Hood* there remained, amongst other things, aspects of my mother which I had internalized not only as 'often protective and loving' but also as the mother who had sent me off, quite unprepared, cruelly exposing me to a most frightening wolf (insect), who might swallow me up/I might swallow.

I shall shortly turn to another piece of data related to *Little Red Riding Hood* which will lead me back to the above data. However, before doing this I would like to summarize the points from my denial paper. Unlike previous analyses of fairy tales, which deal exclusively with the child's unconscious needs in listening to the tale, such story-telling is, in fact, an interactive process, through which the mother expresses her own unconscious wishes, needs and defences regarding her child. One such need, consciously denied, is to sometimes expose the child to a certain degree of cruelty and fright through the tale. With regard to the text of *Little Red Riding Hood* itself, I interpreted the behaviour of mother as unprotective and inadequate and that of Little Red Riding Hood as overobedient and denying.

When I put down my reconstruction of the tale a few months after having read the German version, my aim was to be as true to the original as I could. (My purpose in this was quite other than that of Holland, 1975, of whose work I did not then know. In any case, other than a very preliminary looking-over of the material and comparing of it with the original, I had left it lying.) But in turning back to it now, once more I was puzzled by the same two deviations from the original tale that had caught my attention at the time: in my reconstruction I had repeatedly referred to the '*Körbchen*' (little basket) into which Little Red Riding Hood's mother placed 'bread, a bottle of wine, and ?' But this description was not accurate. To my surprise there was no mention of a basket in the original. (Of course, a basket *is* referred to in many later versions of the tale, and Little Red Riding Hood does appear with a basket in her hand in many drawings. But this is begging the question.) Why did I choose to introduce this detail, rather than another, from later versions? It must have had a very specific personal significance, since I had repeatedly inserted the German '*Körbchen*' into my reconstruction, which was otherwise written in Hebrew, and since I can hardly write German, having come to Israel before I was three and having communicated with my mother almost exclusively in Hebrew, so that German words, when they do occur to me, have the ring of early childhood. As for 'bread, a bottle of wine, and ?' – I kept inserting that question mark because I was certain that there *was* something else, which I could not recall. Unlike other details of whose accuracy I was uncertain, I remained with the vague feeling that it was something of particular significance and therefore felt compelled to make special note ('?') of it. I recall my amazement when I realized that there *was* nothing else in the basket! (Besides, I had written down '*bread* [and] a bottle of wine', when the original said '*cake* and a bottle of wine'. But this slight difference did not preoccupy me at the time.) When I returned to the *Körbchen* and question-mark for purposes of my present re-examination, the feeling of surprise and puzzlement returned. Then, at some point when I was looking at the text, only vaguely attentive, I recalled an incident from childhood, in which the *Körbchen* loomed large. But any connection with the Grimms' tale or my reconstruction of it still remained opaque. Then, a few days later, it suddenly hit me, that the something ('?') that was missing from my basket was the essential connecting link between my childhood memory and my recollection of the Grimms' tale. For in the incident that I remembered, my mother had sent me off with an *empty* basket, quite inadequately equipped for my trip.

I had just turned 6, and we had moved to a house in the village only two months before. That day at school (I was in first grade) the festival of Pentecost [*Shavuót/Bikurím*] was to be celebrated. It was a tradition in the village that every child come to school dressed in white, wearing a floral wreath and carrying a basket filled with seasonal fruits and vegetables from their own gardens. The produce was then sold at the school and the profits donated to a worthy cause. My mother, however, quite new from the city, was not aware that the sale was a serious event. As was her way, she prepared lovely wreaths and prettily decorated baskets, for me and for my brother but with nothing inside, feeling that this was surely not necessary for a performance. What I recall, and very distinctly, is that when we were on the path in our garden, already on our way out my brother, two years my senior, insisted that his basket must be filled. As he was crying and screaming, my mother, suddenly and in exasperation stepped into the vegetable garden, pulled out a whole bunch of very young carrots, and threw them furiously into his basket. The next scene that I remember is me sitting in class, hardly able to contain my tears: all the other children had their loaded baskets in front of them, while I had my pretty but empty basket. Our teacher, Tzipora, went around from child to child, looking over their baskets. By the time she reached me I was crying, then she clasped her hands, saying something (which I still do not recall), and kindly and gracefully taking a fruit from one child's basket and a vegetable from another, until nothing was missing anymore in my basket. But all I recall distinctly is that there was one somewhat rotten apricot lying there in the basket, and that I thought, 'Mummy would *never* have given me *that*!' I had to restore her to perfection.

The two tales from my childhood may already have set the reader thinking that, in my mind, my reconstruction of Little Red Riding Hood and my own personal tales have become strongly associated and intertwined, objects and events belonging to one, having been displaced to another. Like mixing metaphors, I *mistakenly* recalled that my encounter with the *Tümmel* had occurred just as I stepped out of my home on the way to kindergarten, whereas that had been the case in my *Körbchen* tale; I had also, and again mistakenly, recalled that I was carrying a lunch-bag ('food-bag' in Hebrew, and in my home the German expression used was *Brot-Täschchen*, 'bread-little-bag'), whereas in reality (or my recall of it) the basket for food was part of my *Körbchen* tale. In my reconstruction of *Little Red Riding Hood*, I had mistakenly placed bread (the sandwich in the lunch-bag of my distorted *Tümmel* tale) in the basket instead of the cake in the Grimms' original. (As if all this were not enough, my editor, Norma Schneider, pointed out to me that in writing this paper I consistently added a 't' to the word sandwich. Thus it seems that I was condensing a witch from yet other fairy tales: sand*witch*.)

There are, moreover, quite evident parallels between the manifest content of both my childhood tales, which support one another, and which lend support to, and fill gaps in, tracing unconscious motives that guided my textual interpretation of the Grimms' tale: my putting so much emphasis on Little Red Riding Hood's need to be obedient, on her being unloved by her mother, and so on; and it even throws light on my preoccupation with 'denial'. Without going into any further details of my self-analysis, I will offer just one very crude outline of a narrative that combines the two tales, as they cojoined in my mind with 'my' *Little Red Riding Hood* echoing in the background: Mummy has sent me off with a pretty basket containing tasty things that she has prepared for me; but something is very wrong – an insect on the sandwich, nothing in the basket – and she *denies* it! When I was little, just 3 or 4, I still cried out to her, while at the same time joining in in her denial ('the caraway can run!'). By age 6 I had become a mere onlooker, at my brother's protests. And I saw that while he did get his way, it was not lovingly. On the contrary, I had witnessed an event that for me acquired the meaning that when something other than the good she chose to offer was demanded of her, my mother might eventually give, but of her rage as well. I therefore chose to be sent away inadequately equipped, exposed to fright, pain and shame.[2]

As I was putting down the above, with considerable feeling of discomfort and increasing doubts as to whether I would ever so crudely and unfairly expose my (internalized) mother in public, I was suddenly shocked by the realization that precisely this has been the unconscious driving force behind the enterprise. At that time the angry, hurt, vengeful child within me still wished to do something through which I would expose my mother to shame, for all to see, just as she had exposed me to my whole (rather new) class of school-children. But I would overcome my pain and disgrace actively by telling my tale rather than being a passive victim. And in so doing I would place the blame where it is due! I did not follow my first impulse, to stop with the paper. For I knew that an additional stretch of self-analysis would enable me to alter the tone and style of this paper by using my vengefully motivated insights, but relegating that motive to a less prominent place because it is better understood and integrated.

I have not altered this paper. With further processing I have gradually become more in touch with the child within me, the child to whom the shock of awareness, the accompanying shame and guilt – and the vengeful intentions – belonged. Going through these early childhood experiences once again, I could be more in touch not only with my own distress as a little girl but also with my mother's, and now better tolerate and accept her imperfections and my own doubts about her. Inner processing such as I have undertaken, motivated as it was by genuine distress, has led to greater tolerance towards the child within and to progress in acceptance and integration of those aspects of the internalized 'good' and 'bad' mother that are still unintegrated. Thus, what I might otherwise have thrown out in shock, shame and guilt I can now offer to my readers, being fully aware that remnants of vengefulness, punishment through self-exposure and other motives unacceptable to my adult conscience, may still be mildly active in the deed.

It is my stance that has changed. And it is with delight that I have come to realize, and could only now come to realize, that a rare opportunity has come my way in the process of writing this paper. For I have inadvertently, 'before your very eyes', while creating a text – and this time an analysis of a textual analysis – reached an unanticipated inner realization. This has driven me to a stretch of self-analysis, which has affected my self-experience and, in turn, the direction and fate of my text. That such processes exist, and can be reciprocally enriching, for both text and self – is the main thesis of this paper!

But while such processes can lead to an examination of one's inner world, and one's work, unless one persists in working through the difficulties encountered, they can also impede or – as almost happened in my case – even entirely hold up writing. It is not unknown that people tear up many months' work in disgust, or put it away, never to be completed. Yet it is also true that one may return to work that was put away and out of mind for a while and fare better with it then. It is not always necessary or even worthwhile, in terms of time and energies required, to undertake, as I have done, a piece of self-analysis related to one's work, in order to recognize blind spots, overvaluations or misrepresentations of particular points one has made, or even in order to get over a writing block. I have presented my own case in order to demonstrate that there are interactions between writing and unconscious processes and that these may be revealable through self-analysis.

What I hope to offer through this demonstration is a general *procedure for investigating* such interactions, for I believe that such phenomena deserve the careful attention of psychoanalysts, and not only where our analysands are concerned. Further, while we can learn a great deal about the processes involved during sessions, when they are worked on and through during the therapeutic process, such observations have their limitations. There is the need to respect confidentiality, the fact that records of sessions are inevitably incomplete, and lack accuracy even if they are written down or tape-recorded (procedures which, in any case, I would not recommend) – in addition to the truism that a great deal remains implicit and the analysands' statements will always be partially opaque (Spence 1982). The procedure which I have tried to open up here is therefore a complementary method for investigating, using psychoanalysts as object and subject. For the analyst's own notes and drafts are records preserved exactly as originally made and are more directly accessible in terms of their implied meanings than the associations of our analysands. (I have endeavoured to illustrate this in the elaborations on my own notes, which I put in brackets.)[3] Combined with self-analysis, for which our training, experience and interest make us particularly well suited, psychoanalysts could, I believe, offer a body of data and findings not otherwise obtainable.

My presentation has been concerned throughout with ways in which textual and related self-analysis, *whose aims and methods differ*, may interact and even entirely overlap in terms of their *products* – a 'narrative' in either case. This has sometimes led psychoanalysts to apply aims and methods appropriate for textual analysis in their clinical therapeutic work or in self-analysis; it has led to even greater confusion among non-professionals, who often assume that the aims or methods of work in self-analysis or with analysands are the same as those brought to bear in textual analysis. Unless it is one's own, one cannot do a self-analysis directly from a text. Recollections or dreams, on the other hand, lend themselves to *both* self- and textual analysis. There is no distinction in principle to my mind between a psychoanalytically oriented textual analysis of literary texts, communal tales or such personal material as recollections, reconstructions, dreams or phantasies. The aims of all such analyses are similar: to further an understanding of the psychodynamics of the characters or behaviours presented. But while many psychoanalytically oriented literary analyses offer primarily paradigms of characters and of behaviour – beginning with Freud's Oedipus (1955 [1900]) and recently, for example, Green (1982), Nevo (1985) and Segal (1987) – many analyses of private texts primarily aim at unravelling the psychodynamics of a particular person. Because this distinction is essential for my presentation, I shall try to make it as explicit as I can by returning to my illustrations.

Though unconsciously inspired by personal preoccupations related to the tale of Little Red Riding Hood, my intention in the analysis of her denial was to interpret *her* (not my) behaviour. Motivated by intellectual curiosity, I was in fact expanding on Anna Freud's (1936) hypothesis regarding 'denial in word and act' and testing its applicability. In the process of examining various aspects of Little Red Riding Hood's behaviour, I had even subjected my own personal experience with the *Tümmel* to that purpose. My narrative regarding Little Red Riding Hood's denials (and I have only presented a section of that narrative here) emerged following a process of exciting discoveries of various signs in the text which gradually built, in my judgement, into a coherent, consistent and quite comprehensive interpretation of certain aspects of her behaviour. The purpose and methods in my self-analysis were, however, quite different.

The analysis of my *Tümmel* tale was motivated by the feeling of great emotional discomfort upon discovering that it was not simply the lovely tale that it had consciously been for so many years. As my aim was to come to grips with whatever it was that I had not previously faced in relation to that experience, I did not, and could not know, the direction in which my inner exploration would lead me. In this case, therefore, I was associating, rather than looking for signs. And while I can look for signs in any direction I choose, the more unselective my associations, the less choice and control I have over the thoughts and emotions that emerge. For example, following the realization that it was related to my *Körbchen* tale, my feeling of puzzlement regarding the question-mark in my reconstruction of *Little Red Riding Hood* had changed into upset and pain. Such feelings were not unfamiliar in the context of that recollection, although this time they were more poignant and focal – and I aimed to resolve them. If then I, let alone someone not emotionally involved in my tales, were to examine them as *texts*, we would soon recognize parallels between them, and might even reach, through numerous signs in them, a narrative not very different from that which I eventually constructed. But the route would be quite different: *I* had made *no* connection between my two childhood experiences for a considerable time. As a matter of fact, I became preoccupied with my *Tümmel* experience – first, the thoughts and feelings about and around my experience wandering in and out of my consciousness, hitting me emotionally one way and another, and then new closures and insights occurring from time to time. It was only after a few days of a 'mental block' that the *Körbchen* memory came to mind, and even later, after a very intensive preoccupation with it, that my further insight (the meaning of the question-mark for me) followed. There was a considerable period of working through before I began to see (albeit the realization dawned on me suddenly and felt like an immense discovery) that the two experiences were connected, even intertwined, in my inner world.

Thus also, if my personal tales were treated as texts, they could be expanded around the theme of my 'internalized mother' and my responses to her, in a way that would make good narrative sense by commonly accepted criteria. They could help the *analyser understand* something about my psychodynamics, and it could then be 'explained' to me, or if I were that analyser, I might then understand more about myself. But while such a narrative might make good sense to me, without the inner processing it would not affect my self-experience in anywhere near the way that self-analysis does. (If I were in psychoanalysis proper while the tales were coming up, an appropriately tuned analyst might help me along my path if he did not offer me his ready-made narrative on a platter. This complex analytical task has been variously described, e.g. by Arlow 1980, Schafer 1983, Hrushovski-Moses 1985).

Returning to my two childhood tales, it should be evident from what I have said thus far that I do not have the freedom in self-analysis (nor could I in a parallel situation with my analysands) to pursue any aspect of the tales that I might chose. It is whatever emerges, unselectively, that is its product. At the time of my self-analysis I could of course see that personal issues, other than that regarding my internalized mother, were probably hidden in these tales. Indeed, in the process of that analysis I did wander in and out of some of these issues.[4] But they were not at the focus of what was occurring to me at the time, nor of my feelings. In other words, turning to them then because they might make a good narrative would not at all have served my personal aims. On the other hand, had I, or anyone else trained in such an undertaking, treated my personal tales as texts, I (or they) would have had the freedom to pursue various aspects and might have attempted (on the basis of various signs in the texts) to construct a range of narratives, for example around 'my' curiosity, 'my' feeling of emptiness and being filled, indeed, 'my' penis envy: the 'empty basket', my mother who 'inadequately equipped' me, my brother who, after all, got his 'carrots'. Yet, while such psychoanalytically oriented constructions might make good narrative sense, expand the texts, even offer some prototypes of human behaviour – and while such narratives *might* even describe aspects of my psychodynamics, more or less accurately – they would not serve the same purpose as inner processing. For in order for any narrative to become part of the self-experience, one must first be in touch with its emotive specificity and meanings for oneself; the meanings of private metaphors (Arlow 1979) – such as the 'wolf', 'empty basket', 'carrots', and so on – must emerge and become connected.

Finally, the *interactions* as well as the distinctions that I have drawn between textual and self-analysis, lead to a particularly intriguing question: in what sense, and in what ways, can there be interactions between the two types of analyses when one conducts a textual analysis on a personal text? But this is a subject for another discussion.

Notes

1   I would like to thank Dr Erich Gumbel for his fruitful comments on an earlier version of this paper. The research quoted in this paper was made possible with the aid of a grant from the Sturman Center for Human Development of the Hebrew University of Jerusalem.
2   Further expansions on these and other associative links appear in Eifermann (1985, 1987b, c, d).
3   Spence (1982) refers to such elaborations, in clinical reporting, as 'naturalizing' a text.

4 In 'proper' analysis the analyst would recognize in some of these moves aspects of resistance and could then help me remain with the issues I had brought up (Eifermann 1987b).

References

Arlow, Jacob A. (1979) 'Metaphor and the psychoanalytic situation', *Psychoanalytic Quarterly*, 48, 363–85.
—(1980) 'The genesis of interpretation', in Blum H. P. (ed.) *Psychoanalytic Explorations of Technique: Discourse on the Theory of Therapy*, New York, International Universities Press.
Bar-Giora, Rami (1985) 'Lullabies and the psychology of parenthood: a psychoanalytic contribution to the understanding of a problem in the first literary text in the child's life', paper presented at conference on 'Discourse in Psychoanalysis, Literature and the Arts', Jerusalem.
Bettelheim, Bruno (1976) *The Uses of Enchantment*, New York, Knopf.
Eifermann, Rivka R. (1985) 'Teaching psychoanalysis to non-analytical students through work on their own dreams', *Psychoanalysis in Europe*, 22, 38–45.
—(1987a) 'Varieties of denial: the case of a fairy tale', in Edelstein, E. (ed.) *Denial*, New York, Plenum.
—(1987b) 'Fairy tales – a royal road to the child within the adult', *Scandinavian Review of Psychoanalysis*. Also in German, in Storle, J. (ed.) *Das Märchen – Ein Märchen? Psychoanalytische Betrachtung zu Wesen, Deutung und Wirkung der Märchen*, Stuttgart-Bad Constatt, Fromm-Holzboog.
—(1987c) '"Germany" and "the Germans": acting out fantasies and their discovery in self-analysis', *International Review of Psychoanalysis*, 2. Also in German: *Jahrbuch der Psychoanalyse*.
—(1987d) 'Children's games, observed and experienced', *Psychoanalytic Study of the Child*, 42.
Freud, Anna (1936) *The Ego and the Mechanisms of Defence*, London, Hogarth Press.
Freud, Sigmund (1955) [1900] *The Interpretation of Dreams*, in *The Standard Edition of the Complete Psychological Works*, London, Hogarth Press, vols 4 and 5.
Green, André (1979) *The Tragic Effect*, Cambridge, Cambridge University Press.
Grimm, J. and W. (1949) [1819] *Kinder- und Hausmärchen*, Munich, Winkler Verlag.
Holland, Norman N. (1975) *Five Readers Reading*, New Haven, Conn., Yale University Press.
Hrushovski-Moses, Rena (1985) 'Discussion of the paper "Past and present in interpretation" by E. Torras de Beà and J. Rallo Romero', *Psychoanalysis in Europe*, 25, 15–24.

Nevo, Ruth (1985) 'The perils of Pericles', paper presented in a seminar on 'Discourse in Literature, the Arts and Psychoanalysis', at the Center of Literary Studies, the Hebrew University, Jerusalem.

Omer, Dvora (ed. and trans.) (1978) *Fairy Tales of the Magical Palace: A Selection of the Brothers Grimm Tales*, Tel-Aviv, Joseph Schreberk (in Hebrew).

Segal, Ora (1987) 'Joyce's interpretation of dreams', *Hebrew University Studies in Literature and the Arts*, 14, 106–33.

Schafer, Roy (1983) *The Analytic Attitude*, London, Hogarth Press.

Shanon, B. and Eifermann, Rivka (1984) 'Dream-reporting discourse', *Text*, 4, 369–79.

Spence, Donald P. (1982) *Narrative Truth and Historical Truth: Meaning and Interpretation in Psychoanalysis*, New York, Norton.

4

Myth *à la lettre*: Freud, Mann, Genesis and Rembrandt, and the story of the son

MIEKE BAL

'The universal story of the Chaste Youth and the Lustful Stepmother is best known to Western readers in the Biblical account of Joseph's temptation by the wife of Potiphar and in the Greek myth (later embodied in drama) about Hippolytus and Phaedra'; thus begins an article by John Yohannan on Thomas Mann's version of this 'universal story' (Yohannan 1982). Although Yohannan is well aware of the difference between the innumerable 'versions' and traditions, as his earlier book shows (1968), there is no sign of awareness of the scholar's own projections in the very enterprise of his paper. Indeed, the terms in which *myth* in literature has been discussed are terms denoting *eternity* and *truth*, *similarity* and *imitation*, and the term that summarizes these features, 'universal', does appear in Yohannan's first sentence.

Taking the universality of the *story* for granted, the author detaches Mann's text from its discursive contingency. Symptomatic of this move is the very word *story* in Yohannan's title: 'Hebraism and Hellinism in Thomas Mann's Story of Joseph and Potiphar's Wife'. Mann never wrote such a story; perhaps he used one. What he wrote was a voluminous novel of over 1200 pages in which he dealt with what he described as 'only an episode, if an important one, in the life of Jacob's son' (Mann 1984, p. 987). Mann's explicit metatextual polemics (e.g. see pp. 667, 816, 987) and, more importantly, the very choice of a Hebrew myth at the historical moment he wrote the novel, make the attempt, inherent to myth-criticism, to insert the text as another *case* in either tradition of a 'universal content' both misplaced and futile: it says precisely nothing about the book, and what it tries to say is false. There can be no question of trying to deal with the novel as a removal from the historical reality of the day, as many scholars have done (e.g. see Apter 1978); if Mann's novel has a mythical flavour, it can only be accounted for *within* its overall metatextual discussion, which has, as one of its most striking features, a questioning of myth itself, of the tradition of this Joseph-myth, of timelessness and history, of other versions including the Arabic one (Mann 1984, p. 987) and of the ideology of the myth the author deals with. The latter critique is explicitly announced in the Foreword to the novel, where Mann states:

> *Joseph in Egypt* seems to me unquestionably the artistic zenith of the work, if only on account of the humane vindication that I had undertaken in it, the humanization of the figure of Potiphar's wife, the mournful story of her passionate love of the Canaanite major-domo and her *pro forma* husband.
>
> (p. xi)

There is much to be said, indeed, for Mann's claim that this ideological stance has led to artistic mastery, and this is certainly not a coincidence. I will give an example of this assumption later. For the moment, I am interested in Mann's use of the term 'story'. As opposed to Yohannan, he is not referring here to some universal, stable, fixed-for-ever content that can only become discursively different but will still remain the same. He is referring to his own, specific account which he provides with the telling adjective 'mournful' and in which he includes the basically absent character Potiphar himself. By writing about him, including his presence in the story, he signifies his absence differently, elsewhere: in the adjective *'pro forma'* that goes with 'husband'. As a husband, Potiphar is only a signifier, an empty form, and it is the absence of the signified that triggers the story and makes it 'mournful'.

However, if Yohannan uses the word in a different sense, he cannot but be trapped by his own discourse, for the power of the individual over language is limited, and the word 'story' does imply the feature that Mann more readily assumes. For Yohannan, too, privatizes what he believes to be universal. The innocence of the youth is taken for granted, which is not the case in Mann's account. The same holds for the lustfulness of the female character. Calling her a *stepmother*, Yohannan wilfully deviates from the very case he is interested in, for there is no stepmother involved with Joseph – unless one interprets the biblical story as a myth of incest, something that psychoanalysis justifies one to do. But that proves my case rather than contradicting it: the 'universal story' becomes a story of the nuclear family, but then there is no 'chaste' youth any more. The Oedipal youth is not innocent. In other words, Yohannan starts where he should end; taking for granted a certain interpretation of the biblical story, he checks the possibility of interpreting the episode in Mann's novel, where, indeed, Joseph's innocence is as doubtful as the woman's guilt.

There is nothing wrong with Yohannan's study that is not inherently wrong with myth-criticism in general (e.g. Kirk 1972, Vickery 1966). Barthes said long ago that the 'very end of myth is to immobilize the world' (Barthes 1972, p. 155), and according to Rahv the same holds for myth-criticism (Rahv 1966, pp. 109–18). The interest in myth is, according to Rahv, a persistence of romanticism and conservatism occasioned by the fear of history and freedom, of change and making choices, and he concludes: 'the craze for myth is the fear of history' (p. 114). This persistence of the object of study in its approach is quite general; it is clear, for example, in structuralist approaches to myth, like Lévi-Strauss's statement that a myth consists of all its versions (Lévi-Strauss 1963, p. 217), which allows him to proceed to the analysis of what these versions have in common. Edmund Leach, one of Lévi-Strauss's followers in biblical analysis, defends this view in 1983 and refers to any attempt at rehistoricizing and specifying the discursive situation of the texts as 'unscrambling the omelette'. Leach's claim, derived from Malinowski's functionalist view that myths function as charters for social actions, should logically lead to a study of the historical position of myths (Malinowski 1926), but this is not what Leach deduces from it. In myth-criticism as in the structural study of myth, a myth is a myth because, under the layers of dust of historically changing signifiers, it remains the same signifier-independent signified, a universal story. The relationship between myth thus viewed and the concept of collective unconscious is more or less taken for granted. The expression matters only as a symptom of its content, and variation matters only as evidence of similarity. No wonder today's psychocritics rarely bother to study myth for its own sake.

Recent developments in narratology (Felman 1981, Brooks 1984) may help to shed new light on the problem. This 'American narratology' has as its main features a psychoanalytic frame of reference, a priority to discourse and plot as one and the same thing, and a dynamic view of narrative, while historical awareness is frequently thematized. The obvious example is Peter Brooks's characterization of the nineteenth-century novel as structured – that is, within the dynamic view, motivated – by ambition. The idea takes the convincing shape it has in Brooks's analysis of Balzac's *La Peau de chagrin* when it is rephrased in terms like desire, death drive and object choice, all pointing at activities that find their counterparts in narrative dynamic itself. It can gain more interest from the specification proposed by Pavel (1984). It is certainly not a coincidence that psychocritics today mould their view in a narratological – that is in an identifiable and historically specific – discourse. As opposed to early analytic readings, modern critical discourse is only acceptable when its concepts are anchored in the literary discourse itself: concepts like desire as a drive of the plot are acceptable when we have at our disposal, while 'reading for' it, episodes and details that serve as their signifiers.

Although psychocritics have perhaps taken too much for granted that their approach signals the overcoming of formalist narratology, they have made a convincing case for an approach that accounts for narrative as dynamic, and this approach seems to be the appropriate framework in which the concept of myth can be renewed. Renewed it should be, by taking it *and* its object *à la lettre*, as discourse and as symptom.

Myth and transference

The idea of myth in myth-critical discourse has the attraction of truth. Susan Langer, in a statement that is common to myth-criticism, put it in a characteristic way: 'Myths are not bound to any particular words, nor even to language, but may be told or painted, acted or danced, *without suffering degradation or distortion*' (Langer 1953, p. 160; my emphasis). The overall negativity of this statement that describes myth by what it is not, obliterates the difference between the first and the second part of the sentence. Whereas we can agree on the first part, which detaches myths from a definite signifying system, the second part has to be rejected since it implies a positive signified which can suffer damage but can also

remain undamaged. What Rahv described as the fear of history
(Rahv 1966, p. 114) is in Langer's statement quite close to the fear
of the signifier, and, indeed, historicity and discursivity are part of
the same problem. The shifting signifier, inaccessible and versatile,
is as frightening as is the presence of the subject of/in the myth. If
meaning is unstable, it is because of the very split between the
subject that tells the story about itself and the subject it tells about.
The attraction of myth is that its universalism allows the
concealment of this split. The split necessitates eternity, objectivity
and universality in order to help the subject to get rid of time, space
and itself. The idea of myth allows this illusion to be entertained.

If Langer thinks the change of signifying system does not
'distort' myths, it is because there is nothing that can be distorted.
Thus conceived, myth cannot be defined but as an empty screen, a
structure that appeals to the individual subject because of its
pseudo-stability, which helps overcome the feeling of contingency.

In her contribution to a recent issue of *Poetics* on *Psychopoetics*,
Jane Gallop (1984) differentiates a number of things relevant for
our discussion. Commenting on Lacan's comment on Buffon's
statement 'le style, c'est l'homme même', Gallop insists on the
difference between the spirit and the letter, as between the
(American) Humanities and the (French) Letters; as between *man*
and the *other* as the possible content of psychoanalysis; as, could we
now add, between myth as pseudo-transhistorical content and
myth as discourse. A concept of myth according to the 'Humanities' is to be replaced by a concept of myth according to the
'Letters'. Gallop's view is based on Felman's introduction to the
special issue of *Yale French Studies* (1977), where the latter defines
the relation between text and interpretation, or between literary
and scholarly texts for that matter, as non-hierarchical, both in
time and in authority. Felman's brilliant practice of her own view
in *Le Scandale du corps parlant* (1980) shows not only the relevance of
her idea but also the close relation between language and myth.
Her analysis of the theories of speech-acts and the myth of Don
Juan as the *mise en scène* of the paradigmatic speech-act of the
promise, is, indeed, most promising.

Transference is the key-word in Gallop's account of Felman's
point. Interpretation is always an exercise of power; transference is
the structuration of the authority relation; to analyse transference
is to unmask that structuration, to interrupt its efficient operation

(Gallop 1984, pp. 305–6). Analysing the relation of transference displaces the position of the patient from the text onto the critic/reader, and interpretation becomes, then, self-criticism. The text does not become the analyst – neither does, in transference, the analyst – but it occupies, at times, the place of the empty screen, *place tout court*. At other times it occupies the other position with which the first is constantly in dialectic exchange: that of the transferring, projecting patient. Since texts are always also responses to other texts, they cannot but share with the critic/reader the same relation of transference, from which the reader/critic cannot separate him/herself.

The relation between myth and literature is as problematic as the one between phantasy and primal phantasy. On the one hand, myth is a subcategory of literature; on the other hand, it is a more general form of it – Langer *dixit*. If we agree with Lévi-Strauss (1963) that a myth consists of all its versions, we should take the statement to its consequence: there is no myth 'underneath' these versions, there is no myth other than each version, each representation, just as, as we shall see, there is no primal phantasy less personal and less narrative than any other phantasy. The difference between myth and literary text, like that between primal and other phantasies, is to be situated on the level of the transferring subject and its relation to it. The *illusion* of the stable signified allows the user of a myth to project more freely on the screen. But what she/he takes to be a signified, functions as a signifier: a material support borrowed from language – a *letter*. It has no meaning, but it supports meaning, providing the subject's projection with a means to get rid of its subjectivity and thereby grant subjective projections universal status. Therein lies the *interest* in the Habermasian sense of both myth and myth criticism for subjects of sorts (Habermas 1972), including psychocritics.

In the following pages the discourse on myth and the discourse of myth will be analysed as if they were the same discourse. I will expose my reactions to five discursive units, each with a different relation to myth: the scholarly discourse of psychoanalysis on myth; Freud's own mythical discourse; a modern novel by Thomas Mann, with explicit myth-critical intentions, in interaction with a text that Mann and many others have used as source-myth, Genesis 39; and Rembrandt's etching, presumably also based on Genesis 39. The hypothesis of transference and the non-mastery it implies frees the theoretical text from the constraints its status places upon it. If anything, it becomes, through that analysis, more interesting – more lively, literary, narrative. Through this analysis I will slowly and dialectically elaborate my point. That point is that such a dynamic and literary comment can provide a more explicative account of the mythical process than the current approaches can ever lead to.

Myth and psychoanalytic discourse

'Myth' is not a psychoanalytic term. Although the word occurs frequently in psychoanalytic publications, it is never explicitly defined for its own sake. There is no entry on myth in that paradigmatic sample of psychoanalytic discourse, Laplanche and Pontalis' *The Language of Psychoanalysis* (1980). The features it has when used self-evidently, relate it axiomatically to concepts like phantasy. With the latter, it shares connotations of subjectivity, that is of untruth and personal input, projection, identification and the like. At the same time, it has relations, via its universal character, with the more specific concept of *primal* phantasy, with which it then shares connotations of original truth, phylogenesis, transhistoricity and the collective unconscious.

The Freudian concepts of phantasy and primal phantasy as defined in Laplanche and Pontalis' dictionary have, however, perhaps less in common than in contrast. It is in the space left by the tension between these two basic psychoanalytic concepts that the status of the concept of myth as written and unwritten, signified but not defined, can be situated. Between writing and discourse, implicit concepts have no *letter*; they have no such 'essentially localised structure of the signifier' as Lacan defines the letter in his major essay on the letter in which he advises us to take Freudian concepts *à la lettre* (Lacan 1966, p. 259). The concept of *myth*, indeed, has no such letter, in that it has no place in Laplanche and Pontalis' alphabetically ordered series of letters, of concepts placed by letter. On the other hand, it does have letters in the sense of 'material supports which the concrete discourse borrows from language' (Lacan 1966, p. 254), since its signifiers of sorts haunt the analytic text. The conspicuous discursive *lack* in a dictionary, a text which is based on the all-importance of the *definition* as the beginning of discourse on the concept, is symptomatic. The very concept whose use is based on the assumption of universality has no such beginning in the scholarly text. This double absence, then, becomes the *letter* of the concept, its material support by antithesis, its primal signifier. We don't need to take this signifier as referring *only* to its place in the field of the concept that has no origin. It does point, at the same time, to an absence, not of origin but of articulation, hence it is dissolved in related concepts that adopt it. In order to articulate it, then, we must give it a beginning, borrowed from the language of these related concepts.

The following definitions constitute the first piece of discourse to be analysed:

> *Phantasy*: Imaginary *scene* in which the subject is a *protagonist*, representing the fulfilment of a wish (in the last analysis, an unconscious wish) in a manner that is *distorted* to a greater or lesser extent by defensive processes.
>
> (Laplanche and Pontalis 1980, p. 314; my emphasis)

> *Primal phantasy*: *Typical* phantasy *structures* (intra-uterine existence, primal scene, castration, seduction) which psychoanalysis *reveals* to be responsible for the *organisation* of *phantasy life*, *regardless* of the *personal experience* of different subjects; according to Freud, the *universality* of these phantasies is *explained* by the *fact* that they constitute a phylogenetically transmitted *inheritance*.
>
> (p. 331; my emphasis)

Being a narratologist and, for unknown reasons, fond of logical thinking, my reactions to these definitions are the following. The two concepts stand in a relation of specification, hence of implication. Logically, the definition of the first, more general term, 'phantasy', holds also for the second, which is one of its specifications. Surprisingly, the two definitions are both different and to some extent mutually exclusive.

The definition of phantasy has the narratological notions of scene, protagonist and subject. The latter term refers to the split, typical of any autobiographical discourse, between the subject *of* and *in* the phantasy. This eccentricity phantasy shares with both language and representation. It is particularly acute in so-called first-person narrative, but equally, via the concept of projection and that of phantasy itself, in all narrative. Narrative is even *the* type of discourse where *différance* is generally thematized – a feature which allows conceptual reversals like Brooks's junction of 'the narrative of desire' and 'the desire of narrative' (Brooks 1984, p. 37). The double teleology implied in the phrase 'representing the fulfilment of a wish' enhances the new narratology flavour of the definition: both representation and wish coincide in a satisfactory ending. The term 'scene' implies both a plot and its staging, its *mise en scène*. 'Imaginary' and 'distorted' enhance the fictional status of the scene, which makes it still more narrative, in the sense that in English, narrative and fiction are synonymical expressions (Rimmon-Kenan 1983). Note that the distortion, according to syntax, refers to the *manner* of representation, not to the wish or its fulfilment. In other words, the agent of distortion is the focalizor, not the protagonist.

The definition of 'primal phantasy' is quite different in tone. Its beginning is much more static and metalinguistic. If phantasy is a scene, primal phantasy is its structure; if phantasy is literary discourse, primal phantasy is critical discourse. More importantly, the subject, enhanced in the first definition, is disposed of in the second one. The primal phantasy is described in a positivistic discourse which is characterized by the attempt to do away with subjectivity at the cost of personification: primal phantasy is 'responsible' for something that happens to the life of the subject, but 'regardless' of the latter's experience. In terms of the first definition, we could venture that the definition, here, reveals an attempt to get rid of the double subject by elimination of the focalizor who, as the subject of experience, would be capable of bridging the gap between the subject of the unconscious discourse – the scene – and the protagonist. The universality implied in this separation between phantasy and subject, between scene and representation – including distortion – is not argued, not even stated, but *explained*. Its existence, its truth, is taken for granted by the assertion that it is in need of explanation – which indeed it is, but on a different, conceptual level.

Narrativity comes in focus at the end of the definition, precisely when the explanation is given. Hence, narrativity receives an altogether different place here. The phrase 'phylogenetically trans- mitted inheritance' introduces a plot, a dynamic aspect, and two fallacies. The first one consists of the so-called 'third-person narrative', which is the very attempt to get rid of the split between subject and protagonist by eliminating the former, thus breaking with the latter, who becomes the 'third person', radically inac- cessible; the word 'fact' symptomatizes this *objective fallacy* that implies attitudes close to positivism, objectivism and mythical thinking as it is displayed by myth-criticism itself. The second fallacy is the *narrative fallacy* that consists of replacing explanation with story. These two fallacies are needed in order to fit the second definition within the first, while they are not consistent as a set. If phantasy is a *distorted manner of representation of a wish fulfilment*, each embedded verb implying an agent/subject, how can one of its sub-types be universal? If the one is a scene, so must be the other; if the one requires a subject as its discursive agent, how can the other be 'inherited'? The answer provided by the two fallacies is that it can only be on the level of representation, *in casu*, through the idea of primal phantasy itself. That is why narrativity, in the second definition, came in on the metanarrative level.

We now come to grasp why 'myth' needs no definition – indeed, cannot afford definition. It is because it is the paradox itself in which the Freudian argument is caught which tries to explain *structures* by *stories*, or to use Thomas Pavel's terms, to replace *articulation* with *origin* (Pavel 1984), and the inherent subjectivity with the pseudo-objectivity of the 'scientific myth' of phylogenetic explanation/beginning. The replacement of (logical) articulation by (non-falsifiable) origin is an attempt to impose, on notions that are alien to it, a family structure. Ideas, phantasies, get a father and become *sons*.

The conflict between universalism and historicity is thus *staged* (*mise en scène*) in this 'explanation': the utmost universality *is*, in this view, the utmost historicality, via the implicit argument that assumes that the further removed from the present, the older, the truer the story is and the more general its range of application. Within this line of thought, origin counters, replaces articulation. This is exactly how mythical thinking functions. The basic message of myths in this thought is: what *I* think (phantasies, wishfully distorted) *is* the truth *because* it has always been so. The authority of age becomes the historical projection of the un-willingness to assume the historicality of the *I*'s wishes.

Freud's story of the sons

In this respect, there is no more revealing myth, no better case of a primal phantasy *and* of an autobiographical statement, hence no more convincing case of the site of the concept of myth in the space between the phantasy and the primal phantasy of Laplanche and Pontalis' dictionary, than the evocation of the primitive horde and the murder of the father in *Totem and Taboo* (Freud 1946 [1914]; see Appendix 1 at the end of this chapter). The discourse that generates this myth has conspicuous features of both definitions I have analysed above. On the one hand, the myth is veiled by scientific discourse. The subject of the phantasy is hiding behind predecessors, anthropologists who came up with the idea of a primitive patriarchal horde. But this disclaimer of subjectivity is countered by the claim to originality, when Freud corrects and extends the view of the authority, thus assuming subjectivity.

The conflict is *mise en abyme* in the opening sentence of the personal version which is at the same time the outcome, catastrophe and *end* of the whole myth. Freud intervenes with his magic explanation only at the end, when the authority of the predecessor must be replaced with his own. Significantly, the sentence which reveals the origin and truth is surprisingly short. It is provided with an enigmatic footnote: 'One day the expelled brothers joined forces, slew and ate the father, and thus put an end to the father horde' (Freud 1946, p. 183). The passage ends with another footnote referring to another authority whose account of the *same act* is quoted. The difference between Freud's and Atkinson's account is a temporal aspect: whereas Atkinson represents it as a durative act ('combined attacks, renewed again and again') Freud's contribution to the discussion amounts to the turning of this durative act into a *singular event*. No wonder he uses the fairy-tale convention of 'one day' whereas, at the same time, trying to avoid the 'erroneous impression which this exposition may call forth by taking into consideration the concluding sentence of the subsequent chapter'.

There is, again, ambiguity in the use of the spiritual paternity. Freud claims *and* disclaims for this story, which is his most crazy, most creative phantasy, the authority of storytellers like Darwin and Fraser. This was meant to be the most universal story, but in fact it is the most personal one Freud has ever 'revealed'. His use of sources completes the picture. Darwin and Fraser, and Atkinson for that matter, have in common the contamination of their discourse (as quoted by Freud) by their object of study, and the confusion of historical and analogical reasoning. The discursive devices used in this passage – and in the whole book – are borrowed not only from the convention of the fairy tale but also from that of the eighteenth-century fictional novel, where the device of claiming reliable sources has come to signify fictionality.

Indeed, the chapter opens with a sentence that stages the

focalizor whose position Freud wants his readers to share: '*Let us* now *envisage* the *scene* of such a totem meal and *let us embellish* it further with a few probable features which could not be adequately considered before' (p. 181; my emphases). The sentence displays discursive features that embed the definition of the primal phantasy into that of phantasy in general. The plural *and* first-person subject ('us') transfers onto the first definition discussed above, the universality of the second, a move that reconciles it with the first definition's basic subjectivity. Invited to partake in the feast, we become protagonists of the scene *and* focalizors capable of embellishing it according to our personal needs, and hence capable of introducing 'distortions' in the manner of representation. Freud's discourse of this founding myth of the origin of all the myths he is interested in becomes the paradigmatic case of mythical discourse, where phantasy and primal phantasy come together in a pseudo-historical escape from history. Utterly mythical and utterly personal, Freud's father murder scene becomes the myth of myth: *myth-en-abyme*.

Mann's myth versus Man's myth

The relation, or the distinction, between *myth* and *myth-criticism* can be clarified by an examination of the case of Thomas Mann. Thomas Mann's explicit claim that he has attempted to humanize Potiphar's wife in his novel, amounts to a disclaimer. His polemic against the tradition that condemns the woman in the story of Genesis 39 and, through the typically mythical universalistic twist, women in general, is also a reaction to the function of transference implied in the myth. 'Re'-writing a myth is compulsory transference. As Mann complained, the biblical meagre 'what' was lacking the 'how' and the 'why': life's circumstantiality was missing (see Yohannan 1982, p. 431). But this complaint would seem ill-grounded if we take the biblical account at its letter. The proportion between 'life's circumstantiality' and the 'factual' *event* is as unequal as in Mann's novel itself. The chapter in Genesis is characterized in the first place by the amount of circumstantial clauses that literally circumscribe the event, which is, after a long preparation, presented in a few single sentences. The dialectic between the singular and the durative that we have seen at work in the Freudian mythical text is overwhelmed, enclosed, by a predominance of speech events. The latter, as opposed to the former, are not durative but repetitive, narratologically in that they are narrated several times while they occur several times; stylistically in that the declarative verb is repeated in each case, a feature typical of biblical Hebrew but nevertheless functional here in a more specific sense as well.

If Mann reacts to the missing circumstantiality in the Genesis text, then is this not because of a specific aspect of 'life', the one he explicitly claims to be interested in, the woman's subjectivity that is? Indeed, juxtaposing her to the men, to Joseph and to her '*pro forma* husband', Mann transposes a preoccupation of his own onto the screen provided by the biblical story. From the very beginning of this exceedingly long novel, Joseph is presented as a sexually ambivalent character. The first scene represents him daydreaming at night, phantasizing in the moonlight: 'a youth famed for his charm and charming especially by right from his mother, who had been sweet and lovely like the moon when it is full and like Ishtar's star when it swims mildly in the clear sky' (Mann 1984, p. 4). We don't need to guess whether the sometimes explicit femininity of Joseph is Mann's response to the phrase 'and he was beautiful of appearance and beautiful of face' (Genesis 39:6); Mann extensively discusses his view that the relation between beauty and femininity is a subjective association confirmed by intersubjective agreement: 'Joseph, moreover, as he *knew himself*, and as *everybody told him*, was both beautiful and well-favoured – a condition which *certainly* embraces a *consciousness* of femininity' (p. 48; my emphases). The episode with Potiphar's wife is, as Mann claims, an integrated part of Joseph's life, and therefore there is no limit to the projection of features of the ambiguous youth whose status as the 'true son of Jacob' is defined by his very ambiguity, by being an exceedingly attractive man confronting desire in and *as* the other.

Wherever Mann is polemically or otherwise *discussing* the mythical traditions – the Greek, the Arabic, as well as the Hebrew texts that represent the screen – he is not *transferring* onto it but deconstructing the transferences displayed by others. There is no point, then, in taking the entire episode, as it is represented in the novel, as another myth. Much of it amounts to myth-criticism. But Mann cannot escape the mythical dynamics which he tries to undo by replacing it with his conscious preoccupations. He represents an excessively narcissistic Joseph, guilty of *hubris*, too confident in his capacity to defend his somewhat unmotivated chastity. The strangest feature of this character seems to me to be the fact that he loses his charms as soon as he is socially accomplished. Once viceroy of Egypt, he becomes fat, physically middle-aged, pleased with himself, sure of his power. Something must have gone wrong in-between. Indeed, he has lost his ambiguity and the double attraction it guaranteed. Not only all women desired him, but all men as well, including the 'jealous creator and lord, insistent upon sole possession' to whom Joseph's chastity is due. What made the young Joseph so very special was his status as the 'true son', who was identified with his mother and hence the unique love-object of his father. The competition between father and mother, male and female lovers who struggle for the possession of his beauty, is won by the father, or rather, is given up to the fatherly position. Joseph's story ends when he loses his son-ship. He stops being loved by the father when he becomes one himself.

Arguing against the universalistic fallacy of myth-criticism that leads to hatred against women in love, Mann makes his Joseph represent an attempt at a different kind of universality: that which arises when the limits between subjects are suspended. The general recognition of his lovability questions the limits between the self and the others. Being man and woman, loved by men and women, he becomes the screen onto which the other characters project their most problematic feelings. The most characteristic scene in this sense is the generalized defloration-scene (see Appendix 2) that takes place before the famous bed-scene. It represents a case of the junction of artistic and ideological quality. In this talkative text the character of the woman lacks words. Mut-em-enet is pressed by her female friends to tell them why she is so unhappy and sick. Unable to speak, in answer to this request, she gives a party. At dessert, oranges and very sharp little knives are distributed. And when the ladies are peeling their oranges, Osarsiph/Joseph comes in to serve wine. Sheer fright at the sight of such beauty makes all the women cut their fingers, some of them to the bone. 'My loves, what ever has happened to you all? What are you doing? Your blood is flowing', is the reaction of the plotting lovesick virgin. Her exclamatory tone, insincere as it was meant to be, receives sincerity from the contiguous comment. For the narrator continues: 'It was a fearful sight' (Mann 1984, p. 803). Mut-em-enet planned this event with the explicit purpose of making herself understood. She wants her friends to *understand* her love at the very same moment they *know* it; the difference is identification. Where words fail, understanding is only possible through the suspension of subjective limits. They all have to *feel* her love, so that it becomes theirs. Thus the split created by discourse is cured. There is no longer a narrative, a 'third person', an object of gossip.

This strategy fits well with Mann's attempt to humanize the woman by generalizing not her crime but her feelings; by transgressing the denial of female subjectivity. But at the same time, discursive signifiers produce emotional overtones that symptomatize a less explicit truth. Mut expresses her surprise at what *happens*: their blood is flowing. And the narrator partakes in the effect of the event: 'it was a fearful sight'. The moon-nun not only desires sexual initiation, she also fears it. Identification with the female man made the perspective less frightening, but Joseph's refusal was a refusal of that identification. The general defloration he is innocently guilty of is another way of going through the frightful event. This rehearsal for the accusation to Potiphar has, just like the latter, the same aspect of intersubjectivity, of lack of limits between subjects, which is so central in Mann's novel. It enhances and explains the crucial scene.

This aspect of the novel – and many others – are not at all related to the Genesis story. There is no way whatsoever to claim that this text is a 'version' of the 'universal story'. Whereas the latter derives its meaning from the very absence of female subjectivity – the woman acts, but does not focalize – the scene in Mann's novel stages a dramatic generalization of the woman's ambivalent fears. Although he is not explicitly polemic here, I would suggest that Mann's desire to use the Hebrew myth of the Jew in a foreign country, confronted with a foreigner in love with him, for this intense dramatization of emotional community, could only arise from his personal response to the historical moment. While rising Nazism, within a neurotic ideology of maleness, started to make the limits between groups of subjects so absolute as to become those between life and death, the ambivalence, both sexual and ethnic, of the encounter between two ambivalent subjects became an acutely necessary alternative.

In the biblical story the woman obviously functions as a motivator of something else. The text is structured around three notions: talk, possession and the house. The first one is worked out by Mann, the second is not at all central in the novel, while the third is only relevant as setting. The repetition in the Genesis story, of the filling of Joseph's hand with all it can possibly contain, is a

business of men. Joseph's reluctance to transgress is, therefore, an
acceptance of the fathers above him. In Mann's novel the father-
God does claim his abstinence, but for a more indirect reason
involving sexual jealousy and opposing Joseph's narcissistic lack
of realism. The *house* of Genesis is the site of power *and* of bondage.
Joseph goes to and fro between inside and outside; the house
represents danger whereas the outside is of no help; Potiphar
returns to the house from which he had to be absent earlier. The
whole structure which the repetition of the word generates, is *not*
used by Mann. Mann's myth is not the myth of the young man.
Stressing the woman's position and its identity with Joseph's, he
questions the very distinction between the sexes. He uses the story
of the son in order to tell the story of the daughter, while making
subjective identity futile. Thus he introduces as his major theme an
aspect absent from the biblical story.

In Genesis, the house is the mediating signifier between the two
relationships Joseph is involved in. From his deliverance from the
mother's womb to his ascension to worldly power and posses-
sions, the transition is signified, by condensation, in this recurring
word. But it is not *his* house and what happens is not his doing; the
words that narrate it over and over again are not his words. Quite
to the contrary, Mann's Joseph needs no house and talks enough,
too much even. At one point he decides not to talk, but then he acts
instead, if negatively. When on his way to Egypt he has an
opportunity to send a message to his father. He prefers not to do it.
He is so sure of his own power that he accomplishes the very act of
arrogance: he prematurely breaks with his father, with his son-
position, only to become a son again. The analysis of speech-acts
and other acts in both stories show how deeply the two accounts
differ. Mann's decision to attack, to diverge from what he takes to
be his model, shows the function of the mythical screen: Mann *acts
upon it* and cannot help acting beyond his plans.

Rembrandt's myth: jumping to conclusions

If we can follow, through Mann's own statements, his polemical
attitude towards the traditions where he found his mythical screen,
in the case of Rembrandt we have no such evidence. Quite to the
contrary, we must assume that the painter had no conscious wish
to deviate from the myth. In many of his works Rembrandt represents biblical subjects, and although the choice of topics is doubt-

lessly significant, there is no way to challenge his faith in the Holy Writ. Yet his representation of Joseph and Potiphar's wife (Appendix 4) – a subject he took up again in at least two later paintings – is not generally included among his biblical subjects but treated, rather, as a nude (White 1969) or as an eroticum (Ostermann, n.d). This ambiguity in the reception of his little etching of the scene gives no information whatsoever on the artist's stance, and that is so much the better for our discussion. For I have ventured that a myth is a screen for transference. In spite of our good luck in the Mann case, we must, then, accept that in general there is no way we can distinguish between the trans-ference of the artist on the screen provided, say, by the biblical story, and, on the other hand, the transference of the semiotician desperately trying to argue against the stability of myth. But fortunately transference is a dynamic relation, and it is that dynamic that I want to point out now.

If I try to identify the screen in Rembrandt's etching – the empty space onto which I can transfer my phantasies – I come to the conclusion that it consists of, on the one hand, the title and what *I* know of the stories and traditions that title evokes; on the other hand, it consists of three aspects of the image itself: the body, the composition and the position of the spectator. The body of the woman is twisted: the upper part is turned towards Joseph, the lower part is turned away from him towards the lower part of the image. The composition has a specific relation between vertical and diagonal lines. That structure is represented in Figure 1 of Appendix 5. Some of these lines are straight, some are curved, as in Figure 2. The straight line at the bottom right is dominating as a line. The top left vertical is very slight, while the curved lines are less striking as lines. There is a double spectator-position. The external view is directed from the outside into the image. The play of dark and light, characteristic of Rembrandt's work, direct it from the bottom right to the middle/top left (Figure 3). Reaching the thematic centre of the etching, Joseph's head, it reaches the internal, diegetic spectator-position: Joseph's eyes. These look back; although it is unclear in which direction they are turned exactly. Do they look at the body of the woman or at the vertical object where the external spectator-position has entered the image? The ambiguity is represented in Figure 4, where both positions meet.

If I take this minimal description as the screen for my own

mythical transference, I feel justified firstly by its perceptible status, and secondly, by descriptions given by Rembrandt critics (e.g. White 1969, p. 36) which do not lead to the same type of interpretations. Mythical labour starts when the title of the work meets the work-as-screen in the spectator's projection of phantasies. The title, then, functions as a shifter, producing an *Aha-Erlebnis*, which *seems* to be triggered by the representation but is in fact an utterly personal reaction to it.

My response to this etching is inevitably a narratological one. The concept of *focalization*, which has a quite elaborate and specific bearing on the analysis of narrative discourse, can be transposed to some extent onto the analysis of the visual images. This, however, should be done with care. I retain the following features of the concept (for an extensive account of it in language, see Bal 1985):

- In narrative discourse, focalization is the direct *content* of the linguistic signifiers. Here, it is the direct content of visual signifiers like lines, light and dark, composition. Hence, it is already an interpretation.
- In narrative, there is an external focalizor which can, from time to time, *embed* an internal, diegetic one. The relation of embedding is crucial. Here the same distinction holds. The external focalizor, with whose view the spectator is asked to identify but from which the latter is technically distinguished, *embeds* the internal one, the Joseph-focalizor. Hence, they do not *meet* on the same level.
- In narrative the fabula or diegesis is considered to be *mediated*, or even produced, by the focalizors. Similarly, in the case of visual art, the use of the concept implies the claim that the *event* represented has the status of the focalized object produced by focalizors. In the case of a diegetic focalizor (here, Joseph) the 'reality'-status of the different objects painted is variable.
- As a consequence of the last point, the same object or event can receive different interpretations according to different focalizors. Here there can arise ambiguity for the same reasons.
- In narrative discourse the identification of the external focalizor with an internal one can produce a discursive conflation called Free Indirect Discourse. The identification between the external focalizor in visual images with an internal focalizor can similarly give rise to such a conflation.

Nevertheless, there remain differences between visual and discurs-ive narratives. One obvious difference is the relation to time, which makes it possible to see the work of art as a whole, to view all its parts simultaneously. However, I claim that, as soon as one regards a visual work as a narrative, stimulated by its represen-tation, its title or whatever features that suggest narrativity, the basic attitude of the spectator is narratological, that is dynamic rather than static.

I start from what I think is the beginning, from the external spectator-position. Entering the image from the bottom right-hand corner, I stress the diagonal line; hence the woman turns away from me, while I see her sexual parts first. I follow this line as far as Joseph's face and, 'Free Indirect Discursively', look back with him. Now I see the woman's protruding, fat belly; meanwhile I also see the vertical part of the bedstead. Arriving thus at the beginning, I cannot but go back again and I get involved in a to-and-fro movement which makes me aware of the doubleness of my view. I cannot but alternate the external focalization with the internal one, identifying with the outside onlooker and with Joseph, but never at the same time. This is consistent with the technical, logical description of ambiguity (Rimmon 1977, Perry and Sternberg 1968, Gombrich 1968). Ambiguity becomes the leading principle in my reading of the etching, used as I am to considering it as an artistic device.

The two focalizor-positions can be analysed more closely. The ambiguity is different from the famous rabbit-or-duck case in that the principle of embedding is at work here. The hierarchy between the external focalizor and the internal one must be accounted for. There is no direct eye contact between Joseph and the spectator. In other words, we cannot meet Joseph's eyes directly. We see his eyes; he does not see ours. The external focalizor is by definition absent from the image. He is a *voyeur*. Entering at the bottom of the vertical object, it becomes easy to identify the position with that object. The latter's contiguity with the outside, its ending at the very edge of the image makes it a suitable candidate for the function of *mediator*. This mediation produces a case of Free Indirect Discourse. Its strong presence *as* vertical, as opposed to the weak lines of the other vertical object – the door at the other side – suggest to me that I take it as contiguous, too, to another space: the psychoanalytic frame of reference. I can hardly avoid associating it with a *phallus*. More specifically, it comes to stand as a symbol of both the outsider-position and the sceptre that in its

turn signifies power in general and the power inherent to the
position of the *voyeur*. The object represents the outside-viewer *in
absentia*. But then that position becomes gender-specific: the *voyeur*
becomes a man who looks right into the woman's sexual parts.
The function of signifying the absent can be combined with the
inside-focalizor's position. Indeed, there is one conspicuous
absence in the image, signified in its title which states the absent's
presence: Potiphar. The outside focalizor becomes, now, a
motivator. Potiphar's absence is required for the first part of the
event to take place, while his presence, within the mind of both
characters, is required for the second part of the event. The
insistence in the biblical text on this double status of the man in the
closed space of the house, which gets lost in the King James
translation, has been preserved in the Dutch *Statenvertaling* of 1618
and 1619. I have tried to enhance the meeting-places of the Hebrew
text and this Dutch translation in the working translation
(Appendix 3). The historical specificity of Rembrandt's Joseph can
be related, among many other things, to the polemical background
of this very literal translation that was a political act against
Catholicism. I would venture the conjecture that Rembrandt used
this discursive particularity as part of his screen (compare both
translations of verse 11, for example).

   Joseph's ambiguous eyes gain their meaning from the phallic
object's mediating position between inside and outside. He reacts
to the woman – with attraction and repulsion – *and* he reacts to the
object: the father, the fatherly position, the outside position.
Voyeurism is characterized by non-communication; the attraction
of the position is its safety; looking without being looked at, *jouïr
sans l'autre*. The fatherly position is the position of legal rights, of
having-done-it. The father sets the rules, possesses the woman,
excludes the son from sex with her. And it is the position which
belongs to a different *time*, the elder generation to which the son
does not belong. Combining these two aspects of the position, we
can say that Joseph is confronted with the witness of the scene, a
witness which is the internalized law that forbids him to do what,
on the other hand, he seems to be doing: seeing the naked body of
the father's wife.

   Perhaps he is doing more. When we follow the ambiguity as a
signifier further, he seems to be grappling at the body. For his
whole body – his hands, his eyes, his head and his feet – are all
equally ambiguous. The head is turned away, already reaching the

door of escape, but the eyes turn back, looking at the woman *and* at the father, and the hands push away *and* grapple. The reader who is not convinced of the latter conjecture is invited to follow, with a pencil, the line of the 'fold of the garment' the woman holds. This *is* a rabbit-or-duck case. Technically, the woman's hand does hold a fold of the garment. But given the firmness of her grip, should there not be, then, small folds right under her hand? The absence of these folds, although not at all conspicuous, does allow the rabbit to become a duck, for the object the hand holds, then, is hard, no less than the bedstead. While the woman is already grasping the garment for betrayal, the boy is still tempted, phantasizing an event that is ambiguous in its turn: as the passive object of sex, he would both enjoy it and be innocent.

The ambiguity of Joseph's feet frames that of the fold within a 'story of the son'. One foot turns away from the scene, the other points towards it. But what exactly does it point to? To the bottom of the vertical object. In other words, to the aspect of the phallic object which brings together the inside and the outside, the aspects of *voyeurism* and *legitimacy*. At this point, I am going to jump to conclusions. Joseph's attitude is that of an athlete ready to jump. Again, a technical feature which is not conspicuous but nevertheless telling, allows this interpretation. Physically speaking, Joseph's weight rests on the wrong leg. If he wants to go away, in the direction of the door, he should rest on his other leg, since then the woman would pull him back. Why does he not flee in that direction? The door is closed, the house is a *closed-house* as the Hebrew word for prison indicates. There is only escape, for Rembrandt's Joseph, at the other side. The character is preparing to jump from the son-position to the father-position.

In order to clarify this, I go back to the ambiguity of the image as a whole, which started at the doubleness of the focalization. Identifying with the fatherly position, the spectator is committed to seeing what the peeping father/woman-owner sees. The structure of embedding receives its relevance here. *Within* this view, we look with Joseph and notice with fright that the latter *seems* to shrink back from the transgression, but in fact *is* attracted by the perspective. Identifying with the son, the father sees the *other side* of the fold in the garment. Paradoxically, the father's fright can only be understood *and* felt when the outsider enters into the image and identifies, through him, with Joseph. In a different medium, and for a different effect, Rembrandt is using the same device as Thomas Mann in the scene with the little knives. In that case, however, we should wonder what the transference is after, what the problem is that the character-focalizor can only bear when shared with others.

The father looks at the sexual parts of the body; the boy only sees the belly. That belly is fat, ostensively so, and Rembrandt's contemporaries criticized him for it (Emmens 1979). In combination with the status of the focalizor who watches and interprets it, the protruding feature of the belly may be associated with pregnancy (Fig. 5). On the other hand, in combination with the other focalizor, the hairless vagina, the short, fat thighs and the position of the left leg connote a baby (Fig. 6). The meaning of these two different, even contradictory, interpretations of the same body depends on the focalizors. The young boy sees a mother, a woman of the elder generation who, as a primary love-object, attracts him, but who, as belonging to the father, is inaccessible to him. He rejects, if ambiguously, the perspective of being undressed by this naked woman – for that would be both a regression and a transgression. The father, in his direct focalization, sees a baby-girl: a female of the younger generation. In his view, she belongs to Joseph's category: in his frightened phantasy she cannot be but attracted by the handsome youth. The father's anxious jealousy and the son's fear of initiation are represented by the ambiguous structure of focalization of the strangely twisted body that blocks both men's sight.

What about the leap, then? Jumping is skipping. Going to and fro between the two starting points of the readings of the image, the spectator, just like the two focalizors, has been skipping, jumping over, the em-bedded body of the woman. And that is exactly what the two focalizors are concerned with. They are dealing with each other. The father is afraid of the competition with the son, expressed in the childish view of the woman which identifies her with the younger generation, the other side. The son is afraid of the interdiction of the father to compete with him, to gain access to his domain, but he is equally afraid of winning and of losing that competition. Between him and the fatherly position there is the body of the woman: an obstacle in terms of space; initiation in terms of time. What Joseph as an image-internal, hence limited, focalizor cannot know, is that once on the other side, the right side of the image or the right side *tout court*, Joseph will have to assume, with the fatherly position, its ambiguous looking-back at the competing son, and then the whole story begins again.

The embedding position is decisive. In spite of the competing vertical 'fold' – still hidden in ambiguity – it is the thing at the bottom right that clearly has won the competition between the two vertical objects. It is doubly opposed to the door at the upper left. It is, if we may say so, discursively stronger. The door is closed, whereas the sceptre is already *in* the woman's space, delimited by the curtain, and *outside*, at the exit it disposes of and guards. The door is not a viable exit. There is no spectator-position at the top-left-outside: there is no way to turn back, for time moves on and sons become fathers.

Conclusions

If, for simplicity's sake, we assume that both Mann and Rembrandt used the biblical story of Genesis 39 as a screen, it is obvious that they both have aspects in common with the source-myth and nothing, or hardly anything, with each other. On the other hand, they both leave aside several aspects of the Genesis story, which is in its turn doubtlessly very different from its own screen. Thirdly, both Mann and Rembrandt focus on aspects *not* present in Genesis. Fourthly, while Mann shares with Laplanche and Pontalis' definitions a challenge of the distinction between the subjective and the intersubjective, the defloration scene stages that challenge 'horizontally', in a scenic articulation, whereas Laplanche and Pontalis try to obliterate the distinction in a 'vertical' perspective of origin. Freud's myth is in no way related to the story of Joseph and Potiphar's wife; rather, it represents the struggle between positivism and phantasy. However, the problems of the relations between father and son seem to be connected with the relation between positivism and phantasy; for as we have seen, Freud's text shares with Rembrandt's etching a double-levelled representation of the competition between fathers and sons in the fabula and in the discourse that represents it.

My point is not that each occurrence of a mythical signifier is different, for that is commonplace. I have tried to argue that the relation between a mythical unit and its so-called versions is not a relation of interpretation but a relation of transference. Such a relation is dynamic, historically specific and discursive. As a consequence of this first point, a mythical unit is not a unit of meaning but a signifying structure. And it can be, thanks to the fact that the opposite seems to be the case. We are used to referring to myths in terms of what we take to be a summary of their contents. But it is the action imposed onto the myth that *is* the myth. The summary, then, becomes an empty signifier which triggers other signifiers, and the mythical discourse comes into being. In Peircean terms, we can say that an indexical relation between the screen and the myth becomes possible on the basis of the *illusion* of an iconic relation, on whose basis the producer of the new myth thinks she/he can establish an indexical relation, like Mann's polemic response. Mythical thinking which consists of that illusion and the adoption of the universalistic fallacy, is at work in the very discourses which attempt to critically analyse it: myth-criticism and psychoanalysis. If you think that in my discussion of Rembrandt's etching I have not been able to avoid projecting onto it my own subjective preoccupations, entailed both by my experience of the jealous father-woman owner, and of the position of being skipped, and by my feminist position, you get my point.

Note

I am grateful to Danielle Keunen for the drawings in Figures 1 to 6, and to Fokkelien van Dijk-Hemmes for indispensible help with the translation of Genesis 39. Both provided me with the discourse I needed in order to take the myths *à la lettre*. Harai Golomb enhanced my point with a few puns he allowed me to adopt. Ben Broos gave me valuable advice and hints on Rembrandt, his immediate predecessors and the conventions of his time. Brian McHale, and the participants of the conference 'Discourse in Psychoanalysis, Literature and the Arts', gave me precious feedback which helped me to improve my text significantly.

References

Apter, T. E. (1978) *Thomas Mann*, London and Basingstoke, Macmillan.
Bal, Mieke (1985) *Femmes imaginaires: l'ancien testament au risque d'une narratologie critique*, Utrecht, HES/Montréal, HMH.
Barthes, Roland (1972) *Mythologies*, London, Jonathan Cape.
Brooks, Peter (1984) *Reading for the Plot*, New York, Knopf.
Emmens, J. A. (1979) *Rembrandt en de regels van de kunst*, Amsterdam, Van Oorschot.
Felman, Shoshana (1977) 'To open the question', *Yale French Studies: Literature and Psychoanalysis. The Question of Reading: Otherwise*, 55/6, 5–10.

—(1980) *Le Scandale du corps parlant: Don Juan avec Austin ou la séduction en deux langues*, Paris, Seuil.

—(1981) 'Rereading femininity', *Yale French Studies*, 62, 19–44.

Freud, Sigmund (1946) [1914] *Totem and Taboo*, New York, Vintage Books.

Gallop, Jane (1984) 'Lacan and literature: a case for transference', *Poetics: Psychopoetics*, 13, 301–8.

Gombrich, E. M. (1968) [1960] *Art and Illusion: A Study in the Psychology of Pictorial Representation*, London, Phaidon Press.

Habermas, Jürgen (1972) [1968] *Knowledge and Human Interests*, trans. Jeremy J. Shapiro, London, Heinemann.

Kirk, Geoffrey S. (1972) 'Aetiology, ritual, charter: three equivocal terms in the study of myth', *Yale Classical Studies*, 22, 83–102.

Lacan, Jacques (1966) 'L'Instance de la lettre dans l'inconscient ou la raison depuis Freud', in *Ecrits I*, Paris, Seuil, 249–89.

Langer, Susanne K. (1953) *Feeling and Form*, New York, Scribner's.

Laplanche, J. and Pontalis, J. B. (1980) *The Language of Psychoanalysis*, London, Hogarth Press and the Institute of Psychoanalysis.

Leach, Edmund (1983) 'Anthropological approaches to the study of the Bible during the twentieth century', in Leach, Edmund and Aycock, D. Alan (eds) *Structuralist Interpretations of Biblical Myth*, Cambridge, Cambridge University Press.

Lévi-Strauss, Claude (1963) 'The structural study of myth', in *Structural Anthropology*, New York, Vintage Books.

Malinowski, Bronislaw (1926) *Myth in Primitive Society*, London, Kegan Paul.

Mann, Thomas (1984) *Joseph and his Brothers*, Hardmondsworth, Penguin.

Ostermann, G. (n.d.) *Les Érotiques de Rembrandt*, Paris, René Baudoin.

Pavel, Thomas (1984) 'Origin and articulation: comments on the papers by Peter Brooks and Lucienne Frappier-Mazur', *Style: Psychopoetics at Work*, 18(3), 355–68.

Perry, Menakhem and Meir Sternberg (1968) 'The king through ironic eyes: the narrator's devices in the biblical story of David and Bathsheba and two excursuses on the theory of the narrative text', *Ha-Sifrut*, 1, 263–92 (in Hebrew).

Rahv, Philip (1953) 'The myth and the powerhouse', *Partisan Review*, 20, 635–48.

Rimmon, Shlomith (1977) *The Concept of Ambiguity: The Example of James*, Chicago, University of Chicago Press.

Rimmon-Kenan, Shlomith (1983) *Narrative Fiction: Contemporary Poetics*, London, Methuen.

Yohannan, John D. (1968) *Joseph and Potiphar's Wife in World Literature*, New York, New Directions.

—(1982) 'Hebraism and Hellenism in Thomas Mann's story of Joseph and Potiphar's wife', *Comparative Literature Studies*, 19(4), 430–41.

Vickery, John B. (ed.) (1966) *Myth and Literature: Contemporary Theory and Practice*, Lincoln, University of Nebraska Press.

White, Cristopher (1969) *Rembrandt as an Etcher: A Study of the Artist at Work*, 2 vols, London, A. Zwemmer.

—(1984) *Rembrandt*, London, Thames & Hudson.

White, John (1972) *Mythology in the Modern Novel: A Study of Prefigurative Techniques*, Princeton, NJ, Princeton University Press.

Appendix 1

From *Totem and Taboo* by Sigmund Freud (trans. A. A. Brill, M.D., New York, Vintage Books, 1946).

(a)

Let us now envisage the scene of such a totem meal and let us embellish it further with a few probable features which could not be adequately considered before. Thus we have the clan, which on a solemn occasion kills its totem in a cruel manner and eats it raw, blood, flesh and bones. At the same time the members of the clan disguised in imitation of the totem, mimic it in sound and movement as if they wanted to emphasize their common identity. There is also the conscious realization that an action is being carried out which is forbidden to each individual and which can only be justified through the participation of all, so that no one is allowed to exclude himself from the killing and the feast. After the act is accomplished the murdered animal is bewailed and lamented. The death lamentation is compulsive, being enforced by the fear of a threatening retribution, and its main purpose is, as Robertson Smith remarks on an analogous occasion, to exculpate oneself from responsibility for the slaying.

But after this mourning there follows loud festival gaiety accompanied by the unchaining of every impulse and the permission of every gratification. Here we find an easy insight into the nature of the *holiday*. (p. 181)

(b)

By basing our argument upon the celebration of the totem we are in a position to give an answer: 'One day[77] the expelled brothers joined forces, slew and ate the father, and thus put an end to the father horde. Together they dared and accomplished what would have remained impossible for

---

[77] The reader will avoid the erroneous impression which this exposition may call forth by taking into consideration the concluding sentence of the subsequent chapter.

them singly. Perhaps some advance in culture, like the use of a new weapon, had given them the feeling of superiority. Of course these cannibalistic savages ate their victim. This violent primal father had surely been the envied and feared model for each of the brothers. Now they accomplished their identification with him by devouring him and each acquired a part of his strength. The totem feast, which is perhaps mankind's first celebration, would be the repetition and commemoration of this memorable, criminal act with which so many things began, social organization, moral restrictions and religion.[78] (p. 183)

[78] The seemingly monstrous assumption that the tyrannical father was overcome and slain by a combination of the expelled sons has also been accepted by Atkinson as a direct result of the conditions of the Darwinian primal horde. 'A youthful band of brothers living together in forced celibacy, or at most in polyandrous relation with some single female captive. A horde as yet weak in their impubescence they are, but they would, when strength was gained with time, inevitably wrench by combined attacks, renewed again and again, both wife and life from the paternal tyrant' (*Primal Law*, pp. 220–1). Atkinson, who spent his life in New Caledonia and had unusual opportunities to study the natives, also refers to the fact that the conditions of the primal horde which Darwin assumes can easily be observed among herds of wild cattle and horses and regularly lead to the killing of the father animal. He then assumes further that a disintegration of the horde took place after the removal of the father through embittered fighting among the victorious sons, which thus precluded the origin of a new organization of society; 'An ever recurring violent succession to the solitary paternal tyrant by sons, whose parricidal hands were so soon again clenched in fratricidal strife' (p. 228). Atkinson, who did not have the suggestions of psychoanalysis at his command and did not know the studies of Robertson Smith, finds a less violent transition from the primal horde to the next social stage in which many men live together in peaceful accord. He attributes it to maternal love that at first only the youngest sons and later others too remain in the horde, who in return for this toleration acknowledge the sexual prerogative of the father by the restraint which they practise towards the mother and towards their sisters.

So much for the very remarkable theory of Atkinson, its essential correspondence with the theory here expounded, and its point of departure which makes it necessary to relinquish so much else.

I must ascribe the indefiniteness, the disregard of time interval, and the crowding of the material in the above exposition to a restraint which the nature of the subject demands. It would be just as meaningless to strive for exactness in this material as it would be unfair to demand certainty here.

Appendix 2

From *Joseph and his Brothers* by Thomas Mann (trans. H. T. Lowe-Porter, Harmondsworth, Penguin, 1984 [1943])

Again Mut-em-enet had beckoned, and he who now appeared on the scene was the cup-bearer, the pourer of the wine – it was Joseph. Yes, the lovesick woman had commanded him to this service, requesting, as his mistress, that he should himself serve the wine of Cyprus to her guests. She did not tell him of her other preparations, he did not know for what purpose of edification he was being used. It pained her, as we know, to deceive him and deliberately make such misuse of his appearance. But her heart was set on enlightening her friends and laying bare her feelings. So she said to him – just after he had once more, with all possible forbearance, refused to lie with her:

'Will you then, Osarsiph, at least do me a favour, and pour out the famous Alashian wine at my ladies' party day after tomorrow? In token of its excelling goodness, also in token that you love me a little, and lastly to show that I am after all somebody in this house, since he at its head serves me and my guests?'

'By all means, my mistress,' he had answered. 'That will I gladly do, and with the greatest pleasure, if it be one to you. For I am with body and soul at your command in every respect save that I sin with you.'

So, then, Rachel's son, the young steward of Petepre, appeared suddenly among the ladies as they sat peeling in the court; in a fine white festal garment, with a coloured Mycenæan jug in his hands. He bowed, and began to move about, filling the cups. But all the ladies, those who had chanced to see him before as well as those who did not know him, forgot at the sight not only what they were doing but themselves as well, being lost in gazing at the cup-bearer. Then those wicked little knives accomplished their purpose and the ladies, all and sundry, cut their fingers frightfully – without even being aware at the time, for a cut from such an exceedingly sharp blade is hardly perceptible, certainly not in the distracted state of mind in which Eni's friends then were.

This oft-described scene has by some been thought to be apocryphal, and not belonging to the story as it happened. But they are wrong; for it is the truth, and all the probabilities speak for it. We must remember, on the one hand, that this was the most beautiful youth of his time and sphere; on the other, that those were the sharpest little knives the world had ever seen – and we shall understand that the thing could not happen otherwise – I mean with less shedding of blood – than as it actually did. Eni's dreamlike certainty of the event and its course was entirely justified. She sat there with her suffering air, her brooding, sinister, masklike face and sinuous mouth, and looked at the mischief she had worked; the blood-bath, which at first no one saw but herself, for all the ladies were gaping in self-forgotten ardour after the youth as he slowly disappeared toward the pillared hall, where, Mut knew, the scene would repeat itself. Only when the beloved form had disappeared did she inquire of the ensuing stillness, in a voice of malicious concern:

'My loves, what ever has happened to you all? What are you doing? Your blood is flowing!'

It was a fearful sight. With some the nimble knife had gone an inch deep in the flesh and the blood did not ooze, it spouted. The little hands, the golden apples, were drenched with the red liquid, it dyed the fresh whiteness of the linen garments and snaked through into the women's laps, making pools which dripped down on the floor and their little feet. What an outcry, what wails, what shrieking arose when Mut's hypo-critical concern made them aware what had happened! Some of them could not bear the sight of blood, especially their own; they threatened to faint and had to be restored with oil of wormwood and other pungent little phials brought by the bustling maids. All the needful things were done; the neat little maids dashed about with cloths and basins, vinegar, lint and linen bandages, until the party looked more like a hospital ward than anything else, in the pillared hall as well, whither Mut-em-enet went for a moment to assure herself that blood was flowing there too. Renenutet, the wife of the overseer of bulls, was among the more seriously wounded; they had to quench the flow of blood by putting a tourniquet on the wrists to shut off the circulation from the slowly paling and yellowing little hand. Likewise Nes-ba-met, Beknechons's deep-voiced consort, had done herself considerable damage. They had to take off her outer garment, and she was tended and reassured by two of the girted maids, one black and one white, while she raved and raged in a loud voice at everybody indiscriminately.

'Dearest Head Mother and all of you my dear friends,' said the hypocrite Mut, when order had somewhat been restored, 'how could it happen that here in my house you have done this to yourselves, and this red episode has marred my party? To your hostess it is almost intolerable that it had to be in my house that it happened – how is such a thing possible? One person, or even two, might cut their fingers while peeling an orange – but all of you at once, and some of you to the bone! Such a thing has never happened before in the world, and will probably be unique in the social life of the two lands – at least, let us hope so! But comfort me, my sweethearts, and tell me how ever it could happen!'

(pp. 802–3)

Appendix 3

Genesis 39: working translation
Genesis 39: King James translation

Working translation

1. And Joseph was brought down to Egypt and bought him Potiphar, a eunuch of Pharaoh, a leader of the guard, a man of Egypt, from the hand of the Ishmaelites who had brought him from there.
2. And it came to pass [that] Jahweh [was] with Joseph and it came to pass [that he was] a man [whom god] made successful and it came to pass [that he was] in the house of his master the Egyptian.
3. And saw his master that Jahweh [was] with him and all that he was doing Jahweh made successful in his hand.

4. And Joseph found grace in his eyes and he served him and he made him supervisor over his house and all that [was] onto him he gave in his hand.

5. And it came to pass from the time [that] he had made him supervisor over his house and over all that [was] onto him and blessed Jahweh the house of the Egyptian for the sake of Joseph and it came to pass that the blessing of Jahweh [was] upon all that [was] onto him in the house and in the field.

6. And he left all that [was] onto him in the hand of Joseph and not knew he with him anything except the bread that he was eating and it came to pass that Joseph [was] beautiful of appearance and beautiful of face.

7. And it came to pass after these things and lifted up the woman of his master her eyes upon Joseph and she said, lie with me.

8. And he refused himself and said to the woman of his master: behold, my master knows not with me what [is] in the house and all that [is] onto him he gave into my hand.

9. No one [is] greater in this house than me and not kept he back from me anything except you because you [are] his woman and how shall I do this great wickedness and sin against God?

10. And it came to pass when she spoke to Joseph day by day and not he heard to her to lie by her [or] to be with her.

11. And it came to pass on such a day and he went to the house to do his work and no man of the men of the house [was] there in the house.

12. And she caught him by his garment in saying lie with me and he left his garment in her hand and he fled and went outside.

13. And it came to pass when she saw that he had left his garment in her hand and had fled outside.

14. And she called unto the men of her house and said to them saying: see, he made come to us a Hebrew man to laugh at us, he has come to me to lie with me and I called in a loud voice.

15. And it came to pass when he heard that/because I lifted my voice and called and he left his garment with me and he fled and went outside.

16. And she laid his garment by her until came his lord in his house.

17. And she spoke to him according to these words saying: he came to me the Hebrew servant which you made come to us to laugh at me.

18. And it came to pass that I lifted my voice and I called and he left his garment by me and he fled outside.

19. And it came to pass when his master heard the words of his woman which she spoke unto him saying: according to his words did unto me your servant and his nose burnt/his anger rose.

20. And Joseph's master took him and gave him in the closed house, a place where the bound ones of the king were bound and he was there in the closed house.

21. And it came to pass [that] Jahweh [was] with Joseph and extended to him favour/solidarity and he gave him mercy in the eyes of the leader of the closed-house.

22. And the leader of the closed-house gave in the hand of Joseph all the bound ones who [were] in the closed house and all that they were doing there he was the doer.

23. And not the leader of the closed-house was seeing all that [was] in his hand because Joseph [was] with him and what *he* did Jahweh made successful.

King James translation

Chapter 39

And Joseph was brought down to Egypt; and Pŏt-ĭ-phär, an officer of Pharaoh, captain of the guard, an Egyptian, bought him of the hands of the Ĭsh-́meè-lites, which had brought him down thither.

2 And the LORD was with Joseph, and he was a prosperous man; and he was in the house of his master the Egyptian.

3 And his master saw that the LORD *was* with him, and that the LORD made all that he did to prosper in his hand.

4 And Joseph found grace in his sight, and he served him: and he made him overseer over his house, and all *that* he had he put into his hand.

5 And it came to pass from the time *that* he had made him overseer in his house, and over all that he had, that the LORD blessed the Egyptian's house for Joseph's sake; and the blessing of the LORD was upon all that he had in the house, and in the field.

6 And he left all that he had in Joseph's hand; and he knew not ought he had, save the bread which he did eat. And Joseph was *a* goodly *person*, and well favoured.

7 And it came to pass after these things, that his master's wife cast her eyes upon Joseph; and she said, Lie with me.

8 But he refused, and said unto his master's wife, Behold, my master wotteth not what *is* with me in the house, and he hath committed all that he hath to my hand;

9 *There is* none greater in this house than I; neither hath he kept back any thing from me but thee, because thou *art* his wife: how then can I do this great wickedness, and sin against God?

10 And it came to pass, as she spake to Joseph day by day, that he hearkened not unto her, to lie by her, *or* to be with her.

11 And it came to pass about this time, that *Joseph* went into the house to do his business; and *there was* none of the men of the house there within.

12 And she caught him by his garment, saying, Lie with me: and he left his garment in her hand, and fled, and got him out.

13 And it came to pass, when she saw that he had left his garment in her hand, and was fled forth,

14 That she called unto the men of her house, and spake unto them, saying, See, he hath brought in an Hebrew unto us to mock us; he came in unto me to lie with me, and I cried with a loud voice:

15 And it came to pass, when he heard that I lifted up my voice and cried, that he left his garment with me, and fled, and got him out.

16 And she laid up his garment by her, until his lord came home.

17 And she spake unto him according to these words, saying, The Hebrew servant, which thou hast brought unto us, came in unto me to mock me:

18 And it came to pass, as I lifted up my voice and cried, that he left his garment with me, and fled out.

19 And it came to pass, when his master heard the words of his wife, which she spake unto him, saying, After this manner did thy servant to me; that his wrath was kindled.

20 And Joseph's master took him, and put him into the prison, a place where the king's prisoners *were* bound: and he was there in the prison.

21 But the LORD was with Joseph, and shewed him mercy, and gave him favour in the sight of the keeper of the prison.

22 And the keeper of the prison committed to Joseph's hand all the prisoners that *were* in the prison; and whatsoever they did there, he was the doer *of it*.

23 The keeper of the prison looked not to any thing *that was* under his hand; because the LORD was with him, and *that* which he did, the LORD made *it* to prosper.

Appendix 4

Rembrandt, *Joseph and Potiphar's Wife* (1634, Haarlem, Teyler's Museum)

Appendix 5

Structure of Rembrandt's *Joseph and Potiphar's Wife*

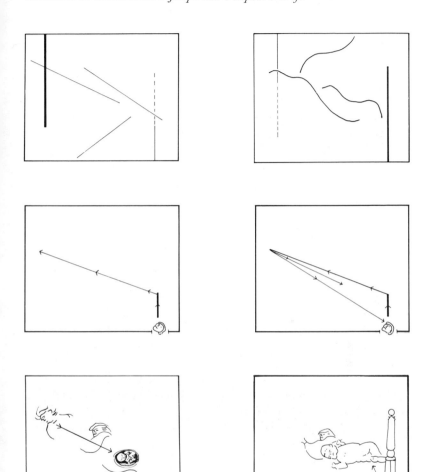

5

Transmission in psychoanalysis and literature: whose text is it anyway?

ELIZABETH WRIGHT

'We apologize to listeners in the London area. The interference was due to a fault in the transmitter.' Transmission is generally thought to be of a fixed and unambiguous message through some intermediary from an authorized source to a passive recipient. Any fault in the system could only occur in the channel of communication connecting addressor and addressee, and it would be considered to be an interference, 'noise' in the circuit, disruptive of 'information'.

The problem of transmission, of what gets through, from what place, and to whom, can be solved very simply, and often is, as in this short text by Thomas Bernhard.[1]

Ein Eigenwilliger Autor

Ein Autor, der nur ein einziges Theaterstück geschrieben hat, das nur ein einziges Mal auf dem, seiner Meinung nach besten Theater der Welt und genauso seiner Meinung nach nur von dem besten Inszenator auf der Welt und genauso seiner Meinung nach nur von dem besten Schauspielern auf der Welt aufgeführt werden durfte, hatte sich schon bevor der Vorhang zur Premiere aufgegangen war, auf dem dafür am besten geigneten, aber vom Publikum überhaupt nicht einsehbaren Platz auf der Galerie postiert und sein eigens für diesen Zweck von der Schweizer Firma Vetterli konstruiertes Machinengewehr in Anschlag gebracht und nachdem der Vorhang aufgegangen war, immer jenem Zuschauer einen tödlichen Schuss in den Kopf gejagt, welcher seiner Meinung nach, an der falschen Stelle gelacht hat. Am Ende der Vorstellung waren nur noch von ihm erschossene und also tote Zuschauer im Theater gesessen. Die Schauspieler und der Direktor des Theaters hatten sich während der ganzen Vorstellung von dem eigenwilligen Autor und von dem von ihm verursachten Geschehen nicht einen Augenblick stören lassen.

(Bernhard 1978, pp. 119–20)

The story is about an author who exercised his will in order to exert total control over the only play he had ever written. Having chosen the best possible theatre, producer and actors he concealed himself in the gallery just before the first performance was due to begin, and set up a machine gun specially manufactured for the occasion: whereupon he systematically fired a lethal shot at any spectator who laughed in the wrong place. The upshot was that by the end of the performance there were only dead spectators left sitting in the seats. All the time this was going on the actors and the director of the theatre had continued their business unperturbed.*

Might there be an alternative to this mode of controlling transmission? One alternative suggests itself by the aesthetic effect of the story: the audience or reader of the story is likely to have laughed consentingly even before asking upon what interpretation of authority this critique of authoritarianism depends. The author of the story has thus achieved by a trick of rhetoric what the author *in* the story, for all his rhetoric (the calculated mastery of the occasion – best theatre, best producer, best actors) was only able to achieve by violence.

The text, then, has demanded a response before we were in a position to make an interpretation. It has caught us out in the act, and the whys and wherefores come afterwards. This is very like the ideal model of the psychoanalytic process, for it is our unconscious that was caught out in the act: we have responded before we know why. Because the text has made us laugh, we are inclined to concede something of its persuasions, to grant it the status of co-analyst rather than try to appropriate its unconscious by digging

---

*This is a paraphrase and not an authorized translation of Bernhard's story. (Ed.)

out a latent meaning. We thus avoid the extreme positions within the text: total power on the side of the violent author and total surrender on the side of the passive audience. An interaction has taken place between text and reader which has altered our view of authority in such a way that we have to take account of a contradiction. The contradiction is that of the classic master/slave problematic: the master in the text is left powerless, for in killing off his audience he has left himself no slaves to invest him with authority. True, the producer and the actors are left, but in this interpretation of the parable they are not relevant: they are no more than the author's pen and paper, his word-processor.

The text, however, has supplied more than an ironic image of this contradiction, and this becomes obvious if one compares it with Shelley's poem *Ozymandias*, a text whose theoretical perspective is grounded in Romantic ideology. In this poem a traveller speaks of finding a ruined statue in the desert, that of an emperor whose city has long since vanished. On the pedestal, on which only the vast legs remain standing, are the words: 'My name is Ozymandias, King of Kings:/Look on my works, ye Mighty, and despair!' To which the traveller adds: 'Nothing beside remains. Round the decay/Of that colossal wreck, boundless and bare/The lone and level sands stretch far away.' This poem, about the Romantic hatred of the tyrant, is limited in its theoretical perspective to the perception of the sculptor, who has 'read' the passions of the tyrant well, because 'the shattered visage' in the sand still reveals a 'frown' and a 'sneer of cold command'. The sculptor is able to show the tyrannical nature of the king, and so theory, such as it is, is confined to the poet/artist (Shelley or the sculptor) as the unveiler of the irony of false authority. Along with this insight we have to carry the Romantic baggage of lonely traveller, desert and ruins, which is certainly no laughing matter.

The modern text, however, *An Author with a Will of his Own*, is directed at the rhetorical situation. Its subject is not just a tyrant, but someone interfering with the communication process. It is about author, text and reader, and about the conditions of the text's production and transmission. The terroristic exercising of authority, as well as the passive acceptance of it, both unnoticed by the institution, have been shown to be self-defeating by our laughter. The laughter, however, is a response to the transmission of a theory, which shows that if, like the author in the story, you deny the joke, assume there is only one meaning, then you lose your audience. For the author *in* the story language is not dialectical, able to be transformed in practice, but dogmatic, resistant to any transformation. The author *of* the story, on the other hand, is not laying down a meaning for his story, for unlike his terroristic counterpart, he allows for the testing out of his own theory in practice. He understands that once authors have relinquished their texts to readers, their theory and practice is under interminable analysis.

In the psychoanalytic situation analysand and analyst are likewise testing out their theories about each other. The transmission of psychoanalytic theory and practice in the training of analysts may be taken as the problem paradigm for the transmission of any knowledge. 'Transmission' is a term currently in favour in French psychoanalytic discourse, where it has emerged as a key problem in the passing on of knowledge from teacher to student in the psychoanalytical institution. The training of analysts involves a 'training analysis', in which the trainee/analysand has to do more than the usual patient, for he or she must occupy a double role of analysand and analyst. The transmission of the therapeutic skill, the professional knowledge, has to come via the operations of that skill, via the application and reception of that professional knowledge. Here at least there is an acknowledgement that transmission is not a matter of fixed and unambiguous messages. Passing on a tradition or a body of knowledge, be it from person to person or from country to country, is fraught with intersubjective effect.

The problematic of transmission looms large when institutions are caught up in the nets of their own power relations. Institutions are systems in which agreed knowledge is taken as a guide for the actions of a group. But although the plans of actions have apparently been authorized by their past success, this is not sufficient to legitimate authority. The newcomer has to be persuaded that his own desire is taken account of, that his acquiescence will lead to emancipation. The key problem of the training analysis – see the recent discussions in Roustang (1983) and Castoriadis (1984, pp. 46–115) – is that of the problem of any teaching/learning situation that takes place in an institution, in that the pupil/analysand is dependent on the teacher/analyst's authority in a present that stretches almost interminably into the future. The situation is thus a real one, not one merely confined to the psychodrama of the classroom/consulting room, for it recreates and perpetuates the childhood situation where a child really depends for its future on its protectors. This amounts to a double-bind: the teacher/analyst is transmitting dependence on authority in practice whilst teaching emancipation from it in theory.[2]

Psychoanalysis finds evidence for this dependence in the phenomena of transference wherein the relationship of analyst and analysand becomes governed by unconscious wishes and phantasies associated with their experiences in early life. This relationship is shot through with two-way effects taking place at an unconscious level: they appear in the analyst as much as in the analysand. For although the analyst has the professional skill, both participants in the drama are up against the institutions of family and state. The phenomena of transference are present whenever there are structures of dependence and authority: inevitably the participants act out either the desire of the institution, submit to authority or, as in Shelley's *Ozymandias*, romantically oppose it. Once the text is framed by the institution, its 'potential space', to use Winnicott's term (1974, pp. 165–82), becomes ideologically suspect, involving a more complex play than that which Winnicott allows for, since he gives the participants, 'mother' and 'child', a place already defined in the power structure.

A pre-deconstructionist writer and dramatist who has grappled most notoriously with the dire effects of transference to the instituted authority is Bertolt Brecht. His writings are a concentrated attempt at the level of both theory and practice to make palpable a system of social relations which defeats all creative self–other relationships, a defeat which the system itself conceals by its stimulation of wants. Brecht's dramaturgy sets out to deconstruct what Marcuse was later to call 'surplus repression', and to show it up as outdated and comically irrelevant to the social good, thus leaving the reader/audience with contradictions and the task of the resolution of them in life's praxis. The reader/audience is to participate in the fun of making new meaning, a process which Brecht referred to intermittently as 'interventionist thinking' (*eingreifendes Denken*). His was a vast and ambitious undertaking, directed at making available 'the pleasure of the text' not only to the single subject but to the class that was being oppressed. This is not merely a case of changing the political content of art, but of changing the relations between producer and consumer. It is here that a generalization can span psychoanalytic and critical/aesthetic discourses: 'interventions' will occur at all points of the communication process. Transmission within an institution must involve the participation of all if the pleasure of undermining the old system is to be constructively mobilized rather than anarchically indulged in. The importance of pleasure is linked with the production of the social: in his 'epic' theatre, later called 'dialectic', Brecht devised a mode of acting and staging whereby the actors, unlike those in Thomas Bernhard's story, *show* the distorted social relations which deny the characters all subjectivity.

In his brief song-ballet *The Seven Deadly Sins of the Petit-Bourgeois*, the seven traditional vices are virtues when viewed from an anti-capitalist standpoint. To demonstrate this, Brecht works with a split subject, the singing Anna I as business manager of the dancing Anna II, the goods being sold. Anna I sings the 'Song of the Sister' (all translations from Brecht are my own):

> My sister is beautiful, I am practical.
> My sister is a little off her head, I am all there.
> We are not really two persons
> But only one.
> We are both called Anna
> We have one past and one future
> One heart and one bank balance
> And each does only what's good for the other
> Isn't that so, Anna?
> Yes, Anna.

> Meine Schwester ist schön, ich bin praktisch.
> Meine Schwester ist ein bisschen verrückt, ich bin bei Verstand.
> Wir sind eigentlich nicht zwei Personen
> Sondern nur eine einzige.
> Wir heissen beide Anna
> Wir haben eine Vergangenheit und eine Zukunft
> Ein Herz und ein Sparkassenbuch
> Und jede macht nur, was für die andere gut ist
> Nicht wahr, Anna?
> Ja, Anna.   (Brecht 1967, vol. 7, p. 2860)

Anna II begins each scene by refusing to submit to the market economy and this results in a transvaluation of values: she shows laziness in promoting injustice, pride in refusing to make her art saleable, gluttony in the assertion of her natural appetite, lust in the refusal to be calculating about the other, and so on. Where Anna II reveals her subjectivity in dance, Anna I criticizes in song her 'sister's' failure to meet the desire of the capitalist Other. A split is thus enacted and transmitted to the audience. It is a parable of the divide that appears between those who toil to produce the goods and those who consume them. The audience is invited to acknowledge this split.

The Brechtian *Gestus*, the calculated pose whereby the actor shows the character's estrangement from the role assigned to him, may be seen as a deliberate unveiling of the transference to the prevailing power structure, the transmission of a political unconscious, showing how both repression and resistance are interlocked in the struggle to find an alternative. The actor, as in the Chinese theatre which inspired the Brechtian 'estrangement effect' (*Verfremdungseffekt*), shows himself conscious of his own movements. Brecht might thus be seen as a radical analyst, enlisting the actors in their dual capacity of analyst/analysand, by making them use gestic means to display repressions which are the result of old unwanted postures, imposed by an asocial system. The actor transmits this repression consciously, where the old-style actor would do it mimetically, hoping to lure the reader into collusion.[3]

Brecht's model of the theatre is equally instructive for critics of the psychoanalytic and the literary institutions. Where authority aims at mimesis, a reproduction of the already established, Brecht wishes to avoid such mimesis, refusing any notions of an expressive realism. It is therefore worth dwelling on what he saw as the paradigm of his new theatre, what he called 'The Street Scene' (Brecht 1967, vol. 7, pp. 546–58). He saw this as the 'natural' epic theatre, taking place at a street corner instead of on the stage. An eye-witness of an accident is engaged in giving a dramatized account of it to a crowd of bystanders. He performs his narrative with the help of gestures, demonstrating how, in his view, the accident occurred:

> The performance of the street demonstrator has the character of a repetition. The event has happened, what is taking place here is a repetition. ... The rehearsed elements become plainly apparent, namely, the text learnt by heart, the whole apparatus and all the preparation.

> Die Vorführung des Strassendemonstrants hat den Charakter der Wiederholung. Das Ereignis hat stattgefunden, hier findet die Wiederholung statt. ... Das Geprobte am Spiel tritt voll in

Erscheinung, das auswendig Gelernte am Text, der ganze
Apparat und die ganze Vorbereitung.

(p. 548)

The street demonstrator has to transmit the repetition of the
accident in a certain complex fashion. As a demonstrator of the
actions of those involved, he has to show the event with a
particular distance, he must not identify with the bearing of the
other but must 'quote' him, so that the audience will see the split
between who speaks and who is spoken:

> He never forgets, nor lets it be forgotten, that he is not the
> subject, but the demonstrator.

> Er vergisst nie und gestattet nie zu vergessen, dass er nicht der
> Demonstrierte, sondern der Demonstrant ist.

(p. 553)

The spectator is to identify with the demonstrator, not the
character he demonstrates, trying to decide in what way the
incident is meaningful:

> The origins of the performance lie in an incident that can be
> judged in different ways, can repeat itself in one form or another
> and is not yet completed, but is bound to have consequences so
> that this judgement is of significance. The object of the
> performance is to make it easier to assess the incident.

> Die Vorführung hat einen Vorfall zum Anlass, der verschieden
> beurteilt werden kann, der sich in der einen oder andern Form
> wiederholen kann und der noch nicht abgeschlossen ist,
> sondern Folgen haben wird, so dass die Beurteilung von
> Bedeutung ist. Zweck der Vorführung ist es, die Begutachtung
> der Vorfalls zu erleichtern.

(p. 558)

The Brechtian actor, of course, will be biased against the
prevailing power structure, revealing its sleight of hand, showing
how capitalist ideology has control over audience and theatre.
Therefore, Brecht maintains, his acting is different from that
practised in the theatre of illusion, because the gestures of the
narrator are not mimetic but interpretative.

For Brecht both natural street theatre and artistic epic theatre
share the fact that the demonstration is done for a social purpose

and has social significance. His theatre is an attempt at a social intervention, an on-the-spot discourse analysis, with an aesthetic effect. Its intention is revolutionary: the prevailing social structure must be felt to be intolerable, acting as a trigger for the critical process of analysis, with author/audience equally involved in challenging the text in their shared roles of analyst and analysand, involving a complex process of double seeing. Together with the 'street demonstrator' they will look at 'character' in its social and historical context:

> To the street demonstrator the *character* of the person demonstrated remains a quantity that does not have to be entirely defined. Within certain limits he can be this way or that way, it does not matter. What interests the demonstrator are his accident-prone and accident-proof qualities.

> Für unseren Strassendemonstranten bleibt der *Karakter* des zu Demonstrierenden eine Grösse, die er nicht völlig auszubestimmen hat. Innerhalb gewisser Grenzen kann er so und so sein, das macht nichts. Den Demonstranten interessieren seine unfallerzeugenden und seine unfallverhindernden Eigenschaften.

> (p. 551)

Brecht and Freud might here be seen in the joint enterprise of looking at the symptoms that are transmitted in the narration of a primal accident, an 'accident' producing different kinds of 'street-users'. Whereas for Freud the traumatic accident of birth produces street-users who are henceforth inescapably accident-prone, for Brecht it is a question of how to change the traffic laws of society so as to make the streets negotiable and help the street-users to become more accident-proof. To become more accident-proof is to become aware of the nature of the ideology which is immediately and secretly responsible for acts within a social structure. In his 'street scene' Brecht unknowingly avails himself of the metaphors of psychoanalysis – accidental event, apparatus, split subject, repetition phenomena, origins – but in doing so he is no merely purveying its themes and theories, he is challenging What goes on having effects, repeating itself in one form or is ripe for demystification.

ample of such ideology at work in the history of medicine can be drawn from accounts of the effects of a of accident. It is here instructive to move from

Brecht's accident analogy to an actual example. Brecht made a street accident the occasion for demystifying a hidden ideology. The demonstration had the practical aim of bringing to light the circumstances surrounding the accident, how the responsibility for it was to be distributed amongst agents and agencies, whether the victim was absent-minded, whether his attention was distracted at that moment and, if so, for what reason. The demonstration may be governed by the question of compensation for the victim. The accident can thus have an ideological explanation revealing hidden pressures. This is precisely what happened when, in the course of the nineteenth century, railway workers came forward to claim compensation for accidents.[4] They complained of a variety of symptoms, such as headaches, dizziness and tremors, for which no organic cause could be found: what was assumed was that their sufferings were due to 'spinal concussion', a 'back-trauma'. This assumption gave rise to a whole mythology whereby the disease was popularized under the term 'Railway-Spine', later changed to 'Railway-Brain' when a disturbance of the cerebral function was thought to have occurred. This mythology became medically more plausible when the disease was assigned the term 'traumatic neurosis' by a German neurologist. It turned out, however, that this so-called male traumatic neurosis shared all the symptoms of male hysteria, then under investigation by Jean-Martin Charcot. But whereas the 'accident' incurred in the cause of work or war was accepted by the medical profession as a material basis for the symptoms of male hysteria, female hysteria continued to be regarded as somehow inherent in the female constitution, if not stemming from the womb, then from an overdelicate sensibility. And this was so despite the statistics of the time, which showed an interesting anomaly: whereas this traumatic neurosis was found to predominate for men in the lower socio-economic groups, it was in the higher groups in the case of women. If the aetiology of hysteria is dependent on a complex relation between gender and class oppression, then, like Brecht's street demonstrator, any potential victim of an accident will be transmitting, for all those that have eyes to see, not only the symptoms of his or her personal repression but also the symptoms of repressive institutions. The 'Railway-Spine' example indicates how an 'accident' can have varying interpretations according to the role and its occupant. The symptoms will bespeak the institution as much as the individual.

Brecht's epic theatre, modelled on the street scene, was designed precisely to supply a built-in critique of institutions in general and the theatre in particular. Yet his case, now a live issue again after a period of canonization in the West and indifference in the East, continues to be a shining example of a failure of theory in practice. His project was to do away with the theatre of illusion as the theatre of the culture-industry and to try to intervene critically at every possible level, that of writing, direction, staging, acting, music and audience response. His estrangement effect was designed to raise consciousness, to show present relationships in the light of the past, so that those of the past could be seen as no longer appropriate. For Brecht the estrangement effect was not merely an aesthetic device, as it was for the Russian Formalists, the seeing of the object with new eyes, but a *social* device, undoing the reification of reality under capitalism. What returns is not just the personal repressed but the political repressed, the collective repression that the culture cannot acknowledge.[5] What is to be transmitted is the awareness of the concealed springs of action. Where for Freud repetition-phenomena are the result of the subject's capture in the social structure according to its personal and suprapersonal history (*Totem and Taboo, Civilization and its Discontents*), for Brecht this structure is negotiable because his-story is the story of capitalism. Brecht's problem was, however, that he underestimated the capacity of the institution to incorporate his revolutionary drama, with the result that the theory is proving more radical than the practice: he is now more written about than performed. The very devices he installed to serve a political intention were turned against that intention. His aesthetics of intervention was defeated because his new theatre could not be realized within the old institution, the problem of transmission *par excellence*. The institution proved too powerful in determining the form of transmission, for it exercises influence over audiences outside the theatre. Brecht underestimated what the audience could do to determine the play.

There is a story told by one of the directors of the Berliner Ensemble (Wekwerth 1980, pp. 114–15) who once conducted an experiment whilst working with a drama school in Sweden. He asked the least gifted student to go onto the stage, where he was to act nothing, do nothing and think nothing. The others were told that a colleague had been asked to show something, and they were to guess what it was. The curtain was raised bit by bit and the lights dimmed. There was a deathly hush while the poor fellow just stood there, doing absolutely nothing. There was five minutes' silence, then ten. After a couple more minutes someone started to laugh and the laughter continued for five minutes. Then there was deep gloom until, after twenty minutes, the curtain finally came down. The audience were asked what they had seen. They said they had experienced the tragedy of man in the age of technology, the loneliness and alienation of the individual. They noted the courage of his resistance, so splendidly acted. He was totally in command, nothing would make him give in. He refused to compromise himself by becoming integrated in such an inhuman system. But then they had laughed because it had become obvious that this man, wearing an expression of total inflexibility, was quite oblivious of the things going on in the city around him and was rejecting them with a tremendous show of refusal, superbly acted. Finally they were overcome by great sadness on account of the plight of the individual in Sweden. Whereupon the stage manager told the audience that nothing at all had been performed.

This story (which I have abridged and translated) makes a good counterpiece to the tale of *An Author with a Will of his Own* in being about an audience with a will of its own. It could be called a 'Found Play': the impulse to project our unconscious desire will produce an illusion of meaning where there is none intended. The author with a will of his own is under a complementary illusion, for in demanding a passive audience, he assumed a pure match between the acting he commanded and the meaning it was to convey. Such collusion between author and reader, actor and audience, producer and consumer, was precisely the target of Brecht's subversive strategies.

He gave directions that the deliberately lush stage-effects were to be countered by placards hung up in the auditorium with the words 'Don't be such a romantic gawper' on them ('Glotzt nicht so romantisch', Brecht 1967, vol. 1, p. 70), and he maintained that the first condition for the success of the 'V-effect' is that 'stage and auditorium must be purged of all that is "magical" and that no "hypnotic fields" come about' ('dass Bühne und Zuschauerraum von allem "magischen" gesäubert werden und keine "hyp-notischen Felder" entstehen', vol. 15, p. 341). But this is easier said than done. As the psychoanalyst, struggling to install his V-effect, knows only too well, the barest of stages and blankest of countenances are enough to produce the transference effect. The psychoanalytic situation can here be seen to relate directly to the real world of artistic production; both show how reality is a matter of construction under not always controllable circumstances.

Marx has written, 'The philosophers have merely interpreted the world in various ways, the point is to change it.' However, there is a current joke in the German Democratic Republic which goes: 'We have been changing the world long enough: the point now is to interpret it again' (quoted by Wekwerth 1980, p. 112). This is a recognition that interpretation and change cannot be taken as separate; otherwise change is no more than a predictable alteration of what has gone before, the expected outcome of a successful plan, with the future already accounted for. To get away from the notion that the text is fixed, one should look not to the Socratic philosopher, lover of wisdom but to the Freudian/Brechtian philo-sophist,[6] lover of subversive speech. The process of transmission is the struggle to decide whose text it is anyway.

Notes

1 Quoted by Rusterholz (1984, pp. 121–2). The translations throughout this chapter are my own.

2 See *Yale French Studies* 63 (1982), which interrogates texts for their implicit pedagogical aims in the pursuance of this problem, and see particularly Johnson (1982, pp. 165–82).

3 See particularly Freud (1953 [1905], vol. 7, pp. 305–10), where he outlines a theory of audience response which depends on the dramatist luring the spectator into an unconscious identification with the character's problems.

4 For what follows I draw on an article by Ursula Link-Heer, 'Männliche Hysterie', *kultuRRevolution*, no. 9 (June 1985), pp. 39–47. I am also indebted to Friedrich Kittler (Freiburg) for drawing my attention to this material and for useful comments on the Freud/Brecht connection. The main sources cited by Link-Heer in support of the material I have used are as follows: Charcot (1887–8), Fischer-Homberger (1975), de la Turette (1894), Schivelbusch (1977).

5 See Jameson (1981) on the concept of an unexpressed utopian reality that underlies all social use of language.

6 Term coined by Joachim Perner in a lecture at the University of Kassel, October 1984.

References

Bernhard, Thomas (1978) *Der Stimmenimitator*, Frankfurt, Suhrkamp.

Brecht, Bertolt (1967) *Gesammelte Werke*, Werner Hecht (ed.) 20 vols, Frankfurt, Suhrkamp.

Castoriadis, Cornelius (1984) *Crossroads in the Labyrinth*, Brighton, Harvester.

Charcot, Jean-Martin (1887–8) [1892] *Leçons du Mardi*, Paris, Publications du Progrès Médical.

de la Turette, Gilles (1894) *Die Hysterie nach den Lehren der Salpêtrière*, Leipzig and Vienna, Hans Huber.

Fischer-Homberger, Esther (1975) *Die traumatische Neurose: Vom somatischen zum sozialen Leiden*, Bern, Stuttgart and Vienna, F. Deuticke.

Freud, Sigmund (1953) [1905] 'Psychopathic characters on the stage', in *The Standard Edition of the Complete Psychological Works*, London, Hogarth Press, vol. 7, pp. 303–10.

Jameson, Fredric (1981) *The Political Unconscious: Narrative as a Socially Symbolic Act*, London, Methuen.

Johnson, Barbara (1982) 'Teaching ignorance: *L'Ecole des Femmes*', *Yale French Studies*, 63, 165–82.

Roustang, François (1983) *Psychoanalysis Never Lets Go*, Baltimore, Johns Hopkins University Press.

Rusterholz, Peter (1984) 'Lesen und Verstehen', *Fragmente*, 11, 113–35.

Schivelbusch, Wolfgang (1977) *Geschichte der Eisenbahnreise: Zur Geschichte von Raum und Zeit im 19. Jahrhundert*, Munich and Vienna, Carl Hanser.

Wekwerth, Manfred (1980) 'Brecht-Theater in der Gegenwart', *Aktualisierung Brechts*, Berlin, Argument-Verlag, pp. 101–22.

Winnicott, D. W. (1974) *Playing and Reality*, Harmondsworth, Penguin.

6

On the melancholic imaginary

JULIA KRISTEVA

Translated by Louise Burchill

Melancholy is amorous passion's sombre lining. A sorrowful pleasure, a lugubrious intoxication constitute as much the banal background from which our ideals or euphoria break away as that fleeting lucidity which fractures the hypnosis entwining two people together. Conscious of being destined to lose our loves, we are perhaps even more bereaved by noticing in our lover the shadow of a loved object, formerly lost. Depression is the hidden face of Narcissus: that countenance which – although it is to carry him off into death – remains unperceived by him during his marvelling self-contemplation in a mirage. We are, in speaking of depression, led once again into the miry environs of the Narcissisian myth. This time, however, it is not brilliant and fragile amorous idealization that we will focus upon but, on the contrary, the shadow cast over the fragile ego, barely dissociable from the other: a shadow cast, precisely, by the loss of this necessary other. A shadow of despair.

Rather than seeking the meaning of despair (which is evident or metaphysical), let us admit that there is no meaning aside from despair. The child-king becomes irremediably sad before proferring his first words: it is being separated from his mother, despairingly, with no going back, that decides him to try and recuperate her, along with other objects, in his imagination and, later, in words. The semiology interested in the degree zero of symbolism is unfailingly led to pose itself questions concerning not only the amorous state but also its sombre corollary – melancholy. Thereby to recognize, in the same movement, that if there exists no writing that is not amorous, then neither does there exist an imagination that is not, manifestly or secretly, melancholic.

Nevertheless, melancholy is not French. Protestantism's rigour or Christian orthodoxy's matriarchal weight show themselves to be more ready accomplices of the bereaved individual – when they do not invite him to a morose revelry. For the Catholic West, sadness is a sin and the wretched citizens of the 'abode of woe' are placed by Dante in the circles of Inferno (Canto III). True though it be that French medievalism presents us with delicately perceived portrayals of sorrow, the Gallic tone, Renascent and enlightened, belongs more to jest than to nihilism: Rousseau and Nerval cut here sad – and exceptional – figures.

Variable according to the religious climate, melancholy is affirmed, if it may be so stated, in religious doubt. There is nothing sadder than a dead God, and Dostoevsky himself was to be troubled by the distressing image of the dead Christ in Holbein's painting, counterposed as it is to the 'truth of the resurrection'. Particularly propitious to this black, melancholic humour are those epochs witnessing the collapse of religious and political ideals: the epochs of crises. An unemployed worker is, admittedly, less suicidal than a jilted woman; but in times of crisis, melancholy imposes itself, lays down its archaeology, produces its representations and its knowledge. Certainly, melancholy in writing has little to do with the clinical stupor of melancholia (even if the two carry the same name in French). Beyond the terminological confusion up to now maintained (what is a melancholia? what is a depression?), we find ourselves here before an enigmatic chiasmus that will not cease to preoccupy us: if loss, mourning, absence set the imaginary act in motion and permanently fuel it as much as they menace and undermine it, it is also undeniable that the fetish of the work of art is erected in disavowal of this mobilizing affliction. The artist: melancholy's most intimate witness and the most ferocious combatant of the symbolic abdication enveloping him – until death strikes and suicide imposes its triumphant conclusion upon the void of the lost object.

Melancholia here designates the clinical symptomatology of inhibition and asymbolia that an individual displays sporadically or chronically, often in alternation with the so-called manic phase of exultation. These two phenomena (dejection–exultation), in less marked forms and in more frequent alternation, constitute the *depressive* temperament of the neurotic. While recognizing the two phenomena to be different, Freudian theory detects in both the same impossible mourning of the maternal object. Question: impossible on account of what paternal failing? Or, because of what biological fragility? Melancholia – for let us take up again the generic term after having distinguished the psychotic and neurotic symptomatologies – has the formidable privilege of situating the analyst's interrogation at the intersection of the biological and the symbolic. Parallel series? Consecutive sequences? Or aleatory intersection requiring specification? Or, again, another relation to be invented?

The depressive: hating or hurt?

According to classical psychoanalytical theory (Abraham 1953; Freud 1957 [1917]; Klein 1950a, 1950b), depression, like mourning, hides an aggression against the lost object and thereby reveals the ambivalence on the part of the afflicted with respect to the object of his mourning. 'I love him/her' (the depressive seems to say concerning a being or object lost), 'but, even more, I hate him/her; because I love him/her, in order not to lose him/her, I install him/her in myself; but because I hate him/her, this other in myself is a bad ego, I am bad, I am worthless, I am destroying myself.' So self-accusation would be an accusation against the other; self-annihilation, the tragic disguising of another's massacre. Such a logic presupposes, it is speculated, a severe super-ego and an entire complex dialectic of idealization and devaloriz-ation, both of oneself and the other; the set of these mechanisms being based upon the mechanism of *identification*. For it is indeed an identification with the loved/hated other – through incorporation, introprojection, projection – that is effected by the taking into myself of an ideal, sublime, part or trait of the other, this becoming my necessary and tyrannical judge. Depression's analysis is, in consequence, conducted through a making manifest of the fact that the self-reproach is a hatred directed against the other and, doubtlessly, the carrier of an unsuspected sexual desire. It is understandable that such an afflux of hatred in the transference carries its risks for the analysand as for the analyst, and that the therapy of depression (even of that attributed as neurotic) skirts schizoid fragmentation.

However, with the treatment of narcissistic personalities,

modern analysts have been led to comprehend a different modality of depression (Jacobson 1977, among others). Far from being a dissimulated assault upon another – imagined hostile because frustrating – sorrow would be the signalling of an incomplete, empty and wounded primitive ego. Such a person doesn't consider himself as injured but as stricken by a fundamental lack, by a congenital deficiency. His grief hides neither the guilt nor failing of a vengeance hatched in secret against the ambivalent object. Rather, his sorrow would be the most archaic expression of a narcissistic wound, unable to be symbolized or named, too precocious for any exterior agent (subject or object) to be correlated to it. For this type of narcissistic depressive, sorrow is in reality his only object; more exactly, it constitutes a substitute object to which he clings, cultivating and cherishing it, for lack of any other. In this context, suicide is not a camouflaged act of war but a reuniting with sorrow and, beyond it, with that impossible love, never attained, always elsewhere; such are the promises of the void, of death.

Is mood a language?

Sorrow is the fundamental mood characterizing depression, and even if manic euphoria alternates with it in the bipolar forms of this state, grief is the principal manifestation betraying the sufferer. Sorrow leads us into the enigmatic domain of *affects* such as anxiety, fear or joy (on the affect, see Green 1971, Jacobson 1977). Irreducible to its verbal or semiological expressions, sorrow (like every affect) is the *psychic representation of displacements of psychic energy* provoked by external or internal traumas. The exact status of these psychic representatives of energy-displacements remains, in the present state of psychoanalytic and semiological theories, very imprecise: no conceptual framework of the constituted sciences (linguistics, in particular) shows itself adequate for the comprehension of this seemingly very rudimentary representation (pre-sign and pre-language). The mood 'sorrow' set off by an excitation, tension or energy-conflict in a psychosomatic organism, is not a *specific* response to that setting it off (I am not sad as a response or as a sign to X and only X). Mood is a 'generalized transference' (Jacobson 1977, pp. 66–107) that marks *all* behaviour and all sign-systems (from motility to elocution and to ideation) without being identical to them nor causing their disorganization. There are grounds to think that what is at play here is an archaic *energy-signal*, of phylogenetic heritage, which in the psychic space of the human being finds itself, however, *immediately* taken into charge by verbal representation and consciousness. Nevertheless, this taking into charge is not of the order of the cathexes said by Freud to be 'bound', admitting of verbalization, association, displacement. We shall say that the representations proper to affects, and notably sadness, are *fluctuating* energy-traces: insufficiently stabilized to coagulate into signs, verbal or otherwise, actuated by the primary processes of displacement and condensation, and dependent nevertheless upon the instance of the ego, they register across this instance the threats, orders and injunctions of the super-ego. So the moods would be inscriptions of energy-ruptures and not simply brute energies. They lead us into a modality of signifiance* that, at the threshold of bio-energetic equilibria, assures the preconditions or the dissolutions of the Imaginary and the Symbolic. At the boundaries of animality and 'symbolicity', the moods – and sadness, in particular – are the ultimate reactions to our traumas, our fundamental homeostatic recourse. For though it be true that an individual, if captive of his moods (a being drowned in his sorrow) reveals certain psychic or ideational frailties, it is just as true that a diversification of my moods (a spectrum of sadness, a refinement of grief or mourning) is the mark of my humanity, assuredly not triumphant but subtle, combative and creative.

Literary creation is that adventure of body and signs that bears witness to the affect: to sadness as the mark of separation and the beginnings of the dimension of the symbol, to joy as the mark of triumph, placing me in that universe of artifice and symbol which I try to make correspond, as best as I can, to my experiences of reality. But this testimony is one produced by literary creation in a medium entirely different from that of mood, the affect being transposed into rhythms, signs, forms. The 'semiotic' and the 'symbolic' (Kristeva 1984, pp. 19–106) become the communicable marks of an affective reality, present, palpable to the reader (I like

---

*Translator's note: '*Signifiance*, as Kristeva uses the term . . . refers to the work performed in language (through the heterogeneous articulation of semiotic and symbolic dispositions) that enables [for example] a text to signify what representative and communicative speech does not say' (L. S. Roudiez, in the Introduction to Kristeva 1980, p. 18).

this book because sadness – or anxiety or joy – is communicated to me by it) and nevertheless dominated, kept at a distance, vanquished.

Presuming that the affect is the most archaic inscription of internal and external events, how does one get from there to signs? We would follow the hypothesis according to which the infant prompted by separation (note the necessity of a 'lack' if the sign is to arise) produces or utilizes objects or vocalizations that are the symbolic equivalents of that lacking (Segal 1957). Subsequently, and from the so-called depressive position, he tries to signify the sorrow that submerges him by producing in his own ego elements that, while alien to the exterior world, are to correspond to that lost or displaced exteriority: we are, then, in the presence no longer of equivalences but of symbols in the proper sense of the word. We shall add to the position of Segal that such a triumph over sorrow is rendered possible by the ego's capacity to identify now no longer with the lost object but with a third instance: father, form, schema. A condition of a position of disavowal or of mania ('No, I haven't lost anything; I evoke, I signify: through the artifice of signs and for myself, I bring into existence that having separated itself from me'), this identification, that may be called phallic or symbolic, assures the subject's entry into the universe of signs and of creation. The father-support of this symbolic triumph is not the Oedipal father but, indeed, that 'imaginary father', 'father of personal prehistory' that for Freud (1961 [1923], p. 31) guaranteed the so-called primary identification. Later, that essential moment in the symbol's formation which is constituted by the manic position lining depression can, in the entirely different circumstances of, for example, literary creation, manifest itself by the constitution of a symbolic filiation (hence the recourse to proper names arising out of the subject's real or imaginary history, of which the subject presents himself as the inheritor or the equal).

Object-depression (implicitly aggressive), narcissistic depression (logically anterior to libidinal object-relations). Affectivity at grips with signs – exceeding, threatening or modifying them. Departing from this picture, the problem that interests me here could be summarized as follows: aesthetic – and, in particular, literary – creation, as well as religious discourse in its imaginary fictional essence, proposes a configuration of which the prosodic economy, the dramaturgy of characters and the implicit symbolism are an extremely faithful semiological representation of the subject's battle with symbolic breakdown. This literary or religious representation is not an *elaboration* in the sense of a 'becoming conscious' of the inter- and intrapsychic causes of moral pain. In this it differs from the psychoanalytic path that proposes itself for the dissolution of this symptom. However, this literary (and religious) representation possesses a real and imaginary efficacy that, cathartic more than of the order of elaboration, is a therapeutic method utilized in all societies throughout the ages. If psychoanalysis considers itself as being more effective, particularly in reinforcing the subject's ideational possibilities, it additionally owes to itself the enrichening to be gained through an added attention to sublimatory solutions of our crises.

I attempt in what follows to outline two variants of these sublimatory solutions – in Nerval and Dostoevsky.

'Black sun' – prosody – esoterism

Gérard de Nerval (1808–55) interweaves with 'le soleil noir de mélancolie'/'melancholy's black sun' a complicity formed of evasion and osmosis, of triumphant flight and voluptuous immersion. 'El Desdichado' (Nerval 1952), which translates from the Spanish as 'the disinherited' or, rather, as 'the despairing', confesses to being 'gloomy', 'bereft' and 'unconsoled'. But he is only the funereal double of that conqueror who has 'deux fois traversé. . .l'Achéron'/'twice traversed. . .the Acheron' and who is no other than the poet Orpheus. The metaphor of the 'black *sun*' for melancholy admirably evokes the blinding intensity of an affect eluding conscious elaboration. A powerful attraction, less than a sentiment, more intense than any word or idea: the narcissistic ambivalence of the melancholic affect alone finds, in order to represent itself, the image of death as the ultimate site of desire:

> Mourir, grand Dieu! Pourquoi cette idée me revient-elle à tout propos, comme s'il n'y avait que ma mort, qui fût l'équivalent du bonheur que vous promettez. Ma Mort! Ce mot ne répand pourtant rien de sombre dans ma pensée: elle m'apparaît, couronnée de roses pâles, comme à la fin d'un festin; j'ai rêvé quelquefois qu'elle m'attendait en souriant au chevet d'une femme adorée, non pas le soir mais le matin, après le bonheur, après l'ivresse, et qu'elle me disait . . .. O Dieu! Je ne sais quelle profonde tristesse habitait mon âme, mais ce n'était autre chose

que la pensée cruelle que je n'étais pas aimé! J'avais vu comme le fantôme du bonheur.

To die, heavens! Why does this idea haunt me at every turn, as if my death was the only equivalent of the happiness you promise. My Death! This word does not, for that, cast a shadow in my thought. She appears to me, wreathed with pale roses, as at the end of a feast; I have sometimes dreamt that she awaited me, smiling, by the bedside of an adored woman, not the evening but the morning, after the happiness, the intoxication, and that she said to me . . .. O God! I know not what profound sorrow occupied my soul, yet it was nothing other than the cruel thought that I was not loved! I had seen happiness's double.

(Nerval 1952, vol. 1, p. 726)

Provoked by separation or rejection, more narcissistic than aggressive, this sorrow considers the lost other as an alter-ego, as a double: is the woman loved because woman or because actress, an artist like our Orpheus?

Rien n'est plus dangereux pour les gens d'un naturel rêveur qu'un amour sérieux pour une personne de théâtre; c'est un mensonge perpétuel, c'est le rêve d'un malade, c'est l'illusion d'un fou. La vie s'attache tout entière à une chimère irréalisable qu'on serait heureux de conserver à l'état de désir ou d'aspiration, mais qui s'évanouit dès que l'on veut toucher l'idole.

Nothing is more dangerous for people naturally given to reverie than a serious love for a person of the theatre; it is a perpetual lie, a sick man's dream, the illusion of a fool. Life clings totally to an unrealisable chimera that one would happily retain as a desire or aspiration, but which vanishes as soon as one wishes to touch the idol.

(on the subject of Restif de la Bretonne, vol. 2, p. 999)

He is to flee this sorrow to refind it elsewhere, in the imaginary country of journeys to the Orient, place of dream and desire:

il y avait de la douceur et une sorte d'expression amoureuse dans cet hymne nocturne qui s'élevait au ciel avec ce sentiment de mélancolie consacré chez les Orientaux à la joie comme à la tristesse.

dans toutes les cérémonies des Egyptiens, on reconnaît ce

mélange d'une joie plaintive et d'une plainte entrecoupée de transports joyeux qui déjà, dans le monde ancien, prédisposait à tous les actes de leur vie.

there was a certain gentleness and a sort of amorous expression in this nocturnal hymn, raising itself to the heavens with that sentiment of melancholy consecrated, by the Orientals, to joy as to sorrow.

(vol. 2, p. 152)

in all of the Egyptians' ceremonies, one recognises this combination of a plaintive joy and a plaint interspersed with joyous raptures that already, in the former world, preconditioned all the acts of their life.

(vol. 2, p. 238)

Finally, he believes death to be refound in his own putting-to-death.

Two essential methods seem to offer themselves to the protagonist enshrouded in gloom as means to displace melancholy's 'black sun'. On the one hand, it is a matter of the esoteric symbolism (Richer 1947, Poulet 1971) that often retakes, amplifies or embellishes the traumatic or maturative moments or themes essential to the psychic economy, these becoming, in this context, initiatory themes. But on the other hand, and above all, the anti-depressant is the 'luth constellé'/'starred lute': the poetic art that transposes the affect into an elliptic, lacunary prosody formed by condensation and allusion (see Jeanneret 1978). Repetitive, often monotonous, this prosody imposes upon affective fluidity a grid as exacting in its deciphering (presupposing a detailed knowledge of mythology and of esoterism) as it is supple and indefinite by its very allusiveness. Who are the *Prince of Aquitaine*, the 'seule étoile morte'/'only dead star', *Phoebus, Lusignan, Biron* . . .? It is, one knows, possible to know; the interpretations consolidate or diverge. But, ultimately, one can read the sonnet without knowing anything of these referents, letting oneself be seized solely by the phonic and rhythmic coherence that marks a boundary relative to the free associations inspired by each word or proper name. One understands thereby that the triumph over melancholy consists as much in the constitution of a symbolic family (ancestor, mythical personage, esoteric community) as in the construction of a symbolic object: the sonnet. This construction, due to the author, replaces the lost ideal in the same movement as it turns melancholy's lugubrious shades into lyrical song incorporating 'les soupirs de la Sainte et les cris de la Fée'/ 'the sighs of the Saint and the cries of the Fairy'. The nostalgic object – 'ma seule étoile est morte'/'my only star is dead' – is transformed into feminine voices incorporated within that symbolic anthropophagy that is the poem's composition, within the prosody created by the artist. It is in an analogous manner that we would interpret the massive presence of proper names in Nerval's texts, particularly in his poems.

Not only do these proper names restitute to him a historical or mythical filiation but they seem to have a quasi-ritual, incantatory value. It is not their concrete referents that these proper names signal – with *signal* opposed here (both for the profane reader as, we would allege, for the hyperlucid Nerval) to 'signify' – as much as it is a massive, incircumventable, unnamable presence. As though they were the anaphora that replaces the unique object: not the 'symbolic equivalent' of the mother but the deictic 'this' that, devoid of meaning, points towards the lost object from which there, at first, emanates 'melancholy's black sun' before the putting into place of the artifice of linguistic signs and, last of all, their archaeology that is the provisionally victorious poem. 'Je criais longtemps, invoquant ma mère sous les noms données aux divinités antiques'/'I cried for a long time, invoking my mother under the names given to ancient divinities' (Nerval 1952, vol. 1, p. 423).

The melancholic's past never passes. Nor that of the poet, that permanent historian not so much of his real history but of the symbolic events which have led his body to signification or, indeed, which threaten to overwhelm his consciousness.

The Nervalian poem has also a highly mnemonic function, 'une prière à la déesse Mnémosyne'/'a prayer to the goddess Mnemosyne', he writes in *Aurélia* (1952, vol. 1, p. 366), especially in the sense of a textual commemoration of both the genesis of symbols and of one's phantasmic life, such texts becoming the artist's real life. ('Ici a commencé pour moi ce que j'appellerais l'épanchement du songe dans la vie réelle'/'Here commenced for me what I will call dream's spilling over into real life', vol. 1, p. 367; and consequently: 'A dater de ce moment, tout prenait parfois un aspect double'/'Dating from this moment, everything at times took a double aspect'.) So, for example, in a passage of *Aurélia*, one can trace the necessary concatenation of the death of the beloved woman (mother), the identification both with her and with death, the putting into place of a space of psychic solitude based upon the perception of a bisexual or asexual form and, finally, the eruption of sorrow encapsulated in the citing of Dürer's *Melancholy*.

> Je vis devant moi une femme au teint blême, aux yeux caves, qui me semblait avoir les traits d'Aurélia. Je me dis: 'C'est *sa mort* ou la mienne qui m'est annoncée!'. . . . J'errais dans un vaste édifice composé de plusieurs salles . . .. Un être d'une grandeur démesurée, – homme ou femme, je ne sais – voltigeait péniblement au-dessus de l'espace . . .. Il ressemblait à l'Ange de la Mélancolie, d'Albrecht Dürer. Je ne pus m'empêcher de pousser des cris d'effroi, qui me réveillèrent en sursaut.

> I saw before me a woman of wan complexion, with sunken eyes, whose features seemed to me to be those of Aurélia. I said to myself: 'It's her death or mine that is heralded!'. . . . I wandered into a huge building, composed of several rooms . . .. A disproportionately large being – man or woman, I couldn't say – hovered overhead . . .. It resembled the Angel of *Melancholy*, of Albrecht Dürer. I couldn't help myself from crying out in terror, which woke me with a start.

> (vol. 1, p. 366)*

Whatever may be the allusions to freemasonry and to initiation – and perhaps in parallel to them – the text evokes (as in an analysis) archaic psychic experiences that few people attain in their conscious discourse. That Nerval's psychotic conflicts were capable of favouring such an access by him to the limits of the being of language and humanity seems obvious. Melancholy, in Nerval's case, is only one facet of these conflicts that would seem to encompass schizophrenic fragmentation. Nevertheless, through its pivotal position in the organization and disorganization of the psychic space, at the limit of the affect and meaning, of biology and language, of asymbolia and vertiginously rapid signification, it is indeed melancholy that dominates the representation. The creation of a prosody and of a highly symbolic text around the 'black mark' or 'black sun' of melancholy is also depression's antidote, a provisional well-being.

*Translator's note: For an English translation of *Aurélia*, see References.

The writing of suffering's pleasures

The tormented universe of Dostoevsky (1821–81) is without a doubt dominated more by epilepsy than by melancholia in the clinical sense of the term.[1] And if Hippocrates identified the two ills, and if Aristotle, in distinguishing them, compared them, current clinical reality considers them to be thoroughly separate entities. None the less, we would keep before us both the dejection that in Dostoevsky's texts precedes or, in particular, follows the fit such as it is described by the writer himself, and to an even greater degree, the hypostasis of suffering throughout his work that, while lacking an immediate or explicit relation to epilepsy, imposes itself as the essential trait of the Dostoevskian anthropology.

So, in Dostoevsky's *Notebooks of the Possessed* (or *of the Devils* – the novel *The Devils* appearing in 1873):

> Fit at six o'clock in the morning (the day and almost the hour of Tropmann's agony). I was not aware of it, waking up at eight o'clock with the consciousness of a fit. My head ached, my body was broken. In general, the fit's aftermath – that is, nervousness, a hazy and, in a certain way, contemplative state of mind – lasts longer now than in preceding years. Before this passed in three days and now not before six. In the evenings especially, when the candles have been lit, a *hypochondriac sadness, without object, like a blood-red tone* (not tint) over everything.
> (Dostoevsky 1955, p. 810; my emphasis)*

Or again, he repeats, 'nervous laughter and mystic sorrow' (p. 812), in implicit reference to the *acedia* of the monks of the Middle Ages. Or again: how to write? 'Suffer, suffer enormously. . . .'

Suffering seems here to be an 'in excess', a force, a sensual pleasure. The 'black mark' of Nervalian melancholy has given way to a passionate torrent: to a hysterical affect, if one likes, the fluid overflowing of which carries away the placid signs and quiescent compositions of 'monological' literature. This confers a vertiginous polyphony to the Dostoevskian text and imposes as the ultimate truth of Dostoevskian man a rebellious flesh that takes its pleasure in non-submission to the Word. Sensuality of suffering's pleasure that has 'nothing of the coldness, nothing of the

*Translator's note: The page references are to the French Pléiade edition. For English translations, see References.

disenchantment, nothing of that having been made fashionable by Byron', but, on the contrary, an 'intemperate and insatiable thirst for pleasures', 'a thirst after inextinguishable life', including 'pleasures of theft, of banditry, the sensual pleasure of suicide' (p. 1154). This exultation of a mood that can turn from suffering to an incommensurable jubilation is admirably described by Kirilov in the moments preceding suicide – or the fit:

> 'There are seconds – they come five or six at a time – when you suddenly feel the presence of eternal harmony in all its fullness. It is nothing earthly. I don't mean that it is heavenly, but a man in his earthly semblance can't endure it. He has to undergo a physical change or die. This feeling is clear and unmistakable. . . . It is not rapture. . . . Nor do you really love anything, oh! it is much higher than love. What is so terrifying about it is that it is so terribly clear and such gladness. If it went on for more than five seconds, the soul could not endure it and must perish. . . . To be able to endure it for ten seconds, you have to undergo a physical change.'
> 'You're not an epileptic?'
> 'No.'
> 'You will be one. Take care, Kirilov. I've heard that's just how an epileptic fit begins. . . . '

(Dostoevsky 1971, p. 586)

And concerning the short duration of this state: 'Remember Mahommed's pitcher from which no drop of water was spilt while he flew round paradise on his horse. The pitcher – that's your five seconds. It's too much like your eternal harmony, and Mahommed was an epileptic. Be careful, Kirilov, it is epilepsy!' (p. 586).

Irreducible to sentiments, the affect is translated here with an extraordinary accuracy in its energy intensity and its existence as psychic representation – lucid, clear, harmonious, but some-what outside of language. The affect is not conveyed by language or, more precisely, when referred to by language, the affect is not bound to it as is the idea. The verbalization of affects (unconscious or not) does not have the same economy as that of ideas (unconscious or not). One can suppose that the verbalization of unconscious affects does not render these conscious (the subject knows no more than previously where his joy or sorrow comes from) but that it causes them to operate doubly: on one hand, the affects redistribute language's order, giving rise thereby to a style;

on the other, they display the unconscious in the characters and acts representing the most forbidden and transgressive motions of the drives. Literature, like hysteria – which for Freud is but a 'deformed work of art' – is a staging of affects on the intersubjective, as on the intralinguistic, level.

It is probably such an intimacy with the affect that led Dostoevsky to his vision according to which the humanity of man resides less in the pursuit of a pleasure or a profit (an idea extending to even Freudian psychoanalysis despite the predominance finally accorded to a 'beyond the pleasure principle') than in the aspiration for a voluptuous suffering. Different from animosity or fury, less in relation to an object, more turned back onto the person himself, suffering would be the threshold of consciousness proper, beyond which there is but the loss of self in the body's obscurity. Suffering: an inhibited death drive, a sadism fettered by the conscience's vigilance and turned back upon an ego, thereafter woeful and inactive:

> My anger, in consequence of the damned laws of consciousness, is subject to chemical decomposition. As you look, its object vanishes into thin air, its reasons evaporate, the offender is nowhere to be found, the affront ceases to be an offence and becomes destiny, something like toothache, for which nobody is to blame.
>
> (Dostoevsky 1972, p. 27)

And finally, this apology of suffering worthy of medieval *acedia*, indeed of Job:

> And why are you so firmly and triumphantly certain that only what is normal and positive – in short, only well-being – is good for man? Is reason mistaken about what is good? After all, perhaps prosperity isn't the only thing that pleases mankind, perhaps he is just as attracted to suffering. Perhaps suffering is just as good for him as prosperity. Sometimes a man is intensely, even passionately, attached to suffering – that is a fact.
>
> (Dostoevsky 1927 [1875], p. 61)

Extremely Dostoevskian, this definition of suffering as liberty affirmed, as caprice:

> I am not here standing up for suffering, or for well-being either. I am standing out for my own caprices and for having them

guaranteed when necessary. There is no place for suffering in farces for example, I know that. It is quite inconceivable in a millennium: suffering is doubt, negation. ... Suffering – after all, that is the sole cause of consciousness. Although I declared to begin with that in my opinion consciousness is man's supreme misfortune, I know that man loves it and would not change it for any gratification.

(Dostoevsky 1972, p. 41)

Dostoevsky or Job

Let us not be precipitate in interpreting these remarks as an avowal of masochism. Isn't it in *signifying* his hate, the other's destruction and, perhaps before all else, his own putting to death, that the human being survives *qua* symbolic animal? A violence, exorbitant yet curbed, leading to the self-annihilation of the ego imposes the emergence of the subject. From a diachronic point of view we are here at the minimal threshold of subjectivity, before an other comes to be demarcated as the object of an amorous or aggressive assault. Now, this curbing additionally allows mastery over signs: I don't attack you, I *speak* (or I write) my fear or my pain. My suffering is the lining of my word, of my civilization. One can imagine the masochistic risks of this civility. The writer is, however, for his part, able to extract from this a jubilation through the manipulation that, upon this base, he knows how to inflict upon signs and things.

Suffering – and its reverse, jubilation, and therefore pleasure in Dostoevsky's sense – imposes itself as the ultimate index of a rupture immediately prior to the (chronological and logical) autonomization of the ego and the other. The rupture in question may be bio-energetic, internal or external, or symbolic – due to an abandonment, a punishment, a banishment: the severity of Dostoevsky's father, reviled by his moujiks and, according to some, murdered by them, cannot be overemphasized. In any case, suffering is the first, or final, attempt by the subject to affirm his particularity in the closest proximity to the threatened biological unity and a narcissism put to the test. So, too, this exaggeration of humour, this pretentious inflation of 'propriety' or peculiarity, states an essential truth of the psyche in the process of constitution or of decomposition, a process which takes place under the gaze of the ego ideal: under the law of an Other, already dominant albeit still not recognized in its omnipotent alterity.

For this very reason, the suffering being found in Dostoevsky recalls the paradoxical adventure of Job which had so struck the writer:

> I am reading the book of Job from which I derive a morbid exultation: I stop reading and pace up and down in my room, an hour at a time, almost in tears. . . . The strange thing is, Anna, that this book is one of the first to have made an impression upon me . . . and, at that time, I was still almost a babe in arms.
> (Dostoevsky 1927 [1875], p. 61)

Job, nourishing himself upon sighs and groans, as though bread and water, was, it will be remembered, a man who, prosperous and faithful to Jahweh, finds himself suddenly beset by various misfortunes. . . . By Jahweh or by Satan? And yet here is this 'man of grief', object of scorn ('If one should address a word to you, will you endure it?', Job 4:2), who is, in sum, sad only because he holds fast to God. That this God be pitiless, unjust to those faithful to him, and even generous to the wicked, does not lead him to break his divine contract; on the contrary, he places his life under the constant scrutiny of God. Striking avowal of the depressive's dependence with respect to his super-ego cum ego-ideal: 'What is man that you (God) should make so much of him' (7:17); 'turn your eyes away, leave me a little joy' (10:21). And yet Job does not accredit God with his true force ('Were He to pass me, I should not see Him', 9:11), and God himself will be required to recapitulate all of Creation before his depressive, to affirm his position as Legislator or as super-ego, for Job to recover hope. Would the sufferer be a narcissist, a man too concerned with himself, attached to his own importance and close to taking himself for an example of transcendence's immanence? However, after having punished him, Jahweh finally favours him and places him above his detractors: 'I burn with anger against you,' God says to them, 'for not speaking truthfully about me as my servant Job has done' (42:8).

In the same manner, suffering – pre-eminent index of humanity – is, in the texts of the Christian Dostoevsky, the mark of man's dependence and, at the same time, of his irremediable difference with respect to a divine law. There is a simultaneity of bond and fault, of fidelity and transgression – such as is refound in the ethical order itself, where Dostoevskian man is an idiot through saintliness, a prophet through criminality.

It would surely be impossible that this logic of necessary interdependence between law and transgression be extraneous to the fact that the epileptic fit is very often triggered off by a strong contradiction between love and hate, desire and rejection of the other. On the other hand, one can wonder if the famous ambivalence of Dostoevsky's heroes, that lead Bakhtin (1973) to postulate a 'dialogism' at the base of his poetics, is not an attempt to *represent*, by the construction of discourses and the conflicts between characters, this opposition lacking a synthetic resolution of the two forces (positive and negative) proper to the drive and desire.

However, break the symbolic bond and our Job becomes Kirilov, a suicidal terrorist. Merejkovsky (1906) is not entirely wrong to see in the great writer the precursor of the Russian revolution. Certainly, he dreads, rejects and stigmatizes it, but nevertheless it is he who knows of its sly advent in the soul of his suffering mankind, ready to betray the humility of Job for the manic exultation of the revolutionary who takes himself for God (such, according to Dostoevsky, being the form taken by atheists' socialist faith). The depressive's narcissism is inverted into the mania of atheist terrorism: Kirilov is the man without God who has taken the place of God. Suffering ceases in order that death be affirmed: was suffering, then, a barrier against suicide and against death?

Suicide and terrorism

One will recall at least two solutions, both fatal, to Dostoevskian suffering – that ultimate veil of chaos and destruction. First there is that of Kirilov, who is persuaded that God doesn't exist but who, in adhering to the divine instance, wishes to raise human liberty to the height of the absolute by that exemplary act of denial and freedom which, for him, is suicide. God doesn't exist – I am God – I do not exist – I commit suicide: such would be the paradoxical logic of this negation of an absolute divinity or paternity none the less maintained in order that I possess myself of it.

Second there is the solution of Raskolnikov, who, as in a manic defence against despair, turns his hate back not onto himself but onto another, denigrated, denied. By his gratuitous crime, consisting in killing an insignificant woman, he breaks the

Christian contract ('Love your neighbour as yourself'); this signifying that he denies his love for the original object ('Because I don't love my mother, my neighbour is unimportant to me, which permits me to eliminate him without worry') and that, departing from this implicit premise, he authorizes himself to realize his hate against an entourage and a society experienced as persecutory.

The metaphysical meaning of these behaviours is, as one knows, the nihilist rejection of the supreme Value, provoking, on the part of Dostoevsky, the believer's revolt against this erasure of the transcendental. The psychoanalyst will additionally see here both the writer's (at least ambiguous) fascination with so much exquisite depression and certain manic defences against this suffering, both of which are moreover cultivated by the writer as the necessary and antinomic linings of his writings. The abandonment of all morals, the loss of the meaning of life, or the terrorism and torture so frequent in our quotidian reality, all recall to us that these ramparts/nihilism/violence are abject. The writer, for his part, chose the adhesion to a religious orthodoxy, and this 'obscurantism', so violently denounced by Freud, is, all things considered, less harmful to civilization than terroristic nihilism – as too, obviously, is the painful and permanent battle to compose a work of art side by side with the innumerable pleasures comprising destruction and chaos.

Religion or the mania born of paranoia – are they the sole counterbalances to despair? Artistic creation integrates and consumes them; works of art leading us thereby to establish less destructive, more pleasurable relations with ourselves and with others.

Psychoanalysis – a laic discourse creating and dissolving the transferential bond – is an apprenticeship in living beyond despair; not by a manic defence countering it, but through a receptivity to it, an endowing of it with meaning. Consolidating the ego in this way, artistic creation allows it to assume an existence upon the basis of its very vulnerability in relation to the other.

This overview of a certain number of depression's facets could not be terminated without evoking the pharmacological advances and the modern biochemical knowledge concerning melancholia's endogenous factors. The hypothesis seems to be gaining ground according to which it is an insufficiency of (nor)adrenalin and serotonin, or of their reception, that hampers the conductibility of synapses and *possibly* conditions the depressive state. However, in the star-shaped structure of the brain, the role of a few synapses could not be absolute (Widlöcher 1983). Such an insufficiency can be counteracted by other chemical phenomena and, too, by different external effects (including symbolic) upon the brain, which accommodates itself to these through biological modifications. Thus without renouncing the chemical role in the battle against melancholia, the analyst has – if he so chooses – at his disposal an extended range of verbalizations of this state and its overcoming, the example of which is presented to us in works of art. Therefore the attention that we bring to bear upon religious or aesthetic discourse in relation to melancholia is not solely a means of rendering our phenomenological description of this symptom more penetrating: by the interpretation that this knowledge allows us to elaborate, by a verbalization as exact as possible of destructive affects, it can also be an essential therapeutic measure.

Note

1 Freud's canonical text on Dostoevsky examines the writer from the point of view of epilepsy, amoralism, parricide and gambling, and only allusively deals with the 'sado-masochism' underlying his suffering (Freud 1961b [1928], pp. 175ff; see also Sollers 1978).

References

Abraham, Karl (1953) 'Notes on the psycho-analytical investigation and treatment of manic-depressive insanity and allied conditions', in *Selected Papers*, New York, Brunner/Mazel, pp. 137–57.
Bakhtin, Mikhail (1973) *Problems of Dostoevsky's Poetics*, Ann Arbor, Mich., Ardis.
Dostoevsky, Fyodor (1968) *Notebooks of the Devils*, Chicago, University of Chicago Press.
—(1971) *The Devils*, Harmondsworth, Penguin.
—(1972) *Notes from Underground*, Harmondsworth, Penguin.
—(1955) *Carnet des démons,* in *Les Démons*, Paris, Gallimard, Pléiade.
—(1927) 'Letter to his Wife, 10 January, 1875', in *Letters to his Wife*, t. II, 1875–80, Paris, Plon.
Freud, Sigmund (1957 [1917]) 'Mourning and melancholia', in *The Standard Edition of the Complete Psychological Works*, London, Hogarth Press, vol. 14, pp. 237–58.
—(1961a [1923]) 'The Ego and the Id', in *The Standard Edition of the Complete Psychological Works*, London, Hogarth Press, vol. 10, pp. 1–66.

—(1961b [1928]) 'Dostoevsky and parricide', in *The Standard Edition of the Complete Psychological Works*, London, Hogarth Press, vol. 21, pp. 175–98.
Green, André (1971) *Le discours vivant*, Paris, PUF.
Jeanneret, Michel (1978) *La Lettre perdue: écriture et folie dans l'oeuvre de Nerval*, Paris, Flammarion.
Jacobson, E. (1977) *Depression: Comparative Studies of Normal, Neurotic and Psychotic Conditions*, New York, International Universities Press.
Klein, Melanie (1950a) 'A Contribution to the psychogenesis of manic-depressive states', in *Contributions to Psychoanalysis*, London, Hogarth Press, pp. 282–310.
—(1950b) 'Mourning and its relation to manic-depressive states', in *Contributions to Psychoanalysis*, London, Hogarth Press, pp. 311–38.
Kristeva, Julia (1984) *Revolution in Poetic Language*, New York, Columbia University Press.
—(1980) *Desire in Language*, New York, Columbia University Press.
Merejkovsky, D. (1906) *Prophet of the Russian Revolution* (in Russian), ed. Pirojov, M.B.
Nerval, Gérard de (1952) *Oeuvres complètes*, Paris, Gallimard, Pléiade.
—(1977) *Aurélia*, London, Aldington, Chatto & Windus.
Poulet, Georges (1971) *Trois essais de mythologie romantique*, Paris, Corti.
Richer, Jean (1947) *Gérard de Nerval et les doctrines ésotériques*, Neuchâtel, Le Griffon d'Or.
Segal, Hanna (1957) 'Note on symbol formation', in *International Journal of psychoanalysis*, 37, 391–7.
Sollers, Philippe (1978) 'Dostoïevski, Freud, la Roulette', in *Tel Quel*, 76, 9–17.
Widlöcher, D. (1983) *Les Logiques de la dépression*, Paris, Fayard.

7

Nadja, Dora, Lol V. Stein: women, madness and narrative

SUSAN RUBIN SULEIMAN

Parler d'amour, en effet, on ne fait que ça dans le discours analytique.

J. Lacan

This essay will be about entanglements – what Lacan would have called knots – entanglements among persons, characters, texts, discourses, commentaries and cross-commentaries, glosses and footnotes and further footnotes to stories real and imagined, scenes seen and recounted, reconstructed, revised, denied; knots between desire and frustration, mastery and loss, madness and reason, illness and cure, men and women. In a word, love. Which some have called transference. Which some have called reading. Which some have called writing. Which some have called *écriture*. Which some have called displacement, slippage, gap. Which some have called the unconscious. Which some have called the discourse of the Other. Which, if it can be spoken (of), written (of) at all, produces knots.

That would be one way to begin. Or I could begin at the beginning, asking questions. How does modern writing move from André Breton's *Nadja* (1964 [1928]) to Marguerite Duras' *Le Ravissement de Lol V. Stein* (1964), and why is that move important? What does it have to do with 'discourse in literature and psychoanalysis' or with women, madness, and narrative? And what do these questions have to do with us?

In an article published ten years ago, Shoshana Felman raised the question of women, madness and the writing and reading of fiction by rereading a story of Balzac's (Felman 1975). The central figures in the story were an army officer who had participated in the Napoleonic wars; a woman he had loved and lost, and whom he found again years later, transformed into a mad creature unable to recognize him or to utter any but a single word ('Adieu', the story's title); and an old, benevolent doctor who is the madwoman's uncle and caretaker, with whose help the officer undertakes to cure her of her madness by recreating the traumatic event (an episode in the French army's retreat from Russia) that precipitated her madness. Felman's reading emphasized two interrelated points: first, that the traditional academic criticism of this story literally *did not see* the woman, being interested only in Balzac's 'realistic' portrayal of the Napoleonic wars; and second, that the story itself is both a dramatization and a subversion of the representational logic which, seeking to cure the woman's madness by means of recognition, re-presentation, attains its aim only at the price of killing her.

Felman's reading of Balzac and of his critics could not have been intelligible, indeed could not even have existed, without the conjunction of three major 'moments' or movements in recent French thought: the psychoanalytic – more exactly, Lacanian – moment, with its emphasis on specularity and the problematics of self and other; the deconstructive moment, with its emphasis on textual rhetoric and textual self-reflexiveness; and the feminist (or, if you will, 'feminine theoretical') moment, with its emphasis on the exclusion of women from traditional discourse, including the discourse of Freudian and Lacanian psychoanalysis. It is precisely at this conjunction – which is not only intertextual but inter-discursive, a multi-dimensional space where literature and psychoanalysis, theory and fiction, meet – that we encounter Nadja, Dora and Lol V. Stein.

Nadja has been called, by Michel Beaujour in an admirable essay, 'the account that an honest man can give of a shattering and failed adventure' (Beaujour 1967, p. 794).[1] The same could be said, with some qualification, about *Le Ravissement de Lol V. Stein* – and yet the distance that separates these two books and these two adventures seems to me much more significant than their resemblances, which are strikingly numerous. In both, a male narrator who says 'I' tells a story, fragmented and discontinuous in its presentation (*récit*) and excruciatingly self-conscious in its mode of telling (*narration*); the story is about the narrator's involvement with a woman, who by 'normal' societal standards is mad, and whose madness constitutes the chief fascination she holds for the narrator. Aside from these internal homologies, the two texts have in common certain significant external features: they are probably the best known and most commented-upon of their author's works, having achieved the status of 'modern classics' (if one can be allowed that antithetical juxtaposition) within a few years of their writing. They both constitute *inaugural* texts – *Nadja* being the first of four autobiographical narratives about the ultimate surrealist adventure, love, according to Breton; *Le Ravissement de Lol V. Stein* being the first of a series of fictions and films in which Duras has reworked, elaborated and expanded a single narrative 'kernel'. Finally, in addition to the outpouring of commentaries which both books have elicited from literary critics and historians, cultural theorists, feminist critics and, in the case of *Lol V. Stein*, from Lacanian analysts including Lacan himself, they have received extensive glosses and reworkings by their own authors.[2]

There is no need to continue the demonstration; these are obviously central texts: central in their authors' *oeuvres*, central in contemporary literary history and central in an intertextual and interdiscursive space of commentary and self-commentary. They are also (and this is not exactly the same thing) *exemplary* modern texts: *Nadja* is *the* surrealist prose narrative, *Lol V. Stein* is (so far, at least) the most important single narrative in which literary modernity and *écriture féminine* are self-consciously merged (see Duras and Gauthier 1974, p. 61).

And *Dora*? Where is *Dora*? Crucial question. In one sense, she – or rather it (Freud's text) – is exactly where the others are, for everything I have emphasized about *Nadja* and *Lol V. Stein* can also be found in *Dora*: self-conscious male narrator, mentally ill woman as main character, inaugural text in a major series (the five case histories), central in its author's *oeuvre* and in the history of modern culture.[3]

At the same time, *Dora* is what separates *Nadja* from *Lol V. Stein*, more radically than their many similarities unite them. I know, I know – *Dora* is not *Dora*, but 'Fragment of an analysis of a case of hysteria', written in 1901, published in 1905, expanded with additional footnotes in 1923 – all well before Breton's *Nadja* saw the light. The space I am referring to, however, is not chronological. Back in the late 1960s and early 1970s, one might have spoken about *la coupure épistémologique freudienne* (see Houdebine 1971). Today we can speak more simply. We can say that *Dora* is the difference between *Nadja* and *Lol V. Stein* as Freud is the difference between Charcot and Lacan. Or we can say that to move from surrealism to *écriture féminine*, modernity must traverse *Dora*, and that to traverse *Dora* is to put into question the subject: the subject of narrative and of sexual difference; the subject of discourse in literature and in psychoanalysis; the subject of desire, of interpretation, of transference.

I

Let us begin, then, once again – once again by citing Shoshana Felman, who I believe was the first to develop the enormously fruitful idea that the analytic experience of transference can also serve to define the experience of literature (Felman 1977). More recently, Peter Brooks has proposed a 'transferential model' of reading in which the relation between narrator and narratee, and between author and reader, is analogous to the relation between analysand and analyst (Brooks 1984). Between Felman and Brooks, however, there is a difference: Brooks's model is classically Freudian: for him, transference is the effect of the *patient*'s desire, to be 'read' by the analyst. Felman's model is Lacanian: for her, transference is also the effect of the *analyst*'s desire. Felman can thus read Freudian interpretation itself through and with Lacan, seeing its blind spot:

> to his great astonishment [this is Lacan talking about Freud, quoted by Felman], he noticed that he could not avoid participating in what the hysteric was telling him, and that he felt affected by it. Naturally, everything in the resulting rules through which he established the practice of psychoanalysis is designed to counteract this consequence, to conduct things in such a way as to avoid being affected.
>
> (Felman 1977, p. 118)

What Freud was blind to, contemporary Freudians have said, was the unavoidable necessity and presence of countertransference, 'the effects of the analyst's own unconscious needs and conflicts on his understanding or technique' (Reich, quoted in Spence 1982, p. 188). Donald Spence, for example, argues that far from being a 'possible source of error, something to be "analyzed away" so as not to contaminate the therapeutic conversation . . ., countertransference may be a necessary part of active listening'

(Spence 1982, p. 284). This, however, is still not the same as the Lacanian view, which sees *transference itself* as the entanglement of two desires. 'Transference', Lacan said in one of his many pronouncements on this subject, 'is a phenomenon in which the subject and the analyst are included together. To divide it in terms of transference and countertransference . . . is never anything but a way of eluding what is involved' (Lacan 1973 [1964], p. 210). What is involved, I would suggest, is not only who desires what and whose desire 'comes first' but also, more importantly, the aim of the clinical encounter itself.

The aim of the encounter is the cure, Freud would say. And in what does the cure consist? In the removal of symptoms and in the construction, or reconstruction, of an 'intelligible, consistent, unbroken' story (Freud 1963a [1905], p. 32). If the sign of true neurotics is their 'inability to give an ordered history of their life' (p. 31), then the analyst's task is to help them achieve that capacity. As Steven Marcus has remarked in his path-breaking essay on *Dora*, 'No larger tribute has ever been paid to a culture . . . which had produced as one of its chief climaxes the bourgeois novels of the 19th century' (Marcus 1975, p. 278) than this faith of Freud's in the healing capacity of coherent story-telling. Donald Spence's influential recent book, *Narrative Truth and Historical Truth* (1982), criticizes Freud's notion that the story thus reconstructed corresponds to historical truth; yet Spence remains totally faithful to the notion that the analytic cure consists in the production of narrative coherence: 'Gaps must be filled; explanations must be supplied; puzzles must be clarified. What we are after, it seems, is a narrative account that provides a coherent picture of the events in question' (Spence 1982, p. 180).

This, however, is where Lacan's notion of transference complicates and entangles things. For it is not at all clear, reading Lacan, that the aim of analysis, or of analytic discourse, is to construct a coherent – that is to say, plausible, finished – story. I would go so far as to say that this is precisely *not* the aim of analytic discourse, according to Lacan.

But I am getting ahead of myself, rushing prematurely from Vienna to Paris. It is imperative to talk of *Dora* – and I realize that my own desire to rush beyond her manifests anxiety of a transferential kind. For more than *Nadja*, even more than *Lol V. Stein, Dora* is a text – and a woman – surrounded by commentaries. In order to reach Dora, will I have to settle for writing commentaries on the commentaries? But what kind of text will that produce? Perhaps it will be hysterical.

At the end of his paper 'The dynamics of transference', Freud speaks about 'the struggle between physician and patient, between intellect and instinct. ... This is the ground on which the victory must be won' (Freud 1963b [1912], p. 114). And in the postscript to *Dora* he says it was because he did not 'succeed in mastering the transference in good time' that he lost the struggle. As many commentators have pointed out, however, starting with Lacan (1952), Freud's real error lay not in failing to master the transference but in trying too hard to master Dora and her story. Indeed, Freud literally tried to ram down Dora's throat the story of her love for Herr K.:

> 'So you see that your love for Herr K. did not come to an end with the scene, but that (as I maintained) it has persisted down to the present day – though it is true that you are unconscious of it.'
> – And Dora disputed the fact no longer.
>
> (Freud 1963a, p. 125)

Dora did not dispute the 'fact', but she opened the next sitting by informing him that it was her last. Marcus's comment on this seems most apt: 'Dora refused to be a character in the story that Freud was composing for her' (Marcus 1975, p. 307).

The most common explanation for why Freud was so intent on forcing this rather unsavory story[4] on Dora is that he himself identified too much with Herr K., a man 'still quite young and of prepossessing appearance', as he put it in a footnote (Freud 1963a, p. 44). Here, then, would be an example of unrecognized countertransference (or more simply, transference) on the part of the analyst. I would suggest, however, that Freud's love story for Dora was inspired not only by his putting himself in Herr K.'s place but also by his putting himself in the place of an omniscient narrator who, having a limited number of 'characters' to work with, must find the most plausible and psychologically motivated solution to their entanglements. In other words, it was the desire for narrative coherence *as such* (based on the only model Freud appreciated, that of the nineteenth-century realist novel, whose privileged subject, as Tony Tanner has shown, was adultery) that may have been a driving force. Freud's own transference, then, was not only to Herr K. but to Balzac – by which I do not mean that Freud desired to write fiction (he vigorously defended himself against that idea, which he considered an accusation), but that, to the extent that he had to construct stories, he desired to possess the authority of a Balzacian narrator.

At the same time, even as he was hammering home his tale of heterosexual jealousy and passion, he set in motion a major 'counter-story', that of Dora's homosexual love for Frau K. – *but it was not a story he told to Dora herself.* This story is elaborated in digressions: first, quite early in the main text (pp. 77–81), then in three long footnotes, which were all already in the 1905 edition (pp. 126, 133, 142). Whereas the heterosexual love-story is addressed to Dora, who is both narratee and recalcitrant protagonist, the alternate, homosexual love story is communicated, as a 'complication' (p. 77), only to the reader.

What links, if any, can we establish between Freud's desire for narrative mastery (what I have called, somewhat facetiously, his transference to Balzac) and his 'splitting' of Dora's story into two versions? There are several possible answers to this question, but here I am going to consider only one, starting from Neil Hertz's illuminating idea that Freud's biggest problem in this case history was his desire not to be confused with Dora herself – not so much because he feared 'feminization' (although that was surely a factor) but because he did not want his *own discourse*, his own knowledge, to be confused with those of the hysteric (Hertz 1983).

This, it seems to me, is the most interesting entanglement of Freud in Dora's case. The desire for narrative mastery would then turn out not only to be a therapeutic desire for the cure but also a personal and intellectual defence against the 'contamination' of psychoanalysis and of the psychoanalyst's discourse by its object. A year before he began the treatment of Dora, Freud already expressed anxiety about mastery in talking about the style of his 'dream book', which he had just finished. He wrote to Fliess:

> Somewhere inside me there is a feeling for form, an appreciation of beauty as a kind of perfection; and the tortuous sentences of my dream book, with their parading of indirect phrases and squinting at ideas, deeply offended one of my ideals. Nor am I far wrong in regarding this lack of form as an indication of insufficient mastery of the material.
>
> (Freud 1985, p. 374)

The 'material' in this case was chiefly his own dreams. In Dora's case, the material was Dora's dreams, Dora's history, and Dora's desire. Freud could not 'sufficiently master' these either, no matter how hard he tried. The 'splitting' of Dora's love story may be read as one indication (a symptom?) of the way in which the case history itself becomes 'hysterical', caught up in what Freud, referring to Dora in another letter to Fliess, called the 'conflicting thought processes ... between an inclination toward men and an inclination toward women' (p. 434).

But perhaps even more interesting, from my point of view, is a single moment in the case history where it is not Freud's *narrative* that is contaminated by hysteria but Freud's own unconscious that seems to become indistinguishable from Dora's. Neil Hertz notices this moment, but fails to notice, I think, what is really significant in it. It occurs during the interpretation of Dora's second dream, the one in which a thick wood (*Wald*), a train station (*Bahnhof*) and a cemetery (*Friedhof*) figure prominently. Associating to this dream, Dora recalls that she saw a similar wood the day before in a picture at an exhibition: 'In the background of the picture were nymphs.' Following this is a paragraph Hertz quotes in its entirety:

> At this point a certain suspicion of mine became a certainty. The use of *Bahnhof* and *Friedhof* to represent the female genitals was striking enough in itself, but it also served to direct my sharpened curiosity to the similarly formed *Vorhof* (vestibulum) – an anatomical term for a particular region of the female genitals. This might have been no more than a witty error. But now, with the addition of 'nymphs' visible in the background of a 'thick wood', no further doubts could be entertained. Here was a symbolic geography of sex! 'Nymphae,' as is known to physicians though not to laymen (and even by the former the term is not very commonly used), is the name given to the labia minora, which lie in the background of the 'thick wood' of the pubic hair. But any one who used such technical names as *Vorhof* and 'nymphae' must have derived his knowledge from books, and not from popular ones either, but from anatomical text-books or from an encyclopaedia – the common refuge of youth when it is devoured by sexual curiosity. If this interpretation were correct, therefore, there lay concealed behind the first situation in the dream a phantasy of defloration, of how a man seeks to force an entrance into the female genitals. (Freud 1963a, pp. 119–20; I have modified the translation somewhat to conform more closely to the original German)

What strikes Hertz as most curious are the last three sentences,

and the logic by which Freud arrives at the very last sentence. Hertz asks: 'is the shift to the masculine pronoun ['any one who used such technical names ... must have derived *his* knowledge'] a way of suggesting that such reading habits, though indulged in by women, are essentially masculine, and hence coordinate with male fantasies of defloration?' He concludes that this would be in line with Freud's persistence in characterizing Dora's love for Frau K. as 'masculine', but that it is above all a sign of Freud's anxiety 'to draw the line between the operations in the hysteric which produce the text of her illness, and those in the analyst which seek to interpret and dissolve that text' (Hertz 1983, p. 73).

I agree with Hertz's conclusion, but I am surprised that he did not notice the astonishing way in which the beginning of Freud's paragraph fails, precisely, to 'draw the line' between operations in the hysteric and those in the analyst. For the really curious slippage in this text is not the use of the masculine qualifier, which in the German construction of the sentence is grammatically *required* ('*Wer* aber solche technische Namen ... gebrauchte, *der* musste seine Kenntnis aus Büchern geschöpft haben' – the 'Wer ... der' construction is obligatory).[5] The really curious slippage is the way *Freud*, not Dora, produces the word *Vorhof* in association with *Bahnhof* and *Friedhof*, and *then* proceeds to say that 'anyone who used such technical names as *Vorhof* and *Nymphen* must have derived his knowledge from books'.[6] At this point, we can no longer be certain whose associations are being interpreted, since Freud has merged his own *Vorhof* with Dora's *Nymphen* to produce the 'phantasy of defloration'. Whose rape phantasy, exactly, is this? And is the position of the subject of the phantasy 'masculine' or 'feminine'? (Dora phantasizes being raped, Dora phantasizes raping; Freud phantasizes Dora phantasizing she is being raped, Freud phantasizes Dora raping, Freud phantasizes being raped, Freud phantasizes raping. . . .)

Psychoanalysis, we have known for a long time, is about the unconscious and about human sexuality. It is also, as Marcus, Brooks and others have reminded us (see especially Brooks 1984) and as any reading of Freud confirms, about the possibilities and limits of narrative. One great virtue of the Dora case – which may explain its apparently endless capacity to generate commentaries and 'rewritings' – is that it dramatizes, as perhaps no other of Freud's writings does, the ways in which the desire of the narrating and of the interpreting subject is caught up, entangled with, contaminated by its object. Freud's multiple entanglements with Dora – on the levels of discourse, of desire and of sexuality – can be read as an allegory of the failure of psychoanalysis, which is at the same time, paradoxically, its greatest success: the failure to achieve complete 'mastery of the material'. Such a reading is, of course, itself necessarily caught up in a process of displacement, the reader/writer, I, contaminated by other texts, other 'sexts' (Hélène Cixous' portmanteau word). Interpreters beware: desire is contagious.

II

If we turn, or return, now to Breton and Duras, it may become clear why *Nadja* lies on one side and *Le Ravissement de Lol V. Stein* on the other of *la coupure épistémologique freudienne*. It may also become clear that what is at stake here is a radical difference that runs *across* and *within* modern writing, at least modern French writing; and that the implications of this difference are not indifferent, either for psychoanalysis or for literature.

That *Nadja* and *Lol V. Stein* are both resolutely *modern* texts is certain: they self-consciously contest and subvert traditional narrative authority and coherence, the authority and coherence on which 'the great tradition' of mimetic fiction is founded and to which Freud, as we have seen, still pledged theoretical allegiance. Where, then, lies the difference? It lies, I shall argue, in sexuality and in the unconscious, in desire, in transference; in the acceptance or refusal of genuine entanglement on the part of the male subject with the woman and her madness.

Nadja opens with a quintessentially analytic question: 'Qui suis-je?'/'Who am I?'. This question is immediately rephrased with a play on words produced by the particular genius of the French language: 'If for once I relied on a proverb, why would it not come down to knowing whom I "haunt"?' (Breton 1964, p. 9). Tell me whom you haunt, I'll tell you who you are, says the proverb. But Breton expresses worry over the word 'haunt', which threatens to 'lead him astray' ('ce dernier mot m'égare'):

It says a great deal more than it means to say, it makes me play, while alive, the role of a phantom, obviously it alludes to what I had to have ceased being in order to be *who* I am ['ce qu'il a fallu que je cessasse d'être, pour être *qui* je suis']. Taken, with only a slight exaggeration, in this sense, it leads me to think that what I take to be the objective, more or less deliberate manifestations of my existence are merely what passes, into the limits of this life, from an activity whose veritable field is wholly unknown to me.

(pp. 9–10; Breton's emphasis)

He then goes on to say what the word 'phantom' means to him:

The representation I have of a 'phantom' . . . suggests to me the finished image of a torment that can be eternal. It may be that my life is but an image of this kind, and that I am condemned to retrace my steps even while believing that I am exploring, to try and know [*connaître*] what I should be able to recognize [*reconnaître*], to learn a small part of what I have forgotten.

(p. 10)

I would suggest that Breton's refusal to take on this role of 'phantom' is tantamount to refusing both the existence of the unconscious ('an activity whose veritable field is wholly unknown to me') and the elaboration of continuous narrative. For to retrace one's steps while believing one is exploring, to try to know for the first time what one should be able to recognize, to learn a small part of what one has forgotten – isn't this one possible description of the enterprise of psychoanalysis? And wouldn't it be one possible description, as well, of a narrative project like that of, say, *A la Recherche du temps perdu*? Breton is not interested in that kind of project. What he wants to discover is his own 'differentiation' from other men (p. 11), not from himself. And he wants to discover his uniqueness not by seeing his life whole, moving through time, but in flashes, unexpected moments of revelation, chance encounters, dizzying coincidences. The whole first part of *Nadja* consists of a string of such coincidences and encounters, presented 'without established order', as they occur in his memory (p. 22).

I will concentrate here on a single encounter, which leads almost directly to the central section of the book, to what Breton calls the 'entrance onto the stage' ('entrée en scène') of his ostensible main character, Nadja. This preparatory, or premonitory, encounter is literally theatrical. Persuaded by the unanimous critical condemnation of a play that it couldn't be all bad, Breton goes to see it – and is marked by it for life: '*Les Détraquées* ['The Deranged Women' – literally, 'off the track'] . . . remains and will remain for a long time the only dramatic work (I mean, written exclusively for the stage) that I will want to remember' (p. 46). His fascination is such that, contrary to his principles, he proceeds to give a continuous, coherent account of the play's plot.

'The action takes place in a boarding school for young girls' (p. 46). It is almost time for the end of the year celebration; the headmistress is feverishly awaiting the arrival of a friend, a certain Solange. After a while, the noise of a carriage is heard:

> An adorable woman enters without knocking. It is she. . . . Blackhaired, brownhaired, I don't know. Young. Magnificent eyes, full of languor, subtlety, cruelty, despair. Slender, very soberly dressed . . . and that touch of the 'déclassé,' which we like so much.
>
> (p. 49)

To cut a long story short, the headmistress and Solange are lovers; Solange injects herself with morphine, 'displaying a marvelous thigh there, just above the dark garter' (p. 49). A ball bounces into the room, followed by a young girl. Curtain. In the second act, the young girl has disappeared. The doctor, having been called, is suspicious – already last year one of the boarders disappeared mysteriously and her body was later found in the well. The search continues. Finally, the headmistress opens a medicine closet and:

> The bloody body of the child appears, head down, and spills out onto the floor. The cry, the unforgettable cry . . . I don't know if the cry I am referring to was the exact end of the play, but I hope that its author . . . did not want to expose Solange to further trials, wishing to spare the character, too tempting to be true, from any appearance of punishment – a punishment which, in any case, it denies with all its splendour.
>
> (pp. 54–5)

As a matter of fact, the play did not end with the cry – and we know this because almost thirty years after the publication of *Nadja*, Breton published *Les Détraquées* in the first issue of his journal, *Le Surréalisme, même*. The play ended with the arrest of the headmistress and Solange, after several long, didactic and moraliz-ing scenes in which the doctor, a psychiatrist, explains to the police commissioner exactly what ailment the women were suffering from ('folie circulaire et périodique') and exactly what they did to the poor girl: 'ces dames pratiquaient le grand jeu'/'these women practised the great game', torturing her with pen-nibs before strangling her in a 'fit of sadistic passion' (Palau 1956 [1921], p. 116). The author of the play, P. L. Palau, explained in a postface that he wanted absolute scientific accuracy and obtained great help from 'the eminent Joseph Babinsky' (p. 120).

Now here is something to sharpen our curiosity, as Freud might say: Breton, neither in the 1928 version of *Nadja* nor in its 1962 revision (after he had presumably read the script), makes any mention of the doctor/*raisonneur* role in the play. In fact, he doesn't merely 'forget' but *actively negates* this role. In the fragment immediately following the plot summary, he returns once again to the play, specifically to the 'gap' between Acts I and II: 'The lack of sufficient indications about what happens after the fall of the ball, about exactly what Solange and her partner might be prey to, in becoming those superb beasts of prey, remains par excellence what confounds me' (Breton 1964, pp. 56–7) – this after stating that he had seen the play two or three more times after the first!

Either what Breton saw was not the play that Palau wrote; or what Breton wanted to see – and remember – was not the play that Palau wrote. For what Breton sees, in his recounting, and what excites and mesmerizes him, is the *spectacle* of female 'otherness': madness, murderousness, lesbianism. In order for the spectacle to produce its voyeuristic pleasure, it has to remain two-dimensional, lacking psychological motivation and depth. The voyeur's pleasure comes precisely from the distance between him and 'the scene', from the gap ('Curtain', at once cut and screen) into or onto which he can project his own phantasies.

The repressed returns, however: in the 1962 version of *Nadja* Breton adds a long footnote giving the reference to the published version of the play. And then he mentions Palau's postface:

> Great was my surprise when I learned that Dr. Babinsky had had a role in the elaboration of *Les Détraquées*. I remember the great neurologist well, having assisted him for a while as a 'temporary intern' in his service at la Pitié. I still feel honored by the kindness he showed me – going so far as to predict a great medical future for me! – and, in my own way, I think I have put his teaching to good use.
>
> (p. 54)

Good use indeed. But who was Joseph Babinsky? The son of Polish immigrants, one year younger than Freud, he had been Charcot's most famous pupil; after Charcot's death he became one of the leading French specialists on hysteria. His chief contribution to the study of that disease was his theory of 'simulation', according to which it was extremely difficult, if not impossible, to tell a 'real hysteric' from one who was merely 'acting' (see Roudinesco 1982, pp. 68–9). We may speculate with some delight on Babinsky's own pleasure in helping Palau 'elaborate' *Les Détraquées*. His name calls to mind another spectacle, however, for he was immortalized, as a young man, in Louis Brouillet's famous painting *Une leçon clinique à la Salpêtrière*. The painting shows the great Charcot lecturing to a group of seated men. To his left, slightly behind him, a young woman stands, half-swooned, throat and shoulders bared, supported at the waist by Babinsky. Her eyes are half closed, her lips slightly parted, as if smiling in sensual bliss. Charcot, ageing, portly, balding, beardless, faces his students while pointing at the woman. Babinsky's face, handsome and bearded, topped by a headful of wavy brown hair, is turned down towards her; his eyes are on her face and throat. (This painting is reproduced on the cover of Bernheimer and Kahane 1985.)

At this point we may digress for a moment to number 11 of the surrealist journal, *La Révolution surréaliste*, which appeared in 1928, the same year as *Nadja* – and the same year as the first French translation of Freud's 'Fragment of an analysis of a case of hysteria'. In this issue we find, among many other interesting things, a short, illustrated article co-signed by Breton and Aragon, entitled 'Le cinquantenaire de l'hystérie'. Among the article's more memorable features are six large photographs drawn from the *Iconographie de la Salpêtrière*, showing Charcot's star patient, Augustine, in various 'attitudes passionelles', lying or sitting, her hair loose, on her bed; and the following question, which contains the only mention of Freud's name: 'Does Freud, who owes so much to Charcot, remember the days when, according to the testimony of survivors, the interns at La Salpêtrière confused their professional duty and their taste for love, when, at nightfall, the patients joined them outside or received them in their beds?' (Breton and Aragon 1928, p. 20). One can only dream about how the author of 'Observations on transference-love' would have responded to this question.

The madwoman observed, theatricalized, photographed, eroticized – this was clearly the aspect of Charcot's legacy to which Breton most deeply responded. Much has been written about the photographs that accompany the text of *Nadja*: their function is to emphasize the documentary quality of the work, its 'anti-literariness', its abhorrence of descriptions reminiscent of the nineteenth-century novel, and so on. No one has suggested, however, that the photographs (which are not all of women, to be sure) may have an affinity with the nineteenth-century observation of hysterics – no one except Breton, that is. In the 1962 preface to *Nadja*, he unites in a single sentence a mention of the photographs with what he calls the 'medical' tone of his narrative:

> Just as the abundant photographic illustration has as its object to eliminate any description...., the tone adopted for the narrative copies [*se calque sur*] that of medical observation, especially neuropsychiatric observation, which tends to keep a trace of all that the examination and the interrogation can yield, without taking the least trouble, in reporting it, to prettify the style.
>
> (Breton 1964, p. 6)

One can question whether Breton did not take quite a bit of trouble over his style, but that's not the interesting thing about this statement. I react above all to the association of 'neuropsychiatric observation' with photographs (Charcot's works on hysteria were all accompanied by abundant illustrations, and Charcot's 'visual' approach to the hysteric has often been noted), and to the words 'examination' and 'interrogation'. For Charcot and the whole school of French neuropsychiatry that followed him, the psychiatric encounter consisted of looking at, pointing to and interrogating the patient.[7] Breton, who at one time thought of becoming a doctor, who had studied with Babinsky, who had spent several months as an 'apprentice' doctor in a psychiatric hospital during the war, had internalized this model to a degree that he was probably not aware of. One of the most famous passages in *Nadja* is the diatribe directed against asylums and psychiatrists (which, for Breton, meant *French* psychiatrists). And yet Breton's own encounter with Nadja, his own recounting of that encounter, his own role and stance and attitude in that encounter, evoke nothing so much as the phantasy embedded in the article on 'Le cinquantenaire de l'hystérie': to 'play doctor' with the madwoman, to know her carnally and otherwise, without ever forgetting *who* one is ('*qui* je suis'). Without becoming entangled with her, without 'ceasing to be oneself', without *haunting* her.

Breton met Nadja on the afternoon of 4 October 1926, on the Rue Lafayette, behind the Opera, during one of his aimless wanderings:

Suddenly, when she is still perhaps ten steps away from me, I see
coming toward me a young woman, very poorly dressed, who
also sees or has seen me. . . . An imperceptible smile may be
wandering over her face. Curiously made up, like someone who,
having started with the eyes, didn't have time to finish, but the
rims of the eyes so dark for a blond.

(p. 72)

And a long parenthesis later: 'I had never seen such eyes.' Inside
the parenthesis is an explanation that such an effect of brightness is
obtained only if one carefully applies the eye-liner under the lid (a
surprisingly 'feminine' piece of information), followed by the
apparently incidental remark ('Il est intéressant de noter à ce
propos . . .') that Blanche Derval in the role of Solange, even seen
from very close up, appeared to have no make-up on. After this,
Breton, who said earlier that to his great shame he never found out
more about Blanche Derval, stops Nadja and speaks to her. She
replies. And so begins their 'failed adventure', whose first and
most intense phase Breton recounts in the form of a diary. This
phase ends nine days after the first meeting, on the afternoon of 13
October in a hotel room in Saint-German-en-Laye, where certain
'scenes of her past life', recounted by Nadja to Breton, almost
'drove me away from her forever' ('ont failli m'éloigner d'elle à
jamais', p. 134). In fact, they do seem to have driven him away from
her, for after this the narrative becomes generalized and atemporal:
'I saw Nadja again many times' (p. 136). Here is where Breton
resembles most the 'neuropsychiatric observer', giving us examples of Nadja's enigmatic drawings (reproduced in photographs), quoting her strange utterances, citing her uncanny ability
to make unexpected associations (like surrealist metaphors?) and
arrive at 'correct' interpretations of surrealist paintings.

This phase of observation ends with a general reflection by
Breton on his fundamental difference from Nadja ('I had, for a long
time already, ceased having an understanding with [*m'entendre avec*]
Nadja. To tell the truth, perhaps we never understood each other',
p. 157). Finally, there comes the last shattering fragment: 'On est
venu, il y a quelques mois, m'apprendre que Nadja était folle' –
'Some people came to tell me, a few months ago, that Nadja was
mad' (p. 159). Breton was very far from her by then, as the
curiously impersonal construction of the sentence indicates. The
next sentence is equally distanced: 'As a result of eccentricities in

which, it seems, she had indulged in the hallways of her hotel, she had had to be committed to the Vaucluse asylum.' The sentence after that raises the disturbing possibility that Breton himself played a determining role in Nadja's madness. This question is deflected by the seven-page diatribe against psychiatrists and asylums, but to his credit Breton returns to it at the end of the fragment. Had he perhaps encouraged her too much along her road to absolute freedom and flaunting of conventions, unaware that she lacked the essential instinct for self-preservation which he and his friends never lost *in fact*? This question is left unanswered. The final section of the book, separated by a blank page, is written after a hiatus of several months, and is addressed to an unnamed woman with whom Breton is in love.

Much has been written about *Nadja* – both the book and the woman – as an embodiment of surrealist ideals. But I feel that the question of Breton's own relation to Nadja, which he himself poses, is the crucial one. Breton's answer, both in the book and in his later commentaries on it, was that the problem was he did not love her: despite all her attractions and seductions, she did not succeed in inspiring in him 'l'amour pur et simple' that the woman to whom the last part of the book is addressed did inspire (Breton 1969, pp. 141–2).

Are we to blame him for this? Certainly not: the ways of love are mysterious, and besides, Nadja was crazy.[8] But we may not be entirely wrong in saying that Breton's conception of 'pure and simple' love – which, by a supreme irony again produced by the French language, he called 'l'amour fou', 'mad love' – precluded precisely the possibility of his being *touched* by madness, or simply by the 'otherness' in femininity. Observed on a stage, distanced from him by the screen of phantasy, female 'otherness' excited him. Close up, he fled from it. The scenes Nadja told him about on 13 October almost drove him away forever, he says, because he judged that they had 'compromised her dignity'. The only one he actually reports, however, has more to it than that:

A story of a punch in the face that made her blood spurt, one day, in a private room at the brasserie Zimmer, a punch in the face received from a man whom she gave herself the nasty pleasure of refusing simply because he was short – and several times she had called for help, not without taking the occasion, before disappearing, of bloodying the man's clothes.

(Breton 1964, p. 134)

The question we cannot fail to ask, I think, is this: was Breton sickened by the loss of Nadja's dignity, or by the image of a man spattered with female blood?

III

This brings me, at long last, to *Le Ravissement de Lol V. Stein*. Published in 1964, thirty-six years after *Nadja*, fifty-nine years after *Dora*, this is yet one more story about a doctor and a madwoman. But the author of the story is a woman, aware of herself writing 'as a woman' – and that, I think, makes a certain difference. The fictional narrator created by Marguerite Duras is a man, Jacques Hold, 36 years old, a doctor, probably a psychiatrist although this is only suggested, not affirmed. He tells the story of Lola Valérie Stein, Lol V. Stein. He tells the story haltingly, uncertainly, retracing his steps while exploring. He says that where he does not know, he imagines; he says that he knows Lol V. Stein the only way he can, by love (Duras 1964, p. 46).

The first scene he imagines, over and over, is the scene of the ball at T. Beach, where Lol watched all night as her fiancé, Michael Richardson, danced with Anne-Marie Stretter. In the morning, he went away with her, and Lol went mad. Mad because she had lost him? Mad because she had lost the sight of him and Anne-Marie Stretter, because she never saw the end of the scene, where Michael Richardson would take off Anne-Marie Stretter's black dress. Deprived of this last image, the ball continues to unfold eternally in 'the cinema of Lol V. Stein' (p. 46).

Jacques meets Lol years after this ball, when she has returned to S. Tahla, her native city, married and a mother. Before recounting the scene of their first meeting, he tells, imagines, another scene, which took place a few days earlier: Lol follows a man through the city to its outskirts, to a lover's rendezvous; the woman he meets is Lol's childhood friend, Tatiana Karl; the hotel where they meet is the hotel where Lol used to meet Michael Richardson. Stretched out in a field of rye, Lol watches through a lighted window while the man and Tatiana make love.

The man was Jacques Hold. A few days later, Lol pays a visit to Tatiana, who is with her husband and her lover. Lol looks at Jacques Hold, who sees her looking at him and wants to 'see her eyes on [him] again' (p. 83). So begins, in the middle of the book, the account of the entanglement which prompted Jacques Hold to begin his narration; which has been present, although unspecified, from the very beginning of that narration ('l'écrasante actualité de cette femme dans ma vie' – 'the crushing presentness of this woman in my life', p. 14); and which perhaps may never end. The entanglement, the love, is chiefly between Jacques and Lol. But it could not come into being, and continue, without the 'third term', Tatiana. Tatiana and Jacques making love, watched by Lol; Tatiana and Lol with their arms around each other, talking, watched and overheard – at Lol's arranging, knowing that she has arranged it *for* him – by Jacques; Lol and Jacques dancing, watched by Tatiana, who does not know; Jacques making love to Tatiana in their hotel room, knowing this time that Lol is watching; Jacques and Lol making love, but Lol calling herself, in the midst of cries, insults and supplications, 'Tatiana Karl and Lol V. Stein'. And once again, Jacques in the hotel room, waiting for Tatiana, his eyes on Lol who has preceded him in the field of rye. The narrative stops here, but it could obviously go on.

Lacan, in what I think is the only piece he wrote about a living author, spoke about *Le Ravissement de Lol V. Stein* in his 'Hommage fait à Marguerite Duras'. 'Marguerite Duras shows that she knows without me what I teach' (Lacan 1979 [1965], p. 133). The apparent arrogance of this statement is attenuated by the sentence just before it, which, despite its tortuous syntax, succeeds in telling us that Lacan agrees with Freud: 'the artist always precedes [the psychoanalyst], who therefore does not need to act like a psychologist [*faire le psychologue*] where the artist shows him the way' (p. 133). To say, then, that I wish to read *Lol V. Stein* 'with' Lacan is not to suggest that Lacan's theories 'apply' to the novel or that this work 'illustrates' his theories. Rather, it is to suggest that each can be read as a commentary on the other – subject to subject, not subject to object. A couple, in sum.

Lacan writes about Jacques Hold that as narrator he is not 'a simple demonstrator of the machine [*montreur de la machine*] but one of its inner springs [*un de ses ressorts*] who does not know everything that holds him in it [*ne sait pas tout ce qui l'y prend*]' (p. 132).[9] When I say that Jacques Hold becomes entangled with Lol, becomes ravished by Lol as he reinvents her own ravishment, I mean precisely that. To be a demonstrator is to be outside, to observe. It is to be where Breton was, where Freud wished to be. Jacques Hold is, and wishes to be, inside; he is *riveted* to Lol: 'Nous voici chevillés ensemble' (Duras 1964, p. 113 – *cheviller*: to peg, to bolt, to pin together). Lol's desire has chosen him. 'Je suis l'homme de S. Tahla qu'elle a décidé de suivre' (p. 113): he is the man of S. Tahla she has decided to follow – and he follows her, across the city and into her dreams. 'Lol rêve d'un autre temps . . .' – 'Lol dreams of another time when the same thing that is about to happen would happen differently. . . . That dream contaminates me' (p. 187). He follows Lol into her memories: 'Lol was looking. Behind her I tried to adjust my gaze so closely to hers that I began to remember, more and more each moment, her own remembrance [*me souvenir . . . de son souvenir*]' (p. 180).

Is Jacques Hold Lol's phantom, the one who haunts her? There is a wonderfully complicated moment in Lacan's 'Hommage fait à Marguerite Duras' where that idea is suggested and where the word 'hanter' occurs; it is complicated because Lacan tells us in the next sentence that this idea is not his but comes to him from Marguerite Duras. And in the sentence after that, he puts it, in his own name, into question. Here is how it goes:

> Cet être à trois pourtant [the triangle of Lol–Tatiana–Jacques], c'est bien Lol qui l'arrange. Et c'est pour ce que le 'pense' de Jacques Hold vient *hanter* Lol d'un soin trop proche, à la fin du roman sur la route où il l'accompagne d'un pèlerinage au lieu de l'événement [the ballroom of T. Beach] – que Lol devient folle.
>
> Dont en effet l'épisode porte des signes, mais dont j'entends faire état ici que je le tiens de Marguerite Duras.
>
> C'est que la dernière phrase du roman ramenant Lol dans le champ de seigle, me paraît faire une fin moins décisive que cette remarque. Où se devine la mise en garde contre le pathétique de la compréhension. Etre comprise ne convient pas à Lol, qu'on ne sauve pas du ravissement.
>
> (Lacan 1974, p. 135; my emphasis)

This three-fold being, however, is indeed arranged by Lol. And it is because the 'thinking' of Jacques Hold comes to haunt Lol with too much solicitude, at the end of the novel, on the road where he accompanies her on a pilgrimage to the place of the event – that Lol becomes mad.

Which, in effect, is suggested by certain signs in the episode, but about which I want to state that I have it from Marguerite Duras.

For the last sentence of the novel, bringing Lol back to the field of rye, seems to me to create a less decisive ending than this remark. Wherein one sees a warning against the pathos of understanding. To be understood does not suit Lol; she is not one to be saved from ravishment.

(My translation)

The first paragraph offers an explanation, even a kind of plot summary: Lol 'arranges' the triangle that will allow her to repeat the scene of the ball (herself as observer, Jacques and Tatiana observed). And because Jacques Hold's 'thinking', his attempt to reinvent Lol's story, comes too close to her, because he 'haunts' her too much with his own solicitude (*soin trop proche*) when he accompanies her on a visit to the scene of the original 'event', she becomes mad.

The second paragraph states that, although in effect there are signs in the last episode (the return to T. Beach) to support this interpretation, Lacan wishes to emphasize that he has it directly from Marguerite Duras.

For as far as Lacan is concerned, says the third paragraph, the final sentence of the novel, which brings Lol back to the field of rye, suggests a 'less decisive' ending. 'Wherein one sees a warning against the pathos of understanding. To be understood does not suit Lol; she is not one to be saved from ravishment.'

I agree. And I dare think, since her name has been invoked, that Marguerite Duras would agree too. Lol does not 'become' mad at the end, not any more than she has been throughout. The warning about trying to understand her is not directed at Jacques Hold but at a reader who would be content with the too easy 'plot summary' offered in paragraph one. Jacques Hold does not need a warning, for he makes no claim to understand Lol V. Stein or to save her from ravishment. For him, nothing ends at the end of the novel, no more than for her. The last sentence (in fact, it's the last two paragraphs that Lacan refers to) is not an ending but a suspension:

Night was falling when I arrived at the Hotel des Bois.
Lol had preceded us. She was sleeping in the field of rye, tired, tired by our voyage.

(Duras 1964, p. 191)

The voyage can continue; nothing says it won't. And Jacques Hold (but let us not forget, behind him, Marguerite Duras) can go on speaking, writing, not what he knows, but what he does not know. For, the very first moment he saw Lol, he understood one thing: 'to have no knowledge at all about Lol was to know her already. One could, I realized, know even less, ever less and less, about Lol V. Stein' (Duras 1964, p. 81).

If Jacques Hold 'haunts' Lol, it is to the exact degree that she haunts him: 'Nous voici chevillés ensemble. Notre dépeuplement grandit. Nous nous répétons nos noms' (p. 113). What does it mean to say 'Our depopulation increases', right after, 'We are riveted together'? And what does it mean to repeat for each other, to each other, to ourselves [*nous nous répétons*] our names, our 'no's', no no's (*nõnõ*)? We are being emptied, riveted together. Our names do not name us, we are not our names.

When (the moment before this) Lol pronounces his name, Jacques is ravished:

> Virginité de Lol prononçant ce nom! Qui avait remarqué l'inconsistance de la croyance en cette personne ainsi nommée sinon elle, Lol V. Stein, la soi-disant Lol V. Stein? Fulgurante trouvaille. ... Pour la première fois mon nom prononcé ne nomme pas.
>
> (pp. 112–13)

Who had ever noticed the inconsistency – the fragility – the lack of solidity – of the person called Jacques Hold, of the person so called, if not she, if not Lol V. Stein, the so-called Lol V. Stein, whose name of 'stone' does not harden her any more than his holds him? She has found in him what no one else has found, recognized in him what no one else has recognized, what he himself didn't see – the absence in his name, precisely that in him which his name does not name. And he does the same for her.

> —Lola Valérie Stein.
> —Oui.
> A travers la transparence de son être incendié, de sa nature détruite, elle m'accueille d'un sourire. Son choix est exempt de toute préférence. Je suis l'homme de S. Tahla qu'elle a décidé de suivre. Nous voici chevillés ensemble. Notre dépeuplement grandit. Nous nous répétons nos noms.
>
> (p. 113)

Two transparencies, two names emptied of solidity, two beings depopulated, riveted together. That is what Jacques Hold's ravishment by and of Lol V. Stein is about.[10]

Lacan, on the last two pages of his 1973 seminar, *Encore*, operates a breathtaking reversal (Lacan 1975 [1973]). Having spent the whole book explaining a few provocative opening statements, such as 'il n'y a pas de rapport sexuel' ('there is no sexual relation', p. 17) and 'il sera à jamais impossible d'écrire comme tel le rapport sexuel' ('it will be forever impossible to write the sexual relation as such', p. 36), he ends by speaking – not for the first time, but for the first time in *this way* – about love. Love, he says, is not a sexual relation, if by that one means the orgasmic reunion of two bodies; instead, it is a momentary, oh so vulnerable *recognition* between two subjects, two split subjects inhabited by lack. It is only this recognition, this encounter of two absences that, as if by miracle, can produce for a moment the illusion that the sexual relation, thus redefined, can cease not being written, *cesse de ne pas s'écrire*. And to displace the negation once again, from *cesse de ne pas s'écrire* to *ne cesse pas de s'écrire* (does not cease being written, writing itself) – that is the (impossible?) aim towards which love tends: 'Tout amour, de ne subsister que du *cesse de ne pas s'écrire*, tend à faire passer la négation au *ne cesse pas de s'écrire*, ne cesse pas, ne cessera pas', 'All love, subsisting on the *ceases not to be written*, tends to displace the negation to *does not cease to be written, to write itself*, does not cease, will not cease' (p. 132).

I will not dot the i's and cross the t's by pointing out the ways in which this magnificently pessimistic and at the same time inspired and inspiring, totally modern yet surprisingly romantic view of love and of its relation to writing responds and corresponds to the pessimistic, inspired and inspiring, magnificently romantic, totally modern vision of love and of *écriture* that Marguerite Duras has pursued in her novels and films since *Le Ravissement de Lol V. Stein*. Instead, I shall end by raising (very briefly) the question of how a feminine discourse – both as criticism and as *écriture* – might situate itself in relation to the discourse of psychoanalysis today. What I tried to suggest, in my reading of Freud, is that the desire to 'master the material' – whether it be dreams, the unconscious, the woman's body, sexual difference or narrative itself – was both the generating impulse and the Achilles' heel of the psychoanalytic project. I also tried to suggest that insofar as it *is* the Achilles' heel, it is a good thing – to be vulnerable, to be open to the risk of pain and death, is the sign of being human. It has also, for a long time and in very specific ways, been the additional sign, in our culture, of being a woman. Women bleed, women give birth, women have holes in them. The discourse of psychoanalysis becomes obnoxious, and noxious, during those moments when, faced with the

openness of women, which it suddenly calls castration, it trans-
forms women into Woman, and Woman into the flawed opposite
of Man.

When he was not being wilfully obnoxious ('La femme n'est pas
toute', etc.) Lacan, I think (I like to think), knew this. Reading
Lacan with Duras, we see emerging the possibility of a psychoanalytic discourse that would not be a discourse of mastery but a
discourse of mutual entanglement. Who writes, or speaks, in the *ne
cesse pas, ne cessera pas* that Lacan leaves us desiring? Who speaks,
or writes, the ravishment of Lol V. Stein? Feminine discourse,
which is not always where one expects to find it, reminds us that
when it comes to being human, we are all in a position of
ravishment (call it lack, if you must); it reminds us that our
brightest hope for survival – call it love – is, against all odds and
through all our divisions, to keep on writing.[11]

Notes

1 All translations from the French are my own. I have consulted with
profit Richard Howard's translation of *Nadja* (New York, Grove
Press, 1960).

2 Breton revised *Nadja* and added a preface and notes to a new edition
published thirty-four years after the original version; and he kept
coming back to it, quoting from it and commenting on it, in
published interviews, in the *Second Surrealist Manifesto* (1935) and in
other writings. Duras has stated in numerous interviews and self-
commentaries that *Lol V. Stein* was the real beginning of a new way of
writing for her (Duras and Porte 1977, p. 90). The three films (*La
Femme du Gange, India Song, Son nom de Venise dans Calcutta désert*) and
two novels (*Le Vice-Consul, L'Amour*) that followed *Lol V. Stein* can
themselves be read as developments and glosses on that book.

3 There is at least one important feature that differentiates *Dora* from
the other two texts: it is a factual, clinical case history, whereas *Nadja*
and *Le Ravissement de Lol V. Stein* are 'literature'; and between the
latter texts there is a difference too, for *Le Ravissement* clearly presents
itself as fiction (the author is a woman, the narrator is a man), whereas
Nadja explicitly rejects the fictional mode and claims to tell 'nothing
but the truth' about Breton's life. These generic distinctions,
although not insignificant, are not relevant to my present argument.

4 Herr K., much older than Dora, was the husband of Dora's father's
mistress. Dora's anger stemmed partly from her sense that she was
being used as a pawn by the three adults.

5 I wish to thank Dorrit Cohn for helping me to analyse this passage in German. See Freud, 'Bruchstück einer Hysterie-Analyse', in *Studienausgabe*, Frankfurt, S. Fischer, 1971, vol. 6, pp. 166–67.

6 This slippage has been noted, in a somewhat different argumentative context, by Madelon Sprengnether (1985, p. 66).

7 This model was fixed and has come down to us in an illuminating multi-volume document, Charcot's *Leçons de mardi à la Salpêtrière*, consisting of verbatim transcripts of the famous 'Leçons'. At each session Charcot would interrogate several patients, addressing didactic remarks to his audience. (For recent selections, see Charcot 1971 and 1974). The *présentation de cas* has remained a central teaching procedure in French psychiatry down to our own day and was used by Lacan as well. Lacan, however, did not address remarks to his public 'above the patient's head' in the latter's presence. For an example of a Lacanian case presentation, see 'A Lacanian psychosis: interview by Jacques Lacan', in Schneiderman (1980, pp. 19–41).

8 She was also poor, and a prostitute on occasion. This introduces the important element of class and social 'respectability' into her relations with Breton, who never ceased living like a good *bourgeois*. Houdebine (1971) remarks that Breton 'missed' not only Freud's epistemological revolution but that of Marx as well.

9 Interestingly, one thing Lacan nowhere mentions is that Jacques Hold is a doctor. Could this have been Lacan's own 'avoidance' of the entanglements of transference?

10 I should note that this reading of *Le Ravissement*, and of Jacques Hold's position in that text, situates me at a critical distance from the influential 'anti-Lacanian' feminist reading proposed by Marcelle Marini. According to Marini's reading, Jacques Hold behaves in typically 'male' fashion by appropriating both Lol's gaze and her story: 'Jacques Hold will live out other scenes of love by giving himself to be seen by Lol, whose gaze remains his surest support: she, confined to her watching-place, will henceforth support by her gaze ... the unchanging splendor of the masculine sex. ... And further-more it is he who controls the discourse whereby he can narrate, at a distance, their story at will, putting himself in the first person while Lol becomes the one he speaks about, the one in whose place he most often speaks in order to sketch her portrait. He is the one who will reconstitute the pieces of the puzzle that is a woman' (Marini 1977, p. 31). In Marini's reading, Jacques Hold remains 'untouched' by Lol, using her to affirm both his sexual and discursive centrality; in that reading, Duras' authorial attitude would have to be seen as *ironic* towards the male narrator. My reading, on the contrary, assumes a significant merging between Duras' authorial voice (and vision) and the voice of Jacques Hold – as if the subversive quality of the novel resided precisely in the 'feminization' of the male narrator, who is

'contaminated' by femininity both on the diegetic or story level (his involvement with Lol) *and* on the discursive level (Jacques' narration is hesitant, uncertain, full of silences, corresponding to Duras' notion of what a 'feminine writing' might be – see Duras and Gauthier 1974). It is important, I think, that Jacques Hold's narrative discourse is *similar* to the narrative discourse of other Duras novels – beginning with *Moderato Cantabile* (1958), which according to Duras constituted a break in her writing – where the narrator is either a woman (*L'Amant*) or else of unspecified gender (*Moderato Cantabile, L'Amour*). One might see in Duras' 'feminization' of Jacques Hold a decentering of the masculine, its displacement towards the margins where femininity (and madness) have traditionally been lodged. This raises some important questions for feminist theory in general and for the practice of 'feminine writing' in particular, which I shall take up in another essay.

11 I have been asked by some who have read this essay in manuscript whether I am 'advocating a Laingian approach where the therapist "shares" in the patient's madness'. In fact, I am in no position to advocate any approach at all, *for* psychoanalysis or psychoanalysts; I can only suggest, speaking as an outsider, what aspects of psychoanalytic discourse strike me as more or less appealing, more or less relevant to feminist thinking about sexual difference and about narrative. My reading of Lacan is itself perhaps subversive, tending to 'feminize' his discourse as Duras feminizes Jacques Hold's. But Lacan, like Duras' narrator/lover, lends himself quite readily to such takeovers. (After finishing this essay I was pleased to see this view of Lacan endorsed in Gallop 1985.)

References

Beaujour, Michel (1967) 'Qu'est-ce que *Nadja?*', *La Nouvelle revue française*, 172, 780–99.

Bernheimer, Charles and Kahane, Claire (eds) (1985) *In Dora's Case: Freud–Hysteria–Feminism*, New York, Columbia University Press.

Breton, André (1937) *L'Amour fou*, Paris, Gallimard.

—(1955) [1933] *Les Vases communicants*, Paris, Gallimard.

—(1964) [1928] *Nadja*, Paris, Gallimard.

—(1969) *Entretiens*, Paris, Gallimard.

—(1971) [1947] *Arcane 17*, Paris, Pauvert.

Breton, André and Aragon, Louis (1928) 'Le cinquantenaire de l'hystérie, 1878–1928', *La Révolution surréaliste*, 11, 20–2.

Brooks, Peter (1984) *Reading for the Plot: Design and Intention in Narrative*, New York, Knopf.

—(1985) 'Constructions psychanalytiques et narratives', *Poétique*, 61, 63–73.

Charcot, J. B. (1971) *L'Hystérie: textes choisis et présentés par E. Trillat*, Toulouse, Privat.

—(1974) *Leçons de mardi à la Salpêtrière* (selections), Paris, Centre d'étude et de promotion de la lecture.

Duras, Marguerite (1964) *Le Ravissement de Lol V. Stein*, Paris, Gallimard, Folio edition.

—(1965) *Le Vice-Consul*, Paris, Gallimard.

—(1972) *L'Amour*, Paris, Gallimard.

—(1973) *La Femme du Gange* (film).

—(1975) *India Song* (film).

—(1976) *Son nom de Venise dans Calcutta désert* (film).

Duras, Marguerite and Gauthier, Xavière (1974) *Les Parleuses*, Paris, Minuit.

Duras, Marguerite and Porte, Michelle (1977) *Les Lieux de Marguerite Duras*, Paris, Minuit.

Felman, Shoshana (1975) 'Women and madness: the critical phallacy', *Diacritics*, 5 (4), 2–10.

—(1977) 'Turning the screw of interpretation', *Yale French Studies: Literature and Psychoanalysis. The Question of Reading: Otherwise*, 55/6, 94–207.

Freud, Sigmund (1963a) [1905] *Dora: An Analysis of a Case of Hysteria*, New York, Collier Books.

—(1963b) [1912] 'The dynamics of transference', in *Therapy and Technique*, New York, Collier Books, pp. 105–16.

—(1963c) [1915] 'Further recommendations in the technique of psychoanalysis: observations on transference-love', in *Therapy and Technique*, New York, Collier Books, pp. 167–80.

—(1985) *The Complete Letters of Sigmund Freud to Wilhelm Fliess, 1887–1904*, Moussaieff Masson, Jeffrey (ed. and trans.), Cambridge, Mass., Harvard University Press.

Gallop, Jane (1985) *Reading Lacan*, Ithaca, NY, Cornell University Press.

Hertz, Neil (1983) 'Dora's secrets, Freud's techniques', *Diacritics*, 13 (1), 65–80. Reprt. in Bernheimer and Kahane (1985).

Houdebine, Jean-Louis (1971) 'Méconnaissance de la psychanalyse dans le discours surréaliste', *Tel Quel*, 46, 67–82.

Lacan, Jacques (1973) [1964] *Le Séminaire, XI: Les Quatre concepts fondamentaux de la psychanalyse*, Paris, Seuil.

—(1975) [1972–73] *Le Séminaire, XX: Encore*, Paris, Seuil.

—(1979) [1965] 'Hommage fait à Marguerite Duras, du ravissement de Lol V. Stein', in Duras, M. *et al.* (eds), *Marguerite Duras*, Paris, Albatros, pp. 131–7.

—(1985) [1952] 'Intervention on transference', in Bernheimer, Charles and Kahane, Claire (eds), *In Dora's Case: Freud–Hysteria–Feminism*, New York, Columbia University Press, pp. 92–104.

Marini, Marcelle (1977) *Territoires du féminin: avec Marguerite Duras*, Paris, Minuit.

Marcus, Steven (1975) 'Freud and Dora: story, history, case history', in *Representations: Essays on Literature and Society*, New York, Random House.

Palau, P. L. (1956) [1921] *Les Détraquées*, in *Le Surréalisme, même*, 1, 73–120.

Roudinesco, Elisabeth (1982) *La Bataille de cent ans: histoire de la psychanalyse en France*, vol. 1, 1885–1939, Paris, Ramsay.

Spence, Donald P. (1982) *Narrative Truth and Historical Truth: Meaning and Interpretation in Psychoanalysis*, New York, Norton.

Schneiderman, Stuart (ed.) (1980) *Returning to Freud: Clinical Psychoanalysis in the School of Lacan*, New Haven, Conn., Yale University Press.

Sprengnether, Madelon (1985) 'Enforcing Oedipus: Freud and Dora', in Garner, S., Kahane, C. and Sprengnether, M. (eds) *The (M)other Tongue: Essays in Feminist Psychoanalytic Interpretation*, Ithaca, NY, Cornell University Press, pp. 51–71. Rprt. in Bernheimer and Kahane (1985).

Tanner, Tony (1980) *Adultery in the Novel: Contract and Transgression*, Baltimore, Johns Hopkins University Press.

8

Tragic drama and the family: the killing of children and the killing of story-telling

BENNETT SIMON

My thesis is, first, that tragic drama deals intensively with conflict within the family and, specifically with the problem of the continuation and propagation of the family that is at war within itself. The conflicts, whether between the husband and wife, or between the generations, or between differing visions of the political loyalties of the family – these conflicts threaten the ability of the family to beget children, to raise children or to allow for an orderly transmission of authority and values from one generation to the next. For our purposes here, I define tragic drama as the study of how the family can both wish to propagate itself and its values and simultaneously act in such a way as to foreclose that possibility.[1] Ancient, Shakespearian and modern tragic dramas deal in characteristic ways with these issues.

The second part of this thesis is that the content of tragic drama, as I here characterize it, carries with it a concern, reflected both in content and in form, about the prospects and possibilities of story-telling. The very conflicts which threaten the continuation of the lineage, the proper sequence of generations, seem to undermine the conditions that make story-telling possible, namely a new generation that is able and willing to hear the tales of the previous generations. My assumption is that the kind of story-telling that is found in extended folk-tale and in more sophisticated oral epics depends upon a confidence in generational continuity, and that the glorious deeds of previous generations are in large measure done so that they may be narrated to the future generations. Further, the sense of time, narrative time, that is present in traditional tales, is one of a continuous flow of time, or perhaps a cyclical and recurring rhythm of time, but a never-ending stream. An epic tale is always part of another tale or other tales. It is preceded by events narrated in other stories and will in turn be followed by other tales and by other audiences to hear the tales. What we do here and now will be, as the Homeric heroes say, 'a song for men in time to come' (Homer, *Odyssey*, 1917, e.g. VIII, l. 580, my translation). The audience hearing the Homeric poem attends to a tale of men performing glorious deeds, and at the same time hearing of the glorious deeds of their own past and already beginning to think of the narrative possibilities of what they are doing. There is a past, present and future, and all are somehow part of the same time warp and woof.

In brief, if there is terrible trouble within the family and a threat from within to the family's existence, we hear of anxiety about narrating and anxiety about time. In *Macbeth*, that most 'dynastic' of plays, where Macbeth can have no progeny but must murder to gain a crown to be passed onto other people's progeny, we find that life is 'a tale/Told by an idiot, full of sound and fury/Signifying nothing' (1963a, V, 5, ll. 26–8). In *Hamlet*, a story of dire threats to the proper relations among the closest of kin, 'the time is out of joint' (1957, I, 5, l. 188). Further, I suggest that the narrative discontinuities and contradictions or the distortions of linear time that are found in many tragic dramas, especially in the greatest ones, can be understood more fully by considering the distortions and contradictions in familial continuity that are represented within the plays.[2] Plays that involve the killing of children betray most clearly anxiety about the prospects for story-telling.

I will briefly consider certain contrasts between early epic poetry – *The Epic of Gilgamesh* (1960) and the Homeric epics (1917, 1920) – and Greek tragedy, and then I will turn to an ancient tragedy, Aeschylus' *The Oresteia* (1959). We will then concentrate on a modern tragedy, Beckett's *Endgame* (1958), keeping in mind that both *The Oresteia* and *Endgame* deal with the destruction of children by parents and of parents by children, thereby threatening the extinction of the line. Cannibalism, child-sacrifice and a child murdering a parent mark the ancient play, while murder by sadism, neglect of helpless children or old people, mark the modern play. What is present *in statu nascendi* in the ancient play, the linkage between child-killing and the silencing of narrative, is full grown and the central subject-matter in the modern play.

From epic to tragic

In a succinct and eminently useful statement of the basic tragic facts of life, one critic has specified (1) death and its inevitability and (2) the necessity of living among one's own kind (Mandel 1961, p. 163; quoted in Nevo 1972, p. 3). We shall utilize this schema to help characterize the different emphases of epic poetry and tragic drama. Epic poetry is organized around the attempt to escape the finality of death, principally via the achievement of immortality by the hero in song and tale, and the immortality that comes with bearing progeny who in turn will be epic heroes. The epic of Gilgamesh and the epic of Achilles, *The Iliad*, most powerfully and most poignantly illustrate these struggles with death and with loss. Tragedy, on the other hand, is still informed and shaped by the ineluctability of death, but faces a new problem: suppose the epic solution is blocked by warfare and hostility within the family, so that no children are left alive, or propagated, to hear about and to carry on heroic deeds. While epic tends to slight the destructive implications for the hero of the killing of the children of the enemy, tragedy portrays the terrible dangers of killing children, whether one's own or even one's enemies. Killing one's enemies' children can be dangerous for the simple reason that the necessary warfare may kill off your own children. Thus tragedy both portrays literal murder of children within the family and poses the dilemma (implicit but not central in epic) of sacrificing one's own children in order to achieve a heroic immortality. Heroic immortality in turn depends on having children alive to appreciate the heroism! Much of Greek tragedy deals with these issues, and Aeschylus' *Oresteia*, Euripides' *The Madness of Heracles* (1959) and his *Medea* (1959) most powerfully illustrate the problems posed by the killing of one's own children.

The oldest heroic epic we possess, the *Epic of Gilgamesh*, is explicit in its attempt to defy death – the hero stung by the loss of his bosom comrade is unable to bear the pain of death and goes on a quest to seek immortality. Gilgamesh presses forward his search and finally comes to the old man, Utnapishtim, the Babylonian Noah (or Noah, the biblical Utnapishtim), the only mortal to have survived the flood and to be granted immortality by gods. Utnapishtim again warns Gilgamesh of the futility of his quest but agrees to help find the plant that will restore youth and guarantee immortality. Gilgamesh manages with great toil to find the plant and bring it up from deep and muddy waters. As he turns to bathe in sweet water, a serpent appears and steals the plant, leaving behind only the skin he, the serpent, has sloughed. Thus the most stalwart heroic effort to defeat ageing and death has been defeated. What is left? What consolations are there? Only the works of the king Gilgamesh, the city of Uruk he built, his fame and, finally, his story:

> This too [Uruk] was the work of Gilgamesh, the king, who knew the countries of the world. He was wise, he saw mysteries and knew secret things, he brought us a tale of the days before the flood. He went on a long journey, was weary, worn out with labour, and returning engraved on a stone the whole story.
>
> *(Epic of Gilgamesh* 1960, pp. 114–15)

Thus, at the end, it is the continuity of story-telling – the old tales he brought back to us and the fresh ones of heroic glory that he created and memorialized – that made Gilgamesh immortal.

The struggle to deny death is more subtle in Homer, but is very much there, and Odysseus of course makes his own perilous journey to a forbidden and forbidding land, Hades, to find out and bring back truths from a wise man.[3] In the course of that journey we learn vividly of the other powerful consolation for the fact of death and, itself a form of immortality, the ability to procreate children who will themselves perform heroic deeds worthy of song. In Book XI Odysseus encounters the shade of Achilles. In lamenting voice Achilles asks him how he could endure to come down to Hades, 'where the senseless dead men dwell, mere imitations of perished mortals'. Odysseus answers him:

> 'Achilleus, no man before has been more blessed than you, nor ever will be. Before, when you were alive, we Argives honored you as we did the gods, and now in this place you have great authority over the dead. Do not grieve, even in death, Achilleus.' So I spoke and he in turn said to me in answer: 'O shining Odysseus, never try to console me for dying. I would rather follow the plow as thrall to another man, one with no land allotted him and not much to live on, than be a king over all the perished dead. But come now, tell me anything you have heard of my proud son, whether or not he went along to war to fight as a champion.
>
> (Homer 1965, XI, ll. 482–93; 'Achilleus' is Lattimore's spelling)

Note the bitterness and renunciation of epic glory, but note too how swiftly follows Achilles' question about his son Neoptolemus ('New-fighter'). Odysseus in the following lines gives a full account of the epic heroism of Neoptolemus, especially in the story of the Trojan horse and the capture of Troy, and also tells Achilles that he is alive and unscathed by battle. Achilles, hearing the news, casts off his gloom, and with giant strides the psyche of Achilles, rejoicing, goes off to the Asphodel Meadows (*mega bibasa; gethosune*) (XI, ll. 538–40). Thus, having a heroic son and a son still alive to procreate sons finally consoles Achilles and releases him from his brooding melancholia.

There is another form of immortality, however, implicit in epic, and that is the sense of time that is conveyed in epic poetry. Homeric epic begins at a particular point in time in what is clearly an endless story – we might even say a continuously recycling story. The 'tale' may begin with an incident in the tenth year of the Trojan War, but it is implicit that heroic tales and deeds have always existed and always will exist. There is no sense of urgency, of temporal finitude. Various literary devices project this sense of time as an unlimited commodity, of the great stretch of generations. Though everyone in the story must die sooner or later, there is the ever-present assumption of continuity, including a continuous audience, an assumption articulated in lines such as 'The generations of heroes are as the leaves of the trees' (Homer 1920, VI, l. 146; my translation) or 'a song for men in times to come'. When we turn to tragedy, we see an intense sense of limit, or urgency – time is not infinitely expansible (see, for example, de Romilly 1968).

Buttressing this sense of a never-ending cycle, or chain of generations, is the epic device of continuous telling. Interruptions of the flow of narration are rare, with the bard occasionally needing a 'refuelling' from the Muse (as in the Catalogue of Ships in *Iliad* II, l. 484), or the narrator within the narration suggesting that the hour is late and perhaps all should retire to their beds.[4] Narratives within narratives are similarly important, as boxes within boxes, in conveying a sense of the intensity of the narrative urge as well as its extension in time. Odysseus narrates large chunks of *The Odyssey*, both at the feast of the Phaiakians and in the scene of his reunion in bed with Penelope. Tragedy introduces a note of anxiety about narration – there are many more pauses, and expressions of anxiety and chariness in speaking. 'But as for the rest, I shall remain silent.

A large ox has stepped on my tongue', exclaims the watchman in the opening of Aeschylus' *Agamemnon* (1954, ll. 35–6; my translation). My hypothesis is that what cannot be told are primarily the details of the intra-familial slaughter and betrayal. Intra-familial strife that threatens the continuity of the family also threatens the continuity of narrating stories about the family and its line.

Overall, in epic the battle is of the hero or heroes – typically the hero and his bosom companion – against an outside enemy. The enemy may be malevolent deities or monsters, another tribe, neighbours who threaten to take over one's own household, even another general within one's own army, but always outside the immediate family.

But when we move to tragic drama we see a 'dramatic' shift of the action and the tension to tales of conflicts, including lethal ones, among members of the same family – husband–wife or parents–children. This is what our critic has called the second tragic fact of life, the necessity of living among one's own kind. Now stories of intra-familial conflict exist in epic, but they are at the periphery of the narrative.[5] In tragedy, however, such stories now move to centre stage. Often we see different mythic versions told in epic, and the tragic versions are likely to select terrible things done between parents and children. Thus, in Homer we hear of Iphigenia as a daughter of Agamemnon and Clytemnestra, but there is no tale of her father sacrificing her.

Epic, overall, does treat of intra-familial conflict and tension, but tends to represent such conflict by *displacement*, or by projection, against an outside agency. One has to interpret the text as having such conflicts as part of their latent meaning, whether the interpretation is a psychoanalytic one or the kind of interpretation provided by variants in the mythic traditions.[6] Tragedy deals with these intra-familial conflicts by *condensation*, by presenting them in compressed, intensified and ineluctable form. One implication of the term *condensation*, with its connection to the mechanism of dream formation, is that each character is also the obverse or opposite of himself or herself. The tragic plot enacts, and the tragic diction suggests, that each woman is also in part man, each man a woman, every victim a victimizer and every master a slave. 'Tragic knowledge' in large part is the awareness of this reversibility in human life and in the human psyche, though often the characters in the drama may not learn this, and only the audience can assimilate such knowledge.

'The Oresteia', child murder, and the 'Ox upon my tongue'

Aeschylus' *The Oresteia* takes up the 'seamy side' of heroic epic by focusing on the domestic tragedy entailed in the Trojan War. In effect, it brings the Trojan War 'home', and the heroic epic war against an outside enemy becomes transmuted into war within the family.[7] It opens with the anticipation of the homecoming of the military hero, Agamemnon, and the unfolding of the terrible avenging fate that awaits him.

The trilogy as a whole is primarily concerned with what is destroying and what can save the House of Atreus. Bear in mind the cry of Orestes in *The Libation Bearers* after he has slain his mother: 'May no wife such as this one share my house. Rather would I perish *childless* (*apais*) at the hands of the gods' (Aeschylus 1959, ll. 1005–6).[8] The house is in danger of extinction, either because it has been killing off children, or else because the last male of the line, Orestes, may not wish to reproduce, or if slain by the Furies, would be unable to reproduce. The murder of a daughter by her father (i.e. the sacrifice of Iphigenia), the revenge of Clytemnestra in murdering Agamemnon and the act of matricide by Orestes all undermine the very survival of the family. Throughout the trilogy there is the pervasive conflict between the sense of children as a threat to parents, or as pawns to be used and manipulated in deadly games between and among adults, and the sense of children as preserving the very values over which the adults are willing to kill each other and their own children. Glory, ambition, power and dominance are 'commodities' and accordingly there are the attendant needs for battle and revenge against those who threaten one's ownership.[9] All of this must somehow be resolved in order that the curse no longer be transmitted and enacted by each generation in turn trying to destroy its own children.

The story-line, and the history of the House of Atreus, contain explicit instances of the killing of children: Atreus slaughtering the children of his brother Thyestes and serving them to his brother at a grim feast of 'reconciliation'; the slaughter of the children of Troy and of the sons of the Achaeans and the sacrifice of Iphigenia so that while justice was being executed on Troy, many, many children would be destroyed. But the poetic imagery constantly brings in child-murder or attack on children as a recurring motif. In the first chorus, the parodos, the stealing of

Helen is analogized to an eagle being robbed of its fledgling. The marriage bed and the nest, or cradle, are merged.[10]

The widening circle of child-destruction is vividly conveyed in the chorus's second image of birds, the omen of the two eagles who attack the pregnant hare (ll. 105–59).

> they [the eagles] lighted, watched by all,
> tore a hare, ripe, bursting with young unborn yet,
> stayed from her last fleet running.
> Sing sorrow, sorrow: but good win out in the end.
>
> (ll. 118–21)

The prophet Calchas interprets the eagles' killing the hare and the unborn babies as the attack of Agamemnon and Menelaus, leading the Greek host, on the city of Troy. By implication, the city pregnant with people, with children, including the unborn progeny of Troy, will be devoured. But he also hints at a grave danger, that Artemis, who is 'kind to the tender young' of all creatures, hares and lions, is 'sick of the eagles' feasting'. He prays that she may not exact her revenge on the Greeks:

> let her [Artemis] not with cross winds
> bind the ships of the Danaans
> to time-long anchorage
> forcing a second sacrifice unholy, untasted,
> working bitterness in the blood
> and faith lost. For the terror returns like sickness to
> lurk in the house;
> the secret anger remembers the child that shall be
> avenged.
>
> (ll. 147–55)

The implications of this omen become progressively clearer as the trilogy proceeds. For the Greeks to devour Troy, it will be necessary that Greek children be devoured – first Iphigenia sacrificed, and then the flower of Greek youth destroyed in battle. By retrospective allusion, the 'second sacrifice' connects up with the history of the house of Atreus, namely Atreus slaying and serving up to his brother Thyestes a feast of Thyestes' own children. The spirals grow wider, for these 'sacrifices' will lead in turn to the murder of Agamemnon and Cassandra, and to Orestes murdering his own mother and her paramour, Aegisthus. These murders threaten to bring about the destruction of all future children of the house of Atreus, all the unborn and unconceived children, by virtue of leaving Electra unmarried and childless and Orestes persecuted by the Furies.

Among the threats of the Furies are attacks on the marrow and the testicles of young men, sucking out and crushing the procreative and life-giving substances (e.g. *The Eumenides*, ll. 179–97, the speech of Apollo expelling the Furies). They will leave the land sterile and fruitless. Thus this omen and its implications set up the 'problem' that *The Oresteia* must also solve – how to end this spiralling so that the murder or abduction of one person's child does not inexorably lead to the murder of all the family's subsequent children.[11]

In lines 184–257 the chorus unfolds the dreadful tale of the sacrifice of Iphigenia. Agamemnon is torn between the fear of letting the army and the expedition waste away in the harbour of Chalcis, forever awaiting a favourable wind, and the dread of sacrificing his own daughter on the altar to Artemis. In effect, he is torn between destroying the 'flower' (*anthos*) of Greek youth, that is one kind of offspring, and destroying a more literal child. Someone's 'flower' must be destroyed, or the 'flower' of his household must be slaughtered and 'deflowered'.[12] The theme of the horror of having to quash one's pity and slaughter one's own child is elaborated. Agamemnon, as many commentators have pointed out, after feeling compelled by necessity to kill Iphigenia, all too eagerly proceeds with the terrible deed.

> Her supplications and her cries of father
> were nothing, not the child's lamentation
> to kings passioned for battle.
> The father prayed, called to his men to lift her
> with strength of hand swept in her robes aloft
> and prone above the altar, as you might lift
> a goat for sacrifice, with guards
> against the lips' sweet edge, to check
> the curse cried on the house of Atreus
> by force of bit and speech drowned in strength.
>
> Pouring then to the ground her saffron mantle
> she struck the sacrificers with
> the eyes' arrows of pity,
> lovely as in a painted scene, and striving
> to speak – as many times

at the kind festive table of her father
she had sung, and in the clear voice of a stainless maiden
with love had graced the song
of worship when the third cup was poured.

What happened next I saw not, neither speak it.

(ll. 227–48)

Note that force must be applied to stifle voice (Iphigenia's) and for the onlookers to be unmoved by pity. There is dread, and there is conflict about the slaughter of one's own child. When we discuss Beckett's *Endgame*, we will see how dispassionate the silencing and murdering of children have become.

In the choral ode describing the sacrifice of Iphigenia we see the dramatization of the tension between the urge to sing and tell, and between being unable to speak or sing. The subject of Iphigenia's sacrifice must be told by the chorus, but they also cannot tell it completely (p. 248). *Oude ennepo*, 'I cannot *sing* as a bard'. These words form a vivid contrast to passages such as the opening of *The Odyssey*, '*andra moi ennepe, Mousa*' – '*Sing*, O Muse, of the man'. Iphigenia used to sing at her father's festive banquets, but now, 'striving to speak', is gagged so that she will not blaspheme or curse. How can one speak the 'unspeakable', and the unspeakable here consists of terrible deeds done within the family, deeds that are the seamy underside of the heroic expedition against Troy.

Consider another instance of interrupted telling. *The Agamemnon* opens with the speech of the watchman, awaiting all these long years the beacon signal that Troy has fallen. Meanwhile, it is clear that the house, the palace, from which he is keeping his watch is in dire straits: 'something's rotten in the state of Argos'. He hints at the problems of having a woman, 'who thinks like a man' as ruling him (l. 11). He says twice in the course of this prologue that he cannot sing and that he cannot tell anymore – first (ll. 15–19), that when he tries to sing, he begins to weep for the fate of the house, and second, that he will keep silent:[13]

The rest I leave to silence; for a huge ox stands upon my tongue. The house itself, if it could take voice, would speak most eloquently. Thus willingly I speak to those who understand, but as for those who do not understand, I have forgotten (whatever I know).

(ll. 36–9)

He *forgets*, another extraordinary 'unepic' piece of behaviour. The Greek text of these scenes and of other parts of the play is strewn with the vocabulary of thwarted or perverted epic telling.[14]

To summarize, we have illustrated briefly the content of *The Oresteia* as dealing with problems of intra-familial strife entailed in epic-heroic deeds, and the killing of one's own children, in conjunction with the difficulty in smooth or continuous narration of tales and details of such strife. Murder the children and you risk murdering the generations and murdering the genealogies.

Beckett's 'Endgame': the killing of children, desire, meaning and story-telling

Vladimir: Suppose we repented . . .
Estragon: Our being born?

Beckett, Waiting for Godot

If the ancient material we have discussed suggests a tension about telling tales when the tales have to do with terrible deeds done within the family, the modern material, Beckett's *Endgame* (1958), builds an entire play around that theme. If ancient drama betrays an anxiety about the possibilities of continuation of the house or the line, it still holds as an almost unspoken value that the race and the house should continue. Even at the gloomiest junctures of ancient drama, such as the chorus in *Oedipus at Colonus*, 'Best is never to have been born' (Sophocles 1950, ll. 1224–5), we find a rapid restitution of the belief in the value of generational continuity. If ancient drama poses a kind of critique of epic story-telling, it still takes for granted a human need and wish for such nourishing and culturally sustaining narratives.

Endgame deals with the end of the human race – no more procreation; indeed, it views the possibility of further procreation as an unmitigated disaster. The assault on conception and birth, so much in evidence in Beckett's *oeuvre*, is also prominent in this play. The play also ridicules and undermines any serious sustained effort at the characters finding or constructing meaning among themselves. Its characters in their interactions have almost totally foresworn sustained desire or passion; even sustained rage or hatred is hard to come by.[15] The audience is quickly induced into the atmosphere of numbness and non-passion, only occasionally relieved by a piece of Beckettian 'gallows humour'. The play as a whole has almost no plot, hardly a story worth summarizing or repeating. Yet curiously enough, at least half of the action of the play consists of an attempt to tell stories, principally one story, Hamm's chronicle. That chronicle involves Hamm's deliberations on the question of whether or not he would let a particular child live or starve to death, and the narration is continuously interspersed with Hamm's self-congratulations of himself as story-teller. While each of these features of *Endgame* has been noted by numerous readers and critics, few, if any, have attempted to draw the connections among the attacks on meaning, desire, birth and children, and the telling of tales. (Most directly relevant to my thesis are Bair 1978; Cavell 1977; Chevigny 1969, esp. her introduction, pp. 1–13; Morrison 1983.)

The attack on meaning associated with *Endgame* is twofold, from within, among the characters themselves, and from without, from the author, who defies audiences and readers to ascribe meaning to the play. The list of meanings – or 'this is really a tale of ...' – ascribed by critics to *Endgame* is quite lengthy and many are of great interest. (A few: a version of *Hamlet*; the Noah's ark story; an intra-psychic drama; a vision of post nuclear holocaust.) Beckett himself threw down the gauntlet when he said he would accept no responsibility for any meanings ascribed to the play: 'If people want to have headaches among the overtones, let them. And provide their own aspirin. Hamm as stated, and Clov as stated, together stated, nec tecum nec sine te' (Beckett 1984a, p. 109). Within the play there is a near poignant moment, an expectation of some feeling beginning to gel between Hamm and Clov. But consider how this development is regarded:

> *Hamm*: ... (Pause) Last night I saw inside my breast. There was a big sore.
> *Clov*: Pah! you saw your heart.
> *Hamm*: No, it was living. (Pause, anguished) Clov!
> *Clov*: Yes.
> *Hamm*: What's happening?
> *Clov*: Something is taking its course. (Pause)
> *Hamm*: Clov!
> *Clov* (impatiently): What is it?

> *Hamm*: We're not beginning to . . . to . . . mean something?
> *Clov*: Mean something! You and I, mean something! (Brief laugh) Ah that's a good one!
>
> (Beckett 1958, pp. 32–3)

The dialogue continues and culminates (if that word can be applied at all in Beckett) in a plea to capture and quickly kill a flea, which could turn out to be the progenitor of the whole human race and start the whole damn thing all over again! Thus the first attempt is quickly to kill any nascent strong feeling (perhaps psychic pain) and any attempt to ascribe significance to their relationship or to their existence. This kind of murder by scorn is quickly followed by an even stronger exterminative frenzy to kill off anything that might procreate any life, especially human life (see also pp. 78–9, the small boy appearing at the end). The equation of the life of the flea with human life here serves not as a plea for the sanctity of all life but as a reduction of human life to the status of insect or animal life. As such, it further numbs the senses about the distinction between life and death.[16] It is as if the characters (or the playwright) concede the truth of certain psychoanalytic propositions that aspects of thinking, such as establishing meaning, significance and connection at even an abstract level are closely tied up with establishing personal significance and meaning at the level of human contact. The truth is conceded by means of scorn and dread of its implications. Acknowledge that any two things have connection or meaning, and once again you'll have started up the whole human race![17]

In another passage we find not murder by extermination but rather the imagery of semi-starvation, non-caring and non-communication in relation to children. Hamm is telling his story, his 'chronicle', the story of a starving man who came begging for bread for his child (that child might, in fact, be Clov). The setting of the tale is an end-of-the-world one, such as after a flood, or the Flood. Hamm disdainfully and contemptuously narrates how he dealt with the man:

> In the end he asked me would I consent to take in the child as well – if he were still alive. (Pause) It was the moment I was waiting for. (Pause) Would I consent to take in the child. (Pause) I can see him still, down on his knees, his hands flat on the ground, glaring at me with his mad eyes, in defiance of my

wishes. (Pause. Normal tone.) I'll soon have finished with this story.

(p. 53)

This story implies a father deeply affected by his son's suffering and trying everything in his power to save his son. Hamm mocks this father's concern and is quite prepared to have the child die and or continue suffering and to have the father continuing to beg on his behalf. This story took place on Christmas Eve and as such is a degradation of the stories of Christ's birth, a mockery of the compassion, love and joy in those accounts.

This same Hamm is the one who first addresses his own father, Nagg, as 'Accursed progenitor' (p. 9). In the sequence following the first narration of Hamm's 'chronicle' (pp. 55–6), Nagg, the 'Noah' of this desolate ark, demands that Hamm, his son, give him his sugar-plum. After an interchange where Hamm finally says that there are no more sugar-plums, Nagg 'curses' him for his cruelty to him, his father:

> It's natural [your refusal]. After all I'm your father. It's true if it hadn't been me it would have been someone else. But that's no excuse. (Pause)
>
> (pp. 55–6)

The father's revenge on the son, then, is the disavowal that there is anything personal in the relationship, especially in the begetting. But the imprecation continues:

> Whom did you call when you were a tiny boy, and were frightened in the dark? Your mother? No. Me. We let you cry. Then we moved you out of earshot, so that we might sleep in peace. (Pause) I was asleep, as happy as a king, and you woke me up to have me listen to you. It wasn't indispensable, you didn't really need to have me listen to you. (Pause) I hope the day will come when you'll really need to have me listen to you, and need to hear my voice, any voice. (Pause) Yes, I hope I'll live till then, to hear you calling me like when you were a tiny boy, and were frightened, in the dark, and I was your only hope
>
> (pp. 55–6)

In this extraordinary portrait of a perversion of parent–infant relationships, we see a glimpse of the 'genetic' or 'developmental' aspects of the characters in the play and their characteristic ways of non-relating. The scorned child ultimately learns not to need the parent, and the parent's vengeful wish is that the grown-up child will sometime need the parent! Even at that point there will be nothing personal, for Hamm will need to hear 'any voice'. The blankness and anonymity of 'any voice' also portends poorly for the possibility of particular voices telling particular tales. Father gets nothing from the son, can give out only curses and has not given much in the past. God, or Jesus, whether *qua* father or *qua* son, is a bastard, and doesn't exist, besides (p. 55).[18] The reciprocity of non-giving and non-caring is indeed the major act of sharing in the play!

Story-telling: death by attrition

In *Endgame* we witness the progressive degradation and dissolution of the fundamental human activity of telling a story. The motives to tell a story are gradually eroded as it becomes clearer that there is no audience interested in hearing and that the story-teller must increasingly talk to himself. The existing progeny do not care to hear their parents' stories, the parents do not wish to hear stories from their children, the parents scarcely care to hear each other's stories, and there will be no progeny to hear any future stories. The very existence of a past worth telling about is in question, with the remote past perhaps having some value (p. 42) and recent past being unspeakable (p. 43). The contents of the stories are principally about mutilation and death, the destruction of creation and of procreation, and involve the murder of strong positive feelings, such as love and tenderness. Tears are belittled or interdicted (e.g. pp. 51, 62, 81). The stories themselves are endless and repetitive, lack any major communicative impetus and at times are almost reduced to a babble.

There are a number of tales narrated within the play, all of them short, except for Hamm's endless 'chronicle'. The first story is told by Nagg to Nell (p. 16), and he laughingly explains their present plight – why they are in ashbins without legs. They had an accident on a tandem bike (activities requiring harmony in this play do not work well!) in the Ardennes, on the way to Sedan. The degradation of feeling, whether sadness, rage, the allusions to the mutilative battles of the First World War, are all signified by the pseudo-appropriate laughter (Cohn 1970, pp. 185–97).

Intertwined with a pained but 'funny' account of the day after their engagement, a boating accident on Lake Como, is Nagg's finally coercing Nell into hearing his 'joke' once again. It is the old joke about the tailor who takes forever to make a botched pair of pants (the narration is replete with bawdy side-jokes) and replies to the customer's complaint by pointing to God, who created the world in seven days and did a much worse job than he, the tailor (Beckett 1958, pp. 22–3). The main 'joke' in the play, then, is not only *about* creation, but the joke *is* creation.[19]

The main story is Hamm's 'chronicle' of the man who came pleading for food and a place to stay for his son. Its narration constitutes a major piece of the action of the play. The bulk of the narration concerns how Hamm made the man grovel, ridiculed him for wanting to save his son, though perhaps he eventually did take the son in:

> It's my little one, he said. Tsstss, a little one, that's bad. My little boy, he said, as if the sex mattered. Where did he come from? He named the hole. A good half day, on horse. What are you insinuating? That the place is still inhabited? No no, not a soul, except himself and the child – assuming he existed. . . . Come now! . . . what he wanted from me was . . . bread for his brat? Bread? But I have no bread, it doesn't agree with me . . . If he's still alive . . . a nice pot of porridge. . . . And then? (Pause). I lost patience. (Violently) Use your head, can't you, use your head, you're on earth, there's no cure for that!
>
> (pp. 51–3)

This is indeed a grim tale, not just about the destruction of the earth but also of the destruction of pity (by ridicule), of caring, of parental affection for children and of any sense of purpose for living on earth. Hamm's act of pity, his resonating with a deep human need and taking in the man and his son, is an act that Hamm says marks his own demise (p. 53)!

As important as the contents of this tale, is its form, especially the relationship implied between the story-teller and his audience. In brief, Hamm's method progressively drives away, numbs, frustrates and throttles whatever audience interest and passion there once may have been. The stories are repetitious, have no end, no climax; if there is an ending (Nagg's joke), the story is repeated endlessly whether or not anyone wants to hear it. Further, we see that the story-teller must either bribe or coerce someone to hear his tale (e.g. p. 48). Story-telling is there set in the frame of failed father–son relationships – Nagg has no wish to hear his son's story – and is also placed in the context of a curse on engendering ('Scroundrel, why did you engender me?', p. 48).

Hamm starts to tell the story as if he is almost finished, or as if *in medias res*, as a caricature of epic-story telling (p. 50). Hamm is a Homer *seemingly* unaware of his audience, unaware of any emotional impact of the story he is about to tell (or has somehow finished telling). He is also able to defend himself against the full emotional import of this story for himself. Story-telling, especially Hamm's chronicle, is a way of both revealing and concealing, in relation to oneself, to other characters and to the audience painful awareness about oneself. What is most deeply yearned for, and deeply dreaded – love and tenderness – is represented in story-telling, but represented at a safe distance and overlaid with enough cynicism, indifference and nastiness to be almost completely disguised. By concentrating on nuances of style, language and delivery, he can avoid the pain of realizing that his chronicle is, in fact, *his own childhood history*, a version of the history of his neglect as an infant that Nagg has told (p. 56)! He tells a tale of what he did unto another, rather than what another (his father!) had done unto him. Hamm can also avoid the dread of experiencing his yearnings for tenderness between father and son, tenderness such as is evinced by the father towards his son in the chronicle. (See Morrison 1983, p. 39, for an elegant discussion of this point, and also Dr Barbara Schapiro, personal communication, 1984.)

Hamm, it becomes clear, has no great need of an audience – he can tell the tale to himself as audience. As both teller and listener, he can be excited, pleased, bored or left exhausted. He comments throughout on his own story-telling; for example, 'There should do it. . . . Nicely put, that. . . . There's English for you. Ah well' (p. 51). Nor does Hamm's story help forge any link between teller and listener, one of the traditional functions of story-telling. It scarcely functions to connect the teller to himself as he keeps losing interest in the telling (pp. 58, 61)!

As Hamm becomes more and more deprived of audience, including himself as audience, he invokes a powerful image of loneliness, the child who must talk to himself:

> *Hamm*: All kinds of fantasies! That I'm being watched! A rat!
> Steps! Breath held and then. ... (He breathes out.) The
> babble, babble, words, like the solitary child who turns

himself into children, two, three, so as to be together, and
whisper together in the dark.

(p. 70)

Even as Clov attempts, ambivalently, to relate to Hamm and his
story and his story-telling, Hamm pushes him away (p. 77), mostly
preferring his own soliloquy and trusting only himself to be an
interested audience. But some need for the minimal relatedness
that is involved in inventing and telling a story persists. Hamm
makes up a story about Clov's departure, even while Clov is still
there (p. 80). Is this also a way of mastering or minimizing the pain
of departure and loss?

Clov and Hamm speak alternately, but not to each other. Clov is
telling *his* story about what had happened to him, is reporting
conversations to himself (e.g. pp. 80–1). Not only does the
audience for the narratives disappear, but concomittantly even the
characters in the story disappear. Hamm stops the narrative with:

I'll soon have finished with this story. (Pause) Unless I bring in
other characters. (Pause) But where would I find them? (Pause)
Where would I look for them? (Pause. He whistles. Enter Clov.)

(p. 54)

The fundamental triangular relationship of story-telling, that
interdependence of story-teller, audience and characters within the
story, is destroyed by the fact of an indifferent teller and an
indifferent audience. The ability to generate characters within a tale
is clearly dependent upon the existence of an audience who cares
about them. That ability is entwined with the necessity of adequate
caring for the generating and sustaining of the life of a child.

In story-telling there is also the perennial issue of *control* between
teller and audience. The optimal condition is one in which there is
some sharing of the control: the story-teller is a 'spellbinder', but
the audience agrees to be spellbound. There is a negotiation
between teller and audience that helps the teller 'hold' his audience.
What we see here is a failed negotiation, and the story-teller can
scarcely even negotiate with himself. The story Hamm is telling,
his chronicle, is about control, about controlling the man, and his
son, and holding that man as a captive audience. The counterpoint
to Hamm's controlling the story and the audience is Clov's wish
for complete order, to get all the fragments of physical objects in

place. Hamm, for his part, wishes to get all the fragments of the story in place (p. 57).

Clov's passion for order is also a passion for death and constitutes another attack on procreation, itself a disorderly process that begets further disorder. Story-telling requires a certain amount of disorder, or 'play', both play as fun, and play as 'give' in a system, in order to survive and propagate itself. In *Endgame* that combination of freedom, imaginative freedom, within a certain amount of constraint is not available to the characters. Similarly, within the vision of the play, procreation is a process that involves too much risk, too much play and the danger of things getting out of control. The attendant passion seems too dangerous. Thus the 'endgame' is also an 'end of games', an end of that elasticity that allows for the creative disorder of procreating children and procreating stories.

When all is said and done, however, there is a certain kind of begetting and reproduction that does take place between the play (or its characters) and the audience. There is a cloning – like the child inventing imaginary companions out of despair and loneliness (p. 70) – one might say a *xeroxing*, within the audience of the frustration, impotence and thwarted yearnings of the characters. There is also some replication of the limited capacity for play that exists among the characters. Beckett, or his play, does succeed in some almost subhuman form of cloning, but not in any deeply gratifying, pleasurable or 'cathartic' mode. It is almost as if the play works like a virus invading a cell and converting (or subverting) the cell's molecular apparatus to the task of replicating the virus rather than the cell. Beckett's effort, both within the terms of the play and within his writings as a whole, is to ensure that anything, once born, is shrunk down to the smallest possible state of existence (or non-existence). However, there is a tension, because while Beckett's characters slouch towards absolute zero, the complete end, it is important that they never quite get there. When a person, or story, within Beckett's work is shrunk down and reduced, it must still continue to exist and replicate, as if within a shrunken womb – replicate the elements of the world it has abandoned or destroyed, replicate the shell of the story that remains.[20]

Notes

1 See Aristotle (1981, pp. 23–5) on tragedy and the family: most of the Greek tragedies were written around six royal houses (e.g. the house of Atreus); terrible events within the family are dramatically the most pitiable; one of the crucial features of dramatic structure is recognition, *anagnorisis*, and recognition of kin is the most powerful form.

2 That is, some of the well known chronological contradictions in *Macbeth* reflect contradictions between the urge to found a house and a line, and the exterminative urges that prevent it. At the end of *Hamlet* the need to restore lawful succession is juxtaposed with the need for orderly telling of the story, especially the tale of heroism. See 1957, V, 7, ll. 331–4: 'draw thy breath in pain/to tell my story'; see also Horatio at V, 7, ll. 363ff. See Tobin (1978) for the thesis that in the modern novel, where there is a disturbance of procreative lineage portrayed in family and doubt about the continuity of the family, time and narration are subject to peculiar distortions.

3 See Frame (1978) on the role of death in the *Odyssey*.

4 The subject of stopping and starting in *epic narrative* deserves detailed treatment in its own right. In literary epic, at the opening of Book II of *The Aeneid* (Virgil 1930), Dido's feast for Aeneas, Aeneas' reluctance to tell of the Trojan War (*horresco referens*) has a number of psychological and artistic motives. My hypothesis is that his hesitation to narrate is proleptic, anticipatory of the fact that the story he will tell of what the Greeks did to the Trojans with the Wooden Horse is the story of what he will do to Dido. Aeneas is the Trojan Horse.

5 Certain characters, such as Phoenix (*Illiad* IX) who is cursed by his father for seducing the father's concubine, or Aiolos, in the *Odyssey*, whose children all live incestuously with each other, flit in and out of the main story-line. Other stories of intra-familial betrayal or terrible behaviour are told or alluded to: the story of Meleager and Althea, a story of Oedipus – Odysseus sees Jocasta in Hades – the murder of Agamemnon by his wife and Aegisthus.

6 See, for example, the versions of father–son rivalry, *bona fide* 'Oedipal triangles', that one can discern in the variants on the Odyssean myths. See the entry 'Odysseus' in *Oxford Classical Dictionary* (1971) and Simon (1973, pp. 555–62).

7 See *Eumenides* (1954, ll. 858–67). Athena appeals to the Furies not to encourage war at home, *Are emphulon*, but rather that war should be 'outside the door', *thuraios esto polemos*.

8 Translation mine. Unless otherwise indicated, the translations are those of Lattimore (1959).

9 The commercial metaphors are most striking at ll. 432–51, *The Agamemnon*, especially the figure of Ares as a money-changer. See *The Libation Bearers*, ll. 503–7, for children 'as the corks that hold up the nets' of the house, and preserve a man's fame after his death.

10 The language of begetting children, nursing, tending and the failure or perversions of these functions is pervasive in *The Oresteia* (Aeschylus 1959). For example, the lion-cub, prematurely torn from its mother's breast (ll. 717–36), Clytemnestra's dream of begetting and nursing a snake in *The Libation Bearers* (ll. 523–53), and the references to intercourse, gestation and miscarriage in *The Eumenides* (Aeschylus 1959). The incidental language of *causality* in the trilogy is typically 'this begets that', especially the language of retributive justice and revenge.

11 I do not discuss here the much vexed question of how to understand the ending and resolution of *The Eumenides*, except to say that it is a 'perverse' solution, in the sense that the psychodynamics of many instances of male perversion involve a 'game' in which there is alternatively and oscillatingly a *denial* of the power of the woman as begetter, nurturer and creature of sexual passion, equipped with a phallus, and an *affirmation* of the dread and awesome aspects of these maternal functions.

12 The Greek text does not play on 'flower' or 'deflower' but does convey a vivid sense of the confusion between the slaughter by sacrifice and the deflowering, whether rape or marriage, of the maiden. See especially Stanford (1983, pp. 126–31). Euripides' *Iphigenia in Aulis* (1959) elaborates the confounding of marriage and of daughter-sacrifice. For grim associations to *anthos* see ll. 658 and 955.

13 Translation mine. L. 16 – *aeidein*, is of course a prime epic term for singing heroic songs – heroic tales fail to provide the solace that might bring sleep; at ll. 36–7 the *mega bous*, the large ox, that has stepped on his tongue is not only a proverbial phrase (see the sources collected in Frankel's note) but, I believe, is also an anticipatory allusion to the slaughter of Agamemnon, as 'the cow' (*boos*), while Clytemnestra is the bull (*tauros*, ll. 1125–6). The Homeric formula for the slaughter of Agamemnon (as at *Odyssey* XI, l. 410) is 'as one cuts down an ox in his manger'. Thus, the *bous* on the tongue of the watchman is a condensation of the story he cannot tell about how his king, who should be a bull (*tauros*), will be slaughtered like a cow, not even like the castrated male (the ox) in Homer. The watchman's refusal to speak is related to the reversal of traditional male and female roles to which he alludes (and to which the ox-cow-bull imagery of the play alludes).

14 Note other allusions to epic singing – forms represented as horrific

and unacceptable – are found at l. 979, where the chorus talks of fear as song, *aoida*, unbidden and unhired; ll. 1186–93, the song of the Erinyes, their choir, drunk on the blood and betrayal within the household.

'Aeschylean silences' in the form of long periods of silence of a character on the stage were well known in antiquity and were parodied in Aristophanes' *Frogs* (1968, ll. 910–46), which is about the stone-like Niobe, silent after the slaughter of all her children by jealous deities. Recent scholarship has begun to suggest the contrast between these silences, other breaks in narrative flow and the epic traditions of telling, including allusions to the 'Beckett-like' silences in Aeschylus. Compare the Aeschylean Niobe with Beckett's mournful 'Reader' in *Ohio Impromptu*. 'No sound. So sat on as though turned to stone. The sad tale a last time told' (Beckett 1984b, pp. 283–8).

15 See Beckett's *Act without Words* (1958), written to be performed following *Endgame*, for a description of how to throttle desire by carefully crafted frustration.

16 This passage is a perverse commentary on Lear's *cri de coeur* about dead Cordelia, 'Why should a dog, a horse, a rat, have life,/And thou no breath at all?' (1963b, V, 3, ll. 308–9).

17 See especially an important article by Bion (1959). Bion (who 'happened' to be Beckett's analyst in the early 1930s; see Bair 1978), uses clinical examples as if drawn from characters straight out of Beckett's plays and novels.

18 See Cavell (1977) for the insight that the biblical tales of Noah and of Christ are evoked as parent–child stories. See also Hamm's curse: 'Infinite emptiness will be all around you' (Beckett 1958, p. 36).

19 Important too is the story of the artist-madman who thought it was the end of the world and could only see ashes and devastation outside the window (p. 44). The frame of *Endgame* of course confirms that the madman's delusion finally comes to be reality.

20 This article is a precis of my forthcoming book, *More than Kin: Psychoanalytic Studies of Tragic Drama and the Family*.

References

Aeschylus (1954) *The Oresteia* (*Agamemnon*; *The Libation Bearers*; *The Eumenides*), *Aeschyli Septem Quae Supersunt Tragoediae*, Gilbert Murray (ed.), Oxford, Oxford University Press.

—(1959) *Aeschylus*, in Grene, David (ed.) and Lattimore, Richmond (trans.) *The Complete Greek Tragedies*, Chicago, University of Chicago Press, vol. 1: *Aeschylus*.

Aristophanes (1968) *The Frogs*, in Rogers, B. R. (trans.) *Aristophanes*, Cambridge, Mass., Harvard University Press, vol. 2.

Aristotle (1981) *Aristotle's Poetics: A Translation and Commentary for Students of Literature*, Golden, Leon (trans.), O. B. Hardison, Jr (Commentary), Tallahassee, University Presses of Florida.

Bair, D. (1978) *Samuel Beckett: A Biography*, New York, Harcourt, Brace, Jovanovich.

Beckett, Samuel (1954) *Waiting for Godot*, New York, Grove Press.

—(1958) *'Endgame': A Play in One Act Followed by 'Act without Words': A Mime for One Player*, New York, Grove Press.

—(1984a) *Disjecta*, New York, Grove Press.

—(1984b) *Ohio Impromptu*, in *Collected Shorter Plays*, New York, Grove Press, pp. 283–8.

Bion, W. R. (1959) 'Attacks on linking', *International Journal of Psycho-Analysis*, 40, 308–15.

Cavell, Stanley (1977) 'Ending the waiting game', in *Must We Mean What We Say?* Cambridge, Cambridge University Press.

Chevigny, B. G. (ed.) (1969) *Twentieth Century Interpretations of Endgame: A Collection of Critical Essays*, Englewood Cliffs, NJ, Prentice-Hall.

Cohn, Ruby (1970) 'The laughter of sad Sam Beckett', in Friedman, M. (ed.), *Samuel Beckett Now*, Chicago, University of Chicago Press, pp. 185–97.

de Romilly, J. (1968) *Time in Greek Tragedy*, Ithaca, NY, Cornell University Press.

The Epic of Gilgamesh (1968), N. K. Sandars (trans.) Harmondsworth, Penguin.

Euripides (1959) *Medea; The Madness of Heracles; Iphigenia in Aulis*, in Grene, David (ed.) and Lattimore, Richmond (trans.) *The Complete Greek Tragedies*, Chicago, University of Chicago Press, vols 3 and 4: Euripides.

Frame, Douglas (1978) *The Myth of Return in Early Greek Epic*, New Haven, Conn., Yale University Press.

Homer (1917) *Homeri Opera (Odysseae Libros)*, Thomas W. Allen (ed.) Oxford, Oxford University Press, vols 3 and 4.

—(1920) *Homeri Opera (Iliados Libros)*, David B. Monro and Thomas W. Allen (eds) Oxford, Oxford University Press, vols 1 and 2.

—(1962) *The Iliad of Homer*, Lattimore, Richmond (trans.) Chicago, University of Chicago Press.

—(1965) *The Odyssey of Homer*, Lattimore, Richmond (trans.) New York, Harper & Row.

Mandel, Oscar (1961) *A Definition of Tragedy*, New York, New York University Press.

Morrison, K. (1983) *Canters and Chronicles: The Use of Narrative in the Plays of Samuel Beckett and Harold Pinter*, Chicago, University of Chicago Press.

Nevo, Ruth (1972) *Tragic Form in Shakespeare*, Princeton, NJ, Princeton University Press.

Oxford Classical Dictionary (1971) Oxford, Oxford University Press.

Shakespeare, William (1957) *The Tragedy of Hamlet Prince of Denmark*, Baltimore, Penguin.

——(1963a) *The Tragedy of Macbeth*, New York, Signet Classic Shakespeare.

——(1963b) *The Tragedy of King Lear*, New York, Signet Classic Shakespeare.

Simon, Bennett (1973) 'The hero as an only child: an unconscious fantasy structuring Homer's *Odyssey*', *International Journal of Psycho-Analysis*, 55, 555–62.

Sophocles (1950) *Oedipus at Colonus*, in *Sophoclis Fabulae*, Pearson, A. C. (ed.) Oxford, Oxford University Press.

——(1959) *Oedipus at Colonus*, in Grene, David (ed.) and Lattimore, Richmond (trans.) *The Complete Greek Tragedies*, Chicago, University of Chicago Press, vol. 2: *Sophocles*.

Stanford, W. B. (1983) *Greek Tragedy and the Emotions: An Introductory Study*, London, Routledge & Kegan Paul.

Tobin, Patricia Drechsel (1978) *Time and the Novel: The Genealogical Imperative*, Princeton, NJ, Princeton University Press.

Virgil (1930) *Aeneid*, Fairclough, H. R. (trans.) London, Heinemann, Loeb Classical Library.

9

Narration as repetition: the case of Günter Grass's *Cat and Mouse*

SHLOMITH RIMMON-KENAN

That narration repeats a story sounds obvious enough; indeed, this seems to be the classical view of narration: reporting, re-presenting, following through a line already there.[1] It is perhaps somewhat less obvious that narration may also repeat not by what it says but by what it does: 'performing', enacting that which gets blocked or concealed by the telling.[2] My interest in texts in which the story is, on the one hand, concealed by narration-as-reporting and, on the other, revealed by narration-as-performance, has led me to psychoanalysis, where such discourses are the daily bread and butter. My intention is not to 'apply' psychoanalysis to literature but rather to show an affinity between the two and to shed a somewhat defamiliarizing light on the literary phenomenon by looking at it through a lens which is akin to it and yet not its own. Interestingly, emphasis on the performative aspect of narration and repetition has received a new slant in both psychoanalysis itself and psychoanalytic literary criticism as a result of Lacanian- and deconstruction-affiliated approaches (Lacan 1977, Laplanche 1976, Felman 1977, Johnson 1977).[3] Thus my attempt to defamiliarize narration in literature by the *rapprochement* with psychoanalysis gets integrated in a complex give-and-take whereby the discourse I draw on has to a certain extent already become defamiliarized by its own drawing on the discourse of literature and literary theory.

Looking back at Freud's writings through the prism of this multi-layered reciprocity, his differentiation between remembering and repeating becomes strikingly similar to my distinction between narration-as-reporting and narration-as-performance. 'We have learnt', says Freud, 'that the patient repeats instead of remembering' (Freud 1958 [1914], p. 154). In repetition compulsion as well as in transference

> The patient does not *remember* anything of what he has forgotten and repressed, but *acts* it out. He reproduces it not as a memory but as an action; he repeats it, without, of course, knowing that he is repeating it. . . . As long as the patient is in the treatment he cannot escape from the compulsion to repeat; and in the end we understand that this is his way of remembering.
>
> (p. 150)

Like the concealing–revealing narrative texts, the analysand reproduces as action that which gets blocked as a memory. His behaviour becomes telling. But whereas the analysand's behaviour – in life as well as in transference – is both verbal and non-verbal, the literary text has only words at its disposal. In it, the manner of telling becomes behaviour, and the performative repetition can be glimpsed through analogies between the process of narration and the events of the story. Bennett Simon (in this book) has traced such analogies between the story of infanticide and the suicide of narration, but – although my own example also concerns murder and perhaps suicide – the phenomenon need not be limited to these themes.

Like the distinction between remembering and repeating, Freud's speculations about the teleology of repetition also prove illuminating for narration.[4] Repetition, it emerges from these speculations, may serve the pleasure principle, but it may also manifest a death instinct. The child's game of throwing the reel away and then pulling it back as an enactment of his mother's departure and return is a successful, constructive, ultimately pleasurable repetition, because by passing from a passive situation of being overpowered by his mother's absence to an active situation where he inflicts the same fate on various objects within his reach, the child gains mastery over the disagreeable experience (Freud 1961 [1920], pp. 9–11). Analogously, repetition in transference is (at least potentially) therapeutic because it brings the original unconscious experience to consciousness, thus enabling the analysand to master it. Over-sameness, rather than difference, dominates in the death-directed repetitions, sameness being akin to the conservative instincts, the urge to return to the inanimate state of undifferentiated matter, to 'the inertia inherent in organic life' (pp. 32, 30).

Narration-as-repetition seems to me to be similarly double-edged: it may lead to a working through and an overcoming, but it may also imprison the narrative in a kind of textual neurosis, an issueless re-enactment of the traumatic events it narrates and conceals. Kristeva (in this book) emphasizes the power of writing to triumph over its 'mobilizing affliction'. The text to be analysed in my own paper, on the other hand, foregrounds the entrapment of narration in the story it tells. I suspect that, as in psychoanalysis, the difference between the two kinds of narrational repetition resides precisely in the proportion of difference within the repetition, but I cannot pursue this hypothesis here.

A complete study of narration as repetition would require an examination of both narration by characters *within* a story and the narration *of* the story, whether by character-narrators or by an undramatized external voice. Thus Emma Zunz, a character within a Borges story which bears her name (Borges 1974), gives the police a false report of the events which led to her killing of Lowenthal, but it is through this false account that she repeats and re-enacts the true Oedipal story of which she is not aware. In their transference-like relationship, Quentin and Shreve, character-narrators in Faulkner's *Absalom, Absalom!* (1972), relive with each other the story of Henry Sutpen and Charles Bon, a story which they reconstruct – or rather construct – in order to understand and master the unknown both outside and inside themselves. And the external narrator in Muriel Spark's *The Prime of Miss Jean Brodie* (1971) repeats in his manner of narration the same tendency to act like providence which the story shows as one of the main failings of the central character. Obviously, I cannot offer here a detailed analysis of these examples – with the similarities and differences between them – nor can I deal with all the narratorial positions which they exemplify. This paper is confined to one narrative, Günter Grass's *Cat and Mouse* (1964), in which the narrator is also one of the story's protagonists.

However, before turning to Grass's novella, I wish to suggest that the narratological categories which seem to me useful for a larger study of narration as repetition also undergo an unexpected

twist or acquire an additional dimension from the very phenomenon they would help to analyse. Reformulated in narratological
terms, with which it is not directly concerned, Derrida's analysis
(1978) of the operation of performative repetition in Freud's *Beyond
the Pleasure Principle* gives rise to an interesting possibility. A
suggestion emerges that while Freud consciously sets himself the
role of external narrator – 'extra-hetero-diegetic', to use Genette's
term (Genette 1972) – his unconscious *fort/da* game with what
Derrida calls the a-thesis of 'beyond the pleasure principle' repeats
Ernst's game and makes Freud in some sense a protagonist-
narrator of his own story rather than a scientific observer of
somebody else's behaviour. While this suggestion does not
collapse the narratological categories (defined by structural criteria, such as the narrator's position in relation to the represented
world), it does add a metaphoric sense in which being outside is
also being inside, and narrating somebody else's story is also
narrating one's own.

Indeed, such a complexity of the narrative situation is a striking
feature of *Cat and Mouse*. Whereas Pilenz purports to give an
account of Mahlke's life – 'but this is not the place to tell my story
... here I am speaking only of you [Mahlke]' (Grass 1964, p. 90),
he says (with variations) on several occasions – it is precisely his
own story that he turns out to be telling. 'As it is', he says even
earlier, 'I can't help writing, for you cannot keep such things to
yourself' (p. 76). Just as he feels compelled to write, addressing his
narrative at least partly to his victim Mahlke,[5] so he feels compelled
to tell his story to Father Alban with whom he discusses religious
matters like 'the sacrament of *penance*' (my emphasis): 'I tell him
about Mahlke ..., about cat and mouse and *mea culpa*' (p. 73). But
my main point is that even the confession is only a screen. In the act
of narration Pilenz manages to evade or attenuate his guilt, and the
narration consequently becomes a repetition of the same behaviour
that made it necessary. Pilenz (unwittingly?) tells one story in order
to conceal another, and it is the other story that returns in the very
act of narration. Rather than confessing the (figurative and
probably also literal) killing of Mahlke, Pilenz's narration kills
Mahlke yet again.

The primal sin which Pilenz narrates (but also attenuates, as we
shall see later) is his enticement of a cat to jump on Mahlke's huge
Adam's apple in the middle of a handball game at school. For
Mahlke this is the traumatic scene which marks him by his

deformity and shapes his whole life as an attempt to conceal it – covering it with pompons, screwdrivers, a stolen medal and then his own medal won at war – and paradoxically exposing, foregrounding, that which he is trying to conceal. But the scene is also traumatic for Pilenz: it is his role as a cat, as an aggressor, that he will keep repeating throughout his relations with Mahlke as well as in their narration. Catlike, Pilenz pursues Mahlke to church only in order to watch the mouselike Adam's apple bobbing up and down during prayer and communion (p. 17).[6] Catlike, Pilenz follows Mahlke everywhere, even to the boat where he knows Mahlke wants to be alone in order to hide the stolen medal (p. 72). When Mahlke stops coming to the barge with the other children, Pilenz feels the relief of not having 'to chase after him the whole time' (p. 81), a negative which betrays the persistence of his earlier pursuit.[7] Indeed, the cat-and-mouse motif, as well as references to the traumatic scene itself, constantly recur in the novella, like a relentless repetition compulsion.

But Pilenz does not only chase after Mahlke. He also kills him twice figuratively before being responsible for his actual death. At school one of the classmates draws a caricature of Mahlke as the Redeemer, ridiculing both his external appearance and his obsession with the Holy Virgin. Pilenz sponges Mahlke's Redeemer countenance off the blackboard, seemingly protecting Mahlke against ridicule but also effacing him. The sinister aspect of Pilenz's action becomes prominent in conjunction with a later scene where the narration does not even attempt to disguise the wiping out as a friendly gesture. In the latrine of a Labour Service camp, Pilenz finds Mahlke's initials carved in a pine board and under them, in Latin, the beginning of Mahlke's favourite sequence: *Stabat Mater dolorosa* .... And so, 'one day after I had been chopping kindling in the battalion kitchen, I took the ax and hacked Mahlke's favorite sequence out of the board and eradicated your name' (p. 99). Ironically, the absence becomes more present than the former presence, 'for the empty patch of wood with its fresh fibers spoke more eloquently than the chipped inscription' (p. 100). Mahlke returns not only through the presence of his absent name but also through stories which are repeatedly told around the camp. The text Pilenz eradicates is thus replaced by other texts, and the oral narratives seem to compensate for and spring from the eliminated name. Isn't this a *mise en abyme* of *Cat and Mouse* where Pilenz's narration also springs from the loss, the eradication, of the person whose story it narrates?

But, as Pilenz says a bit earlier, 'a writer mustn't get ahead of himself' (p. 72), and it is to the literal eradication of Mahlke that I turn now. After the headmaster denies Mahlke, the glorious returning soldier, the habitual permission to tell his story to the school assembly, Mahlke deserts the army in despair and has to hide from the military police. Pilenz does everything to prevent him from reaching a safe shelter. Mahlke first goes to mass and when Father Gusewski expresses his worry that the deserter might do something rash, Pilenz answers, 'Don't worry, Father. I'll take care of him' and 'you'd better keep out of it, Father' (p. 114). But Pilenz has a strange way of taking care of his friend, rejecting every escape possibility Mahlke suggests, including the cellar at Pilenz's house, deceitfully insisting that the military police have already come looking for him, and suggesting that Mahlke hide in the ruined ship. On the way to the ship Mahlke has a symbolic Last Supper, devouring so many gooseberries that he gets stomach cramps and feels he shouldn't swim. But Pilenz insists that they must make haste, lies that he has rented the boat for only an hour and a half (p. 122) and rows Mahlke to the fatal ship. Mahlke dives with his food cans, but the opener, we learn to our shock, has remained with Pilenz, and only when it is too late does Pilenz shout to the vanished Mahlke to come up and retrieve the opener (p. 125). Thus Mahlke will have nothing to eat in his hiding place. Yet Pilenz returns only on Saturday morning, not on the same evening as agreed (p. 126), making it practically impossible to save Mahlke.

This is the story that emerges from *Cat and Mouse*. But how does Pilenz narrate it? Attenuation of incriminating evidence, insistence on his role as a friend, and shifting responsibility from victimizer to victim are all mobilized to turn this seeming confession of guilt into its denial.

The crucial facts are omitted or attenuated in the narration of both the original scene and the final 'murder' scene which repeats it. Active verbs are attributed to the cat in rendering the original scene, creating the impression that the cat jumped of its own accord: 'The cat practised'; 'Still practising, the cat came closer'; 'the caretaker's black cat tensed for a leap'; 'the cat leaped at Mahlke's throat' (p. 8). This is followed by an alternative version, but even the correction begins by a false identification of the performer: 'or one of us caught the cat and held it up to Mahlke's neck, or' – and here comes the real story, almost drowned behind the false ones which preceded it – 'I, with or without toothache, seized the cat and showed it Mahlke's mouse' (p. 8). Note that even here Pilenz limits his role to *showing* the mouse to the cat, not to putting the cat on Mahlke's neck, as transpires from another statement which reveals this and then uses a further denial technique (p. 83; this will be discussed later).[8]

Equally evasive is the narration of the events concerning the can opener in the fatal last scene. During the rowing, Mahlke is said to be 'clutching the wrapped can opener' (p. 120) and then 'playing negligently' with it (p. 122). No transferal of the opener to Pilenz is reported. Instead, Pilenz repeatedly recalls his warning to Mahlke to take the can opener with him (p. 123), and then – following the omission of the main event – comes the narration of the aftermath: 'then I took my foot off the can opener. The can opener and I remained behind' (p. 124). Similarly, three dots of omission stand for the death-suicide-murder at another juncture where the explicit emphasis is on Pilenz's innocence: 'Was it my fault if Mahlke later ...' (p. 76).

The evasion of responsibility is accompanied by an insistence on Pilenz's role as a friend even when the event narrated is a betrayal of Mahlke. Thus the erasing of Mahlke's caricature from the blackboard is told as an act of friendship, and the scenes leading to Mahlke's death insistently repeat, 'rain is a binder'.

Not only does Pilenz present himself as a friend while narrating acts of betrayal, he also accuses his victim of causing his own victimization. Thus in the scene that prefigures all other scenes, it is not the cat who is presented as the aggressor but the mouse who is blamed for tempting the cat to leap: Mahlke's Adam's apple lures the cat (p. 9) and so Mahlke is responsible: it is he (or his mouse) that 'had tempted me to put the cat on his neck' (p. 83). Similarly, in narrating the final scene, Pilenz does not assume responsibility for Mahlke's disappearance but blames Mahlke for not saving himself: 'You might have knocked [on the barge, from within]' (pp. 124–5), says the cat to the mouse.

A similar form of shifting responsibility is role-reversal. While in fact it is Pilenz who pursues Mahlke, the narration often presents Mahlke as pursuing Pilenz, both as a living companion and as a haunting ghost. In youth, Mahlke's presence is so powerful that even during a period of separation it keeps dominating Pilenz's thoughts: 'but not to see you was not, and still is not, to forget your fearful symmetry' (p. 92). Similarly, when Pilenz discovers Mahlke's name in the latrine in the Labour Service camp, he is desperate, feeling that there is no escape from Mahlke:

but all it meant to me was that even in the Labour Service I couldn't get rid of Mahlke. ... For while I relieved myself, you gave me and my eyes no peace: loudly and in breathless repetition, a painstakingly incised text called attention to Mahlke, whatever I might decide to whistle in opposition. ... Mahlke's text drowned out all the more or less wittily formulated obscenities which ... gave tongues to wooden boards.

(pp. 98–9)

After his death Mahlke torments Pilenz in his silence (p. 125), in his all too present absence, and Pilenz's whole life is shaped by Mahlke's disappearance: he keeps looking for him in a meeting of war survivors, he carries on endless confessional conversations with Father Alban and he writes the document we read.

What Pilenz presents as Mahlke's active haunting is the obverse of his own repetition compulsion. For Pilenz's life is shaped by the need to evoke again and again scenes from his past with Mahlke, both in his imagination and in his writing: 'Let us all three celebrate the sacrament *once more and forever* (p. 114; my emphasis),[9] 'Although I have never again to this day set foot in a rowboat, we are still sitting face to face' (p. 120), and so on. But beyond this insistent re-evocation, the narration also repeats the story in the sense of doing again what it narrates, and since what it narrates are acts of persecution and murder, the narration can be seen – as I have already suggested – as killing Mahlke again rather than as evoking and expiating past crimes.

The performative aspect of Pilenz's narration as repetition is emphasized by analogies between story and narration in three central episodes, all of which also display a self-conscious treatment of the act of writing. The first is the opening scene of the novella, the primal sin which is symptomatic of the whole chain of repetitions. The cat's leap, the climax of this episode, is a gradual process: the cat 'sauntered diagonally across the field ... meandered about ... showed a white bib ... practised ... came closer ... tensed for a leap ... leaped' (pp. 7–8). The cat takes its time, and so does the narrator, interspersing the account of the dramatic events with bits of information about the tournament, the operation of the crematorium close by, Pilenz's toothache, the movements of the plane across the sky. An analogy thus emerges between the behaviour of the cat and that of the narrator, and the analogy soon shifts from the relatively harmless common quality of delaying to that of persecuting. Immediately after the cat episode, the text moves from narrating the story to talking about narration:

> And now it is up to me, who called your mouse to the attention of this cat and all cats, to write. Even if we were both invented, I should have to write. Over and over again the fellow who invented us because it's his business to invent people obliges me to take your Adam's apple in my hand and carry it to the spot that saw it win or lose.
>
> (p. 8)

That Pilenz is compelled to take Mahlke's Adam's apple repeatedly in his writing hand does not only mean that writing is a perpetual reliving of the traumatic scene but also that writing, in this case, is equivalent to the act it narrates: to write about the leap of the cat is to leap like a cat, to write about persecution is to persecute once again.[10]

The next analogy between story and narration also concerns delay and persecution, and it occurs in the middle of the novella. Involved are Mahlke who is escaping to the barge with the recently stolen war medal and Pilenz who is following him. Pilenz's pursuit is constantly slowed down. First, he is detained by Father Gusewsky, who inquires about his brother, then he misses a tram, later he has to get rid of Tulla and of some younger boys who are keen on swimming with him and, finally, when he is on his own, he makes no haste, swimming breast stroke, stopping to contemplate the clouds. Like Pilenz the boy, Pilenz the narrator holds up the account of the pursuit by constant digressions concerning the war and the involvement of various classmates in it as well as his conversations with Father Alban as an adult. Interestingly, these digressions treat narration-time and story-time as contemporaneous, a quasi-metaleptic technique which endows the rendering with a self-conscious aura: 'I may as well tell you between two strokes – the water will hold me up – that this was the last Sunday before summer vacation. What was going on at the time?' (p. 72). Later, trying to prevent the narration from getting ahead of itself, he interrupts it with, 'No, not yet. Once again, before it is too late, let me turn over on my back and contemplate the great clouds shaped like potato sacks' (p. 73). A more acute awareness of the status of writing emerges when the analogy between story and narration is formulated explicitly:

As I swam and as I write, I tried and I try to think of Tulla Pokriefke, for I didn't and still don't want to think of Mahlke. That's why I swam breast stroke, and that's why I write that I swam breast stroke. ... I was no longer swimming away from Tulla, but swimming toward Mahlke, and it is toward you that I write: I swam breast stroke and I didn't hurry.

(p. 72)

A similar repetition of the story by the narration occurs towards the end of the novella when Pilenz accompanies the deserting Mahlke on his escape-route to the barge and in fact drives him to his (probable) death. Short sentences re-enact Pilenz's and Mahlke's breathless wandering through the labyrinthine streets, and Pilenz's question, 'How am I going to get out of here?' (p. 117), is made to refer both to the agonizing situation in which he found himself as a boy and to the intricacies of the writing-process. The reference to writing soon becomes more explicit: 'Who will supply me with a good ending?' (p. 126). However, there is no good ending for a narrative whose story is governed by repetition. The *novella* thus ends with a narration of repeated attempts on Pilenz's part to search for the absent-present Mahlke, and it is this present absence at the heart of the repetition that motivates the need to repeat the story again by narrating it.

The analogy between story and narration, emphasizing the performative aspect of repetition at the beginning, middle and end of the novella, is put in a nutshell by the poignant question Pilenz asks about the very nature of stories: 'Are there stories that can cease to be?' (p. 96). This question, I believe, is not only an expression of desire on Pilenz's part to free himself from haunting guilt, but also an unconscious wish to put an end to their protagonist, that is to repeat the guilt-provoking action. But the concealed story, like the lost protagonist, keeps returning. Contrary to Pilenz's wishes, stories one dare not face cannot cease to be, and *Cat and Mouse* will repeatedly bear witness to the story Pilenz would rather not tell.

Notes

1 a) 'Narration', 'text' and 'story' are used as technical terms, equivalent to Genette's 'narration', 'récit', and 'histoire', respectively (Genette 1972).

b) The image of the line is borrowed from Miller (1980, p. 109).

2 The notion of 'performing' and, later in my paper, of 'performative' repetition, is derived from Austin (1962), but it is used in the somewhat loose sense in which it was adopted by a few psychoanalytic literary critics, e.g. Felman (1977) and Johnson (1977).

3 Felman and Johnson emphasize the operation of repetition in the act of reading or interpretation.

4 For a use of Freud's theory of repetition and the death instinct, in order to illuminate the structure of plot, see Brooks (1977, 1984).

5 As will be seen in several quotations later in the paper, Pilenz often switches to 'you' – sometimes even in mid-sentence – when talking about Mahlke.

6 The attribution of the role of cat to Pilenz and that of mouse to Mahlke becomes problematic as the novella progresses. Indeed, the two sometimes change roles, and the cat-and-mouse motif – foregrounded by the title and the sketch on the cover, drawn by Grass himself – becomes ambiguous. This ambiguity emerges in the sequel of my study, but it is not discussed in and for itself. I leave it subordinate to the matter at hand and refer the reader to a brilliant chapter on this novella in Ruth Ginsburg's yet unpublished Ph.D. thesis, *The Anti-Carnivalesque: A Variation of the Grotesque* (Jerusalem, 1985). This is also the occasion to express my gratitude to Ruth Ginsburg for arousing my interest in Grass's text as well as for drawing my attention to many points I may have missed without her.

7 A similar statement occurs somewhat later: 'No, I didn't look after him. Unbelievable, you think?' (p. 92).

8 Incidentally, Mahlke always believed that it was another schoolmate, not Pilenz, who put the cat on his neck (see p. 84).

9 Note that the sacrament is itself a repetitive ritual and that it concerns the *return* of the Son of God.

10 a) This last meaning probably emerges behind Pilenz's back *qua* narrator – which may partly explain the strange metaleptic appeal to the real author at this point: 'the fellow who invented us'. Another explanation may be an attempt on Pilenz's part to shift the responsibility to someone else: it is not he but the one who invented him who is responsible for his acts (which may be another way of describing a compulsion). I have to admit, however, that neither explanation is fully satisfactory and that the function of Pilenz's awareness of himself not as a writer but as a fictional character remains a mystery to me.

    b) The repetitive aspect of the narration may have uncanny implications for Grass's view of the tendency on the part of many German post-war writers (including himself) to write about Germany's role in the war. Since quite a few studies of *Cat and Mouse* discuss the political dimension (though not the aspect I mention here), I shall refrain from analysing it.

References

Austin, J. L. (1962) *How to Do Things with Words*, Oxford, Clarendon.

Borges, Jorge Luis (1974) 'Emma Zunz', in *Labyrinths*, Harmondsworth, Penguin.

Brooks, Peter (1977) 'Freud's masterplot: questions of narrative', *Yale French Studies: Literature and Psychoanalysis. The Question of Reading: Otherwise*, 55/6, 280–300.

——(1984) *Reading for the Plot*, New York, Knopf.

Derrida, Jacques (1978) 'Coming into one's own', in Hartman, Geoffrey (ed.) *Psychoanalysis and the Question of the Text*, Baltimore, Johns Hopkins University Press, pp. 114–48.

Faulkner, William (1972) *Absalom, Absalom!* New York, Vintage Books.

Felman, Shoshana (1977) 'Turning the screw of interpretation', *Yale French Studies: Literature and Psychoanalysis. The Question of Reading: Otherwise*, 55/6, 94–207.

Freud, Sigmund (1958) [1914] 'Remembering, repeating, and working through', in *The Standard Edition of the Complete Psychological Works*, London, Hogarth Press, vol. 12, pp. 145–56.

——(1961) [1920] *Beyond the Pleasure Principle*, New York, Norton.

Genette, Gérard (1972) *Figures III*, Paris, Seuil.

Grass, Günter (1964) *Cat and Mouse*, New York, Signet.

Hartman, Geoffrey (ed.) (1978) *Psychoanalysis and the Question of the Text*, Baltimore, Johns Hopkins University Press.

Johnson, Barbara (1977) 'The frame of reference: Poe, Lacan, Derrida', *Yale French Studies: Literature and Psychoanalysis. The Question of Reading: Otherwise*, 55/6, 457–505.

Kristeva, Julia (1987) 'On the melancholic imaginary', in this volume.

Lacan, Jacques (1977) *Ecrits*, New York, Norton.

Laplanche, Jean (1976) *Life and Death in Psychoanalysis*, Baltimore, Johns Hopkins University Press.

Miller, J. Hillis (1980) 'The figure in the carpet', *Poetics Today*, 1 (3), 107–18.

Simon, Bennett (1987) 'Tragic drama and the family: the killing of children and the killing of story-telling', in this volume.

Spark, Muriel (1971) *The Prime of Miss Jean Brodie*, Harmondsworth, Penguin.

10

Narrative recursion

DONALD P. SPENCE

Twas a dark and stormy night. The band of robbers huddled together around the fire. When he had finished eating, the first bandit said, 'Let me tell you a story. It was a dark and stormy night and a band of robbers huddled together around the fire. When he had finished eating, the first bandit said, "Let me tell you a story. It was a dark and stormy night and . . ."

We begin with a simple piece of recursion – the subject of the tale becomes the teller – and almost before our eyes, the story becomes impossibly complex. What starts off as an almost banal story very quickly escalates into a highly complicated narrative, its complexity marked by the fact that we can transcribe only a very small number of embeddings before we run out of distinguishing quotation marks. Thus we have manufactured a tale which must be told, not written, a tale in which the narrative voice keeps moving farther and farther into the fantastic and away from the conventional bounds of time and space. By the fifth embedding, it is no longer clear who is speaking or in whose mind he is being imagined. He could be a creation of the first narrator – or is he only the responsibility of the next-to-last narrator and therefore free in some significant manner, capable of, let us say, turning on the original teller and surprising him (and us) with some unseen twist of plot?

The recursive narrative (a genre of which this is one example) has an uncanny feel about it which may account for its success with children and for our sense that some kind of mischief is afoot. But it is more than just a curiosity; as I will try to show, the recursive structure lies at the heart of much of our experience in 'real life' and at the heart of many significant clinical phenomena. I will also argue that narrative recursion is a necessary part of narrative persuasion, and this comes about, in part, because it makes a bridge between fact and fiction and gives us a sense that the story we are being told is more than just a story and that it contains an important measure of lived truth – that is, wisdom.

The role of repetition

Something that happens over and over comes to acquire a certain kind of lawfulness and expectancy; we can think of the motions of the planets, the beating of the heart or the variations of the seasons. 'Man is a pattern-seeking animal', writes the anthropologist Benjamin Colby:

> At the subliminal level he continually seeks patterns or regularities in his environment and unconsciously organizes such regularities in a mental structure. I propose the hypothesis that, in hearing the narratives of others, one derives patterns from them and constructs cognitive templates for future use in telling his own stories. These templates must be stored in some organized way, to be called forth by schemata (rules, formulas, programs) or by some other means, at a higher level of mental organization, according to different behavioral situations.
>
> (Colby 1966, pp. 796–7)

If such patterning is *discovered* in what seems to be a random collection of happenings, the fact of repetition helps to validate the discovery. But there are some important qualifications to this rule which must also be considered. If repetition is too obvious or too mechanical, it acquires a distinctly non-human quality and Freud touched on this property in his paper on the uncanny (Freud 1955 [1919]). Frankenstein's monster and Chaplin's factory worker seem dehumanized in direct proportion to their mechanical qualities: what is a machine if not a repetitive device? Thus a narrative which depends too strongly on rote repetition very quickly loses its explanatory force; we are suspicious of repetition when it becomes too stylized and feel more comfortable with a pattern of repetition with variations.

A second problem bears on the difference between twice and anything greater. One repetition in music, for example, seems natural and satisfying; two repetitions seem wrong, unmusical and unbalanced; three or more, the clear sign of a broken record. A similar rule applies to certain kinds of behaviour. We may take the exam a second or even a third time, but there is something neurotic or worse about four or more tries; does this kind of perseveration remind us of mechanical repetition and, for that reason, of human failure?

Quite a different rule applies to a theme and variations. In both music and real life there is almost no limit to the number of permutations we can listen to or watch for; thus we seem to enjoy sameness, perhaps even need it, when combined with difference. Here is where narrative recursion comes into play. A recursive narrative is both same and different, both repetitive and distinctive. Indeed, our first impression may be one of random change, and only after much study will we uncover the recursive principle which provides the repetitive pattern. But in contrast to a theme and variations, a recursive pattern is much more strictly determined because the extent of transformation is defined by the underlying recursive operator. Thus a recursive narrative not only appeals to us because it depends heavily on the principle of repetition but, in addition, because a single recursive operator will *completely determine* the shape of the data. For this reason, a recursive solution to a particular narrative carries with it the same sense of conviction generated by a deductive proof.

There are some additional reasons why recursive narratives have a particular relevance to clinical observations. In the first place, a recursive operator can generate a complex universe of data points in a manner that closely resembles the way in which a latent wish, in Freud's dream theory, can produce the manifest dream. What is more, it significantly strengthens Freud's model. The core argument in *Die Traumdeutung* (Freud 1953 [1900]) is somewhat weakened by its reliance on a primary-process system which contains an unlimited number of transformation mechanisms. The near-infinite degrees of freedom contained in these mechanisms makes it possible to relate anything to anything. But if the transformations are made the property of the recursive operator, then the argument becomes much stronger. In a paper on Freud's Botanical Monograph dream, I showed how the dream can be better understood (and, I think, more rigorously explained) as the consequence of transformations of one or more canonical propositions (Spence 1981). Later in this paper, I will show how these transformations fit the more general class of recursive operators.

A second attraction stems from the fact that the search for the underlying recursive operator parallels the search for an unconscious phantasy or early memory. In none of these cases is the underlying operator intuitively obvious or superficially apparent from the manifest data. In every case, we search for a latent argument which, when transformed in a particular way, will generate the manifest data, and as noted, these transformations can take many different forms. But if we can discover a truly recursive operator, then we have an explanation which is not only exhaustive but reversible; given the operator, it should follow that *anyone* could generate the dream. Thus we not only have explained the dream, but we have a way of validating our explanation.

In the third place, there is a resemblance between recursion and clinical repetition – in particular, repetition in the transference. It appears on close inspection that the original conflict or phantasy or early experience is almost never literally repeated in the transference; rather, what we see is a series of variations on a single theme. But closer inspection reveals that these variations are not casual or quixotic but, quite the contrary, tightly controlled and overdetermined. Suppose the patient has learned that uncontrolled anger leads to rejection. His anger at the therapist, if only in phantasy, can lead to fears of being abandoned, and in the early stages of treatment he may find ways of provoking the therapist and making this 'rule' come true. It takes little imagination to see that the single operator, anger $\rightarrow$ rejection, can generate a bewildering confusion of clinical happenings, depending on how the therapist responds, the extent to which he interprets the 'rule', and a host of other factors.

To illustrate the relevance of recursion to the transference, suppose we make the interpretation that whenever the patient feels angry he will fear rejection. Suppose the patient reacts to this interpretation with anger during the session – a quite plausible consequence – and then silence. We probe the silence and discover that he is daydreaming about dropping out of the analysis and taking a long vacation in the South Seas. We suggest – or rather, we interpret – that he is leaving before we leave him. He anticipates rejection and, to protect himself, he plans to leave first. Thus his phantasy tends to corroborate our interpretation. Now suppose he becomes openly angry on hearing the interpretation and storms out of the office. At the next session we might say that once again he has validated our interpretation and the recursive operator has once again appeared: anger is dangerous; it leads to rejection; and he rejects before he can be rejected.

It can be seen that the single argument, anger → rejection, can be used to account for (a) the patient's current life, (b) his reaction to the first interpretation (the statement of the general principle) and (c) his reaction to the second interpretation (the explanation for his phantasy of the South Seas). We might predict that similar (but not identical) reactions will occur on subsequent occasions until the patient has recognized the truth of the argument. But notice that no two repetitions are exactly alike and that the underlying recursive operator is not immediately obvious from the manifest content. Anger can be expressed in a wide variety of different ways, just as rejection can be signalled or threatened or anticipated in a number of different disguises. A recursive explanation captures both the overall pattern of similarity and the lack of mechanical, dehumanizing repetition.

Recursive properties

Before going into more clinical detail, it might be good strategy to lay out the essential characteristics of recursive process and structure and distinguish them from repetition. We can contrast the tale of 'A dark and stormy night,' a fragment of which we quoted at the start of this chapter, with the story of the bear who went over the mountain ... to see another mountain ... to climb another mountain ...

In the case of the bear, we have repetition but not recursion. Each addition simply carries us further along the same narrative level (ignoring the occasional mountains to be crossed). The bear in the first clause will be the same as the bear in the nth and the nth + 1 clause, and the narrative voice is constant throughout. Repetition of this kind quickly loses its appeal because it does not generate enough variety; repetition of the recursive sort, as we have noted, is always changing. Felman describes it well by comparing it to a spiral. 'The spiral consists of a series of repeated circlings in which what turns is indeed bound to *re-turn*, but in which what circularly thus returns only returns so as to miss anew its point of departure. ... The successive turns and returns to the spiral *never meet*' (Felman 1977, p. 178; original emphasis). Thus the narrator at the third level of 'A dark and stormy night' will never appear again, no matter how long we continue the story, and no telling will slavishly repeat any other telling; there may be resemblances but no carbon copies. The bear, on the other hand, is always with us, no matter how long we continue the story.

I think it is the spiral pattern, the almost but not quite closing the circle, that gives a particular poignancy to any recursive narrative because it will never, by defnition, return 'home'. In this way, too, it resembles real life. At the same time, it also contains an obvious pattern and thus can be reduced to a restricted number of operators. We now must examine how repetition leads to diversity.

The secret lies in the essential property of the recursive structure – the fact that the repetition is always operating on itself. Hofstadter gives the example of a radio news programme in which we are suddenly shifted to a foreign correspondent (Sally Swumpley in Peafog, England) who then plays us a tape from a local reporter doing an interview with a local citizen (see Hofstadter 1979, p. 128). The recursive operator in this case is the device that switches us to another audio source, but we may be unaware of the recursion because we are listening to content and there seems nothing similar in the three changes of voice. It may often require inside knowledge of a particular text to discover which recursive operators are at work; once again, the pattern is not immediately obvious.

Now consider another example from Hofstadter:

> The proverbial German phenomenon of the 'verb-at-the-end,' about which droll tales of absent-minded professors who would begin a sentence, ramble on for an entire lecture, and then finish up by rattling off a string of verbs by which their audience, for whom the stack had long since lost its coherence, would be totally nonplussed, are told, is an excellent example of linguistic pushing and popping [i.e. recursion].

(p. 130)

This specimen, it would appear, becomes recursive in the very act of describing recursion. The recursive operator, 'verb-at-the-end', is brought into play on three occasions in the description – at the end of the first clause ('. . . at-the-end'), at the end of the second clause ('. . . begin a sentence') and at the end of the third clause ('. . . entire lecture'). The first clause is completed with the last clause, the second by the next-to-last, and the third by the second-to-last.

The narrative parallel of Hofstadter's Germanic sentence can be found in the tale begun by one narrator who introduces a second who introduces a third. So far, we have another version of 'A dark and stormy night'. But now we introduce an interesting variation. Suppose when the third narrator finishes his story, the telling is taken up by the second narrator; when he finishes his tale, the original narrator brings us to the end. This variation has been described by Brooks as a structure of boxes within boxes and he identifies both good and flawed versions. Brooks lists Mary Shelley's *Frankenstein* among the former: 'Where Walton's narrative encloses Frankenstein's narrative which encloses the Monster's narrative; when the Monster has finished his narrative, Frankenstein then finishes his, then Walton concludes' (Brooks 1984, p. 351). A flawed version is represented by Conrad's *Heart of Darkness*: the first narrator introduces Marlow, who then begins the tale of Kurtz, but this story is so murky and ambiguous that it has neither beginning nor end; thus it is hard to tell when we move back into the outer boxes.

The Germanic sentence and the Frankenstein story are special forms of narrative recursion which depend on symmetrical entering and exiting of the nest of boxes, but unless the symmetry is perfect, we never come back to the beginning level. Because their formal nature is somewhat artificial, they are rarely found in actuality. The flawed version – Conrad's *Heart of Darkness* – is a much more representative sample, and it echoes reality in two ways: because its form is not perfectly symmetrical and because, as a result of this central ambiguity, it never stops being retold. As Brooks makes clear, the puzzle at the heart of the *Heart of Darkness* motivates a series of retellings – a series of attempts to make sense out of why Marlow made his trip upriver and an attempt to explain the mystery of Kurtz. In trying to unravel the original mystery, we repeat the original act of narration and generate another recursion: each critic and commentator can be represented as another Marlow who repeats the original expedition to make sense out of the unknown. The recursive operator at work here is the attempt to turn a chaotic piece of action which takes place in an exotic setting, into a piece of narrative truth.

When we move from fictional to clinical examples, we often add further recursions in which language becomes action and content becomes form. In the clinical example just cited, the operator is first stated as an interpretation (rejection leads to anger). It then appears in action in the transference when the patient feels rejected on hearing the interpretation and responds with anger. The transition from language to action is a special property of clinical recursion and one reason why the underlying operator or argument is often hard to identify. And a shift of mode from language to action or from content to form also cuts down on the senseless repetition which would make the pattern seem mechanical and unnatural.

It should also be noted that this shift is particularly characteristic of transference interpretations because it often happens that the subject of the interpretation becomes the object of the interaction, and the *response* to an interpretation, when properly decoded, can be used to further support the *claim* of the interpretation. In cases of this kind we can think of the operator (e.g. rejection → anger) as holding true within a certain environment of words or actions, much as the parameters of a sub-routine are expected to maintain their value only within the local domain where the sub-routine is called into play. The specific 'values' of the argument – the specific expressions of anger and rejection – are continually changing, and to further complicate the equation, the 'form' of these variables will sometimes be linguistic and sometimes behavioural. Thus the expression of recursion in the clinical situation is even more complex than it appears in the mathematical case where values may change but form remains constant.

It was Freud's particular genius to recognize that continuity could be maintained in a shift from language to action, from repeating to remembering and from behaviour in the transference to behaviour in the past. He realized that change of mode does not necessarily imply a change in theme, and he found ways of identifying the underlying pattern. The key to discovery often lies in finding the underlying recursive operator which never appears in its pure form but which, once identified, is seen to make possible the puzzling bits and pieces which seem to have nothing in common. Once the operator is discovered, everything else falls into place; until the operator is found, everything seems chaotic.

In the paper on the Botanical Monograph dream, I showed how a botanical metaphor could be used to find uniformity among the three triggering associations (Spence 1981). Carrying this argument forward, we could say that the underlying recursive operator in that dream takes the following form: treat everything as if it were a botanical specimen, and when in doubt, dissect. I have shown how Freud pulls apart the dream 'specimen' (his term) leaf by leaf (one association at a time). The rule that each piece of the specimen is equally informative leads to his confusion about primary and secondary associations. And finally, the botanical metaphor leads to an emphasis on the visual aspects of the dream and a tendency to treat the remembered parts in a highly concrete manner – much the way we might approach a dried leaf or plant.

We are also aware of the interplay between form and content, and we noted that this is a frequent property of clinical recursions. All the time he is describing the botanical *content* of the dream, Freud is approaching it in a botanical *manner*. His search for botanical associations (names of flowers, for example, and memories of his days as a student of botany) is carried out by applying the botanical metaphor: treat the dream as if it were a specimen, leave no part unexamined, and when frustrated in your search for meaning, divide and dissect (i.e. associate to smaller and smaller pieces). The recursive operator thus helps to explain both his central associations to the dream and his manner of approaching their meaning.

For another example of an underlying recursive operator, consider Barbara Johnson's essay on Poe, Lacan and Derrida (Johnson 1977). We first discover that 'it is the *act of analysis* that seems to occupy the center of the discursive stage and the *act of analysis of the act of analysis* that in some ways disrupts that centrality, subverting the very possibility of analytic mastery' (p. 149). The grammatical construction strongly hints at the recursive structure; the act of analysis must be recursive because only such an operator has the means to operate on itself. Johnson's subsequent discussion makes the parallel even more plain: 'In the resulting asymmetrical, abysmal structure, no analysis – including this one – can intervene without transforming and repeating other elements in the sequence, which is thus not a stable sequence, but which nevertheless produces certain regular effects' (p. 149). Once again, we have theme and variations, sequence but not repetition, because each time the operator (the act of analysis) is put to work, the field of action is slightly different from what it was before. Note, too, that in this discussion of Johnson's analysis, we are also carrying out an act of analysis, and in the process, we are bringing the operator into play a third time around.

A second recursive operator can be discovered in Poe's 'The purloined letter' (see Johnson 1977). In the first scene, in the Queen's chambers, an embarrassing letter is stolen by the minister when he substitutes a worthless letter in its place. In the second scene, the stolen letter is retrieved by Dupin by use of *the same ruse*. The application of the first substitution allows the minister to steal the forbidden letter; the second application operates on the results of the first. What is more, the second recursion undoes the results of the first, and once again, we find that fiction tends towards a symmetry that is rarely present in real life.

A clinical example

The hours we now examine in detail took place near the end of the fourth year of a traditional analysis of a young, professional man. During this period the problem of free association came into focus in a particularly persistent fashion, and as more attention was given to this issue, it became clear that to freely associate meant, for the patient, to be out of control and to risk a serious invasion of his privacy. He would typically defend against this danger by giving long narrative accounts of his life outside the session, and because he could specify detail, incident and, where necessary, cause and effect, he gave the appearance of always having the material under firm control and never running the risk of being taken by surprise. His narrative presentations could be seen as the opposite side of truly free association.

In the first hour of the period we will examine, the patient was telling one of his more usual narratives about an incident at work. He was describing one of the people who worked in an adjoining office. The office was on the floor above, and one day when the patient was busy, this person, feeling cold, had taken it upon herself to raise the thermostat, warming not only her office but all other offices in the building. The patient was first puzzled as to why the temperature was climbing, and only after rechecking the thermostat did he realize that the tenant had probably come downstairs into the patient's outer office to alter the setting. The patient described this action as a case of 'crossing his boundary', and the recursive pattern I want to draw attention to is the sequence of one boundary crossing leading to a second, leading to a third, and so on, *ad infinitum*.

After discovering that the thermostat had been raised and after deducing that it was the person upstairs who had made the move, the patient responded by going up to her office (when she was not there) to leave her a note. At the same time, he (the patient) noticed a pile of journals on her desk and noticed, in particular an article by me, his analyst – an article he had never seen but which interested him and aroused the phantasy that perhaps he, the patient, was mentioned in the article. He carried the journal down to his office in order to copy it, and he described this move as making a boundary crossing in retaliation to the first crossing. He skimmed through the article (by me, his analyst) and came across one section which, he felt, seemed to make reference to one of his symptoms; he concluded at this point that I must have written this section with him in mind.

I raised the question whether this perceived reference could also be seen as a *third* boundary crossing and whether he felt that his privacy had been violated. He denied feeling upset; quite the contrary, he felt pleased to see himself in print. The fact of the matter was that my article had not (to my knowledge) been written with the patient in mind, but of course it was perfectly possible for him to find himself in it and to feel gratified. And it should also be noted that the sequence of two boundary crossings just before the article was discovered may have framed my interpretation of the discovery in such a way that I was led to see it, too, as a possible boundary violation, and that had the incident occurred in another context, I probably would have given it quite a different interpretation.

After telling me about finding the article and skimming it quickly, the patient went on to acknowledge that he had, indeed, violated the 'space' of the person upstairs. He then became aware of the link between his action and the initial incident with the thermostat. He began to talk about the need to speak to the person upstairs and establish proper guidelines, thus setting out to remedy the situation through negotiation rather than enact another boundary violation. The chain was broken. It could be argued that the first break occurred when the patient rejected my interpretation; that his decision to see my article in a positive (enhancing) rather than a negative (violating) light made it possible for him to distance himself from the theme of boundary violation and from that particular recursive operator.

I would also argue that breaking the chain has important implications for the future course of the analysis. So long as free association is framed as a kind of boundary violation, and so long as one violation demands another (as in the first and second incidents), then the patient will never comply with the Basic Rule because to expose his private self is to invite phantasies of invading mine, and this either could not be tolerated (by him) or would not be allowed (by me). Truly free association only becomes possible when we can analyse away the violation frame and replace it by another; free association then becomes possible when seen in a different light.

We now are in a position to consider the overall pattern of boundary crossings and look more carefully at the underlying recursive operator. We first notice that where the boundary lies depends on who is calling the shots and whose privacy is being violated. It seems clear that in the first incident the person upstairs was not necessarily conscious of having stepped over a line; intent on getting out of the cold, the boundary is invisible to her and seen only by the patient. In the second incident the patient was not conscious of crossing a line until he reflected on the overall pattern; only when he was able to empathize with the person upstairs as the owner of the journal did he see it as a boundary violation. Does the recursive operator lie in the material or in the mind of the observer? Once pointed out, it seems quite clear and, as we noted above, the sequence of two violations led me to discover a third even where the patient did not agree. Can we consider his rejection of my interpretation a denial in the usual sense, or is it more correct to say that my interpretation was fanciful and unduly influenced by the first two incidents?

It seems quite clear that if boundary violation is a recursive operator, its status is quite different from the operator contained in 'A dark and stormy night' or the one presented in Poe's 'The purloined letter'. But it is also clear that the psychic reality of the first, once it was identified, becomes every bit as compelling as the reality of the second and third. If I see a neighbour's move to trim the hedge as a violation of my boundary, I am more likely to imagine (or even carry out) a similar kind of violation against his. To the extent that retaliation often takes the form of retaliation in kind, an underlying operator, once identified, tends to generate an escalating sequence until broken – by an interpretation, by a discussion, or by violence. But suppose that I see the neighbour as trying to carry out a neighbourly act by saving me some work; I may then reciprocate by finding a favour to do for him. Notice that although the action stays the same, the meaning attached to it is different, and it is the meaning that determines the future course of events.

The analytic attitude (to use Schafer's useful phrase; see Schafer 1983) is based in part on the assumption that a single recursive operator often lies behind what seem like a bizarre series of events and that once the operator is revealed, the overall pattern becomes clear. It also assumes that applications of this operator often exist in pairs, with reaction to one expression of the operator revealing either the same operator in retaliation (as in the example just discussed), or some transformation of the operator – perhaps its opposite. The pairing was well illustrated in Poe's 'The purloined letter': the initial ruse used by the minister to steal the letter was identical to the stratagem used by the detective to recover it. More usually, of course, the pairing is quite unconscious and it is the task of the analysis to reveal the logic behind the pairing and bring it under the patient's control.

I will argue that to identify the underlying operator adds immeasurably to the conviction of the therapeutic narrative being constructed by patient and analyst, and that its plausibility is strengthened even more by the discovery of Felman's spiral pattern. A series of recursive applications, each of which is a partial response to the one before but each of which is transformed just enough so that we have no reason to be suspicious of too-mechanical a repetition, carries its own kind of wisdom and its own kind of conviction.

One final thought about boundary crossings needs to be discussed. The interchange with my analytic patient happened to take place at the time when I was writing this paper and therefore sensitized to the role of recursion in the clinical process. I have no way of proving the point, but I am 99 per cent convinced that the recursive frame constituted by the act of writing the paper predisposed me to listen to the patient's associations in a particular manner and to be more than usually aware of underlying recursive operators which could be derived from the clinical material and could be seen to circle in and out of the patient's awareness. Just as the analyst whose father is dying is more than usually sensitive to themes of death and mortality in his patient, so my preoccupation with the recursive narrative and my need to find examples to illustrate my argument almost certainly helped me to listen to the material in a certain way and, in fact, to generate an example which could be used in the paper. Whether this represents an act of creative listening or an unwarranted intrusion, only the patient can say.

But the point is clear. What Gadamer has called our 'horizon' of pre-understanding will necessarily colour whatever we are looking at and listening to, and my search for recursive operators wherever I could find them, a search motivated by the needs of the paper I was writing, undoubtedly produced a certain horizon of interpretation. The series of events described by the patient could have been interpreted in a number of different ways, and the similarities among them are not strong enough to lead us inevitably to one and only one interpretation. Because we are usually dealing with a theme and variation, as opposed to mechanical, stereotyped repetitions, the commonality among the variations is more a matter of artistic agreement than a matter of Yes or No. Thus it may happen that the interpretation which relies on an underlying recursive operator may be aesthetically compelling but not quite as clear-cut as the hand before your face.

We are also saying something more. If recursion is actually at work, manifesting itself in a spiral of repetitions which results in a theme and variations, then it follows that we will have multiple occasions to test any particular hypothesis. Aesthetic judgement may be involved, but we can also point to a certain kind of replication which allows the interpreter to work in a hermeneutic fashion, back and forth, from hypothesis to illustration to revised hypothesis. Because the recursive operator, by definition, generates a series of semi-repetitive patterns, it allows the investigator an opportunity to serially refine his hypothesis, and in that way come ever closer to approximating the underlying reality. This kind of procedure, relying as it does on a series of ever more refined guesses which are illuminated or falsified by the unfolding clinical material, is clearly an enormous advance over the usual psycho-analytic pattern match which is typically based on a new hypothesis for each occurrence (Spence 1982). What is more, the recursive operator and the possibility for repeated confirmations is significantly more convincing than the more usual procedure of using the patient's associations to validate an interpretation; to use data of this kind only opens the door to claims of suggestion and compliance (Grünbaum 1984).

But the critic might ask, to what extent is the pattern really there? To what extent are you using various forms of artistic licence to suggest a pattern which would not stand up to careful scrutiny? You speak of theme and variations – when does a variation exceed its limits and become simply an unrelated specimen?

The answer would seem to lie in the strength of the pattern

match and also – and this is the more important criterion – in the conditions under which each new pattern appears. We have seen in the clinical example how one boundary crossing evoked another; we have also seen how a break in the chain, brought about either by insight or interpretation, either produced an immediate disappearance of the pattern or shifted the pattern from action to words. Future investigations of recursive narratives may well reveal typical time patterns which can be used to further support the assumption of an underlying recursive operator. Once a pattern has been established, it should be possible to shift its mode of presentation by an appropriate interpretation; if the interpretation succeeds, the operator should move from action to words, and this shift of mode would be another confirmation that the interpretation was correct.

One might apply this rule to literary criticism and, in particular, to commentaries on the *Heart of Darkness*. As we have seen, successive interpreters have been cast in the role of Marlow in so far as they continue his attempt to penetrate the central mystery while never quite succeeding. This failure to achieve an acceptable interpretation is manifested by the emergence of still another critique; when this fails, it too is followed by its successor, and so on, *ad infinitum*. But suppose that one day there appeared the perfect interpretation, one that discovered the true core of the heart of darkness and rendered it transparent, once and for all. The recursive chain should now be broken and commentaries would cease to appear. What is more, the change in pattern would be identified as a significant literary event and would become the subject of a new literature; in this fashion, the recursive mode would have shifted from words (a string of commentaries) to action (a shift in activity).

We have identified two attributes of interest. First, the recursive spiral tends to continue to operate on itself until it is identified and interpreted; second, a break in the spiral tends to be followed by a shift in mode of representation (to borrow a phrase from *Die Traumdeutung*). What I have called the Sherlock Holmes tradition is a case in point. It seems as if the model of the case history has been uncomfortably close to the typical detective story in which we are first introduced to an unusual collection of symptoms and complaints which baffle everyone but the author; these are gradually unravelled, tracked down and decoded; and then the ultimate solution is unveiled. This solution is usually presented as the *only* solution and the author presented as the ultimate authority.

The Sherlock Holmes tradition can be seen as an underlying recursive operator which has operated silently, beneath the surface of the literature, to produce a string of similar-sounding case reports which present only some of the data; which favour arguments from authority; and which discourage alternative explanations. They are notably bankrupt as archives and unsatisfactory as explanation. Now that this pattern has been uncovered and its implications discussed, the spiral seems to be in the process of breaking down – one consequence of correct interpretation. As the genre is beginning to change, the Sherlock Holmes tradition is less enacted and more discussed, and here we have an example of change in mode of representation. As discussion leads to insight and greater awareness of the underlying recursive pattern, there will be attempts to reformulate the genre of case reports and to remedy some of its traditional deficiencies. As the new genre becomes generally accepted and put into practice, it too will drop out of sight and a new spiral will unfold.

Self-analysis

We have drawn attention to the continuity between action and words and to Freud's fascination with the way in which a particular theme continues to be expressed, in spite of – or perhaps because of – a change of voice. The continuity is doubly hard to detect: first, because of a change in mode of representation; second, because the underlying recursive process presents us with a set of variations which may not seem all that similar. But despite the difficulties, the search for similarity continues and in some quarters has become almost second nature; this is the Freudian age, and all of us – believers or sceptics – are continuously influenced by the Freudian metaphor. We are only beginning to recognize its recursive properties.

Consider now the primary Freudian recursion: self-analysis. The search for meaning in your dreams, symptoms, parapraxes and all the other revealing aspects of your behaviour is recursive because the search for meaning is always being applied to a new text, and because the fruits of each search become part of the material to be searched anew on the next spiral. The recursive operator – loosely defined as the quest for continuity and significance – is multiform and polymorphous; it represents more of an attitude than a set of rules to be followed. Grounded in the unconscious – whether metaphor or structure – it is also grounded in a quest for reasons, and approaches behaviour as a set of happenings to be *explained*, not merely suffered. The Freudian metaphor takes very seriously the idea that life is art, composed with as much care and possessing as many truths; the spiralling use of self-analysis to uncover these truths is one of the striking features of our time.

Self-analysis is also flawed, precisely because it is always operating on itself. Because previous discoveries are always added to the text to be clarified and understood, the sheer amount of material to be examined is accumulating faster than it can be understood. And because there is no neutral place to stand outside the spiral, there is no easy way to take a critical look at previous uncoverings; they are now as much a part of me, the observer, as any other part of my past. The reflective life is also a complicating life and can very easily lead to a paralyzed existence; once begun, self-analysis tends to feed on itself and the yield decreases as the questions multiply.

Residues of self-analysis have some peculiar properties. We have seen how quickly, in 'A dark and stormy night', the fourth or fifth narrator becomes free of the original author; in much the same way, the fruits of reflection in a prolonged self-analysis can rather quickly become free of the constraints of reality. Because reflection is feeding on itself, there is frequently no chance to check a conclusion against an outside opinion. No one else is privy to the evidence, and to recapitulate the chain of reasoning amounts to reconstructing an entire life, an effort that would require more time than is available. As a result, most conclusions go unchecked.

How can we characterize the fruits of these analyses? They are experiences too, but a particular kind – for the most part, entirely interior and, for the most part, never made public. The fruits of dialogues never seen or heard by anyone else, they have no tangible proof of existence, and yet they burden the owner as much as, or perhaps much more than, the more ordinary and visible en-counters with life. Invisible changes in one's sense of self, recursively colouring one's view of the present and coloured, in turn, by further reflections on this same presence, the results of a self-analysis can be thought of as a series of invisible reincar-nations. Where the eastern religions specify a change in form as an accompaniment to a change in existence and where death is supposed to intervene between each change in form, the western reincarnation operates below the surface and is largely invisible to outsiders. If his exterior seems more or less the same, it is doubly disconcerting to find the inner voice of a good friend to be significantly different from what it was twenty years ago, and to find, in addition, that these changes were not the result of external reality, with its inevitable ups and downs, but the fruits of an inner struggle which was carried on voluntarily and willingly by the subject himself.

So far we have been talking about asymmetrical self-analyses which spiral further and further away from their beginnings. Can we also identify symmetrical recursions – boxes within boxes – which purposely move down only a fixed number of levels and then reverse the process to end up where they began? The second phase might be characterized by an attempt to seek fewer answers, to consider the possibility that a shovel is sometimes a shovel, and that a chance happening is merely an accident or a simple mistake. To operate in this fashion is to adopt what might be called a post-Freudian metaphor which assumes, contrary to Einstein, that sometimes God does play dice with the universe and that not everything can be explained. This change in outlook – more resigned or more seasoned, depending on one's point of view – is one of the obvious correlates of old age and presents us with one of the more obvious ways to manage a self-analysis, leave it behind and learn from it as opposed to being enslaved by it. Certain autobiographies have this flavour; at a certain stage they read as if the author has learned enough and is satisfied to rest on what he knows. The recursive operator has been changed from a search after meaning to being content with appearances.

We are slowly beginning to realize that this second phase – being content with appearances – is not necessarily an anti-Freudian stance. We have called it a post-Freudian metaphor because it grows out of the Freudian age and can be seen to represent a further stage of development. Rather than relentlessly question all happenings and search for their deeper meanings, it shows an awareness of when the Freudian search may yield something useful and when it represents simply a reflexive reaction. It shows an ability to move back and forth between a naïve respect for appearances and a suspicion that something more important is hiding behind them. It can be distinguished from the dogmatic, anti-Freudian stance in the sense that a search for hidden meanings is always considered but not always carried out; flexibility is the key. And it raises the important question of criteria. Because to admit that more than one approach is possible, we must have standards for deciding when appearances are not sufficient and, conversely, when a search for hidden causes is not satisfactory. The post-Freudian metaphor opens up the issue of alternative modes of explanation, an issue which had been pretty well sealed over since the beginning of the Freudian age.

To say that not everything can be explained raises once again the possibility of not knowing, and this condition carries unpleasant connotations. It was never confronted during the Freudian age because of the belief that the answer could always be found, buried beneath layers of surface distortions and behind years of experience. But it was this belief which increased our toleration of the bizarre and the problematic and which fuelled the spiralling recursions of self-analysis and the orthodox forms of psychotherapy and psychoanalysis. These recursions frequently only postponed the inevitable, and put off as long as possible the possibility that perhaps there is, in some situations, no good answer after all. The modern, post-Freudian theory of dreams makes this position quite clear (see McCarley and Hobson 1977). This theory argues that the stream of images we experience during the night are the result of random firings of the pontine reticular neurones. These images are then subjected to the sense-making properties of the forebrain and we wake up with a semi-believable narrative which, in turn, is further streamlined by the familiar functions of secondary revision. It will be interesting to see when a similar theory is applied to the contents of free association, because here too the appearing structure may be the final common pathway of many contributing factors and not evidence of one underlying pattern. The fact that the patient or the analyst can make sense of these productions says nothing about the presence of an overall structure.

To begin to admit that for some events there is no explanation and that the surface of the world is frequently devoid of meaning is to come face to face with a terrible possibility. This is the challenge posed by the post-Freudian metaphor, and the terror behind this challenge accounts for many of the more recent efforts to salvage the system at whatever cost (see Wasserman's determined critique of the post-Freudian theory of dreams; Wasserman 1984). To be faced with an unknowable world brings us back, once again, to the spiritual crisis of the Middle Ages, when it was recognized that the hand of God was not accountable for everything, and to the crisis of the Renaissance when the power of the alchemists began to give way to the search for real causes by the new breed of experimentalists (see Vickers 1984).

If the terror is recognized for what it is, can we put a stop to the ever-spiralling recursions of the Freudian search? To change operators in midstream or from time to time is a formidable undertaking which calls for a special sensitivity to failures in the traditional approach, to a sense of when the yield of the traditional Freudian stance falls below a certain threshold, and when we learn more from admitting ignorance than by its denial. Art has paved the way: the symmetrical recursions cited by Brooks, in which the first part of the narrative is repaired by the second and we end the story on the level where we began, give us a pattern which we might want to apply to real life. Part of the picture has been sketched by Erikson in his view of the life cycle; you may remember that later stages have a certain tendency to recapitulate the earlier periods (Erikson 1954). But much more work is needed to find ways in which symmetrical recursions may appear in real life, and how the model of boxes within boxes may be a useful metaphor for fact as well as fiction.

Recursive interference

It seemed clear, as we looked at the role of boundary crossings in the case just cited, that replication has a significant influence on conviction. As the examples multiplied which could be attributed to a single recursive operator, and as the relation between sequence of operators, their interpretations and the resulting modes of representation became more obvious, we had evidence for what might be called an example of replicated persuasion – the hermeneutic counterpart of independent verification in the experimental sciences.

Sooner or later, of course, the active operator runs its course and can no longer account for enough of the data points to be used as a feasible hypothesis. We have seen how this may happen following a correct interpretation; we have not said enough about the problems of searching for a new operator. A difficulty immediately arises because to carry out this search requires a shift from deductive to inductive reasoning, accompanied by the awareness that suddenly the degrees of freedom are significantly enlarged.

Good clinical work would seem to be marked by skill in both activities – the good clinician is not only able to identify the variations of a theme but also able to generate a theme from unfolding clinical material even when it has no obvious form or content. Because it is easier to stay with a proven theme or an established recursive operator, the temptation is always stronger to look for yet one more variation, and a fit between two pieces of clinical material can almost always be arranged. It is also tempting to stay with a proven theme because nothing succeeds like success.

When the recursive operator is self-analysis, it is particularly impervious to change of approach. We have seen how the fruits of this procedure are increasingly screened from public view; as a result, there is no obvious moment when a given operator has run its course because, at any one time, in any one life, there are always things that need explanation and there are always cyphers to be decoded. There is no obvious reason why another spiral should not be attempted – particularly when there is no obvious alternative. The post-Freudian metaphor is still felt to be a mistaken approach – heresy at its worst, and a Romantic retreat at its best. In other papers I have considered some of the grounds for such a metaphor and some of its implications for clinical practice (Spence 1984, 1986). Here, however, more needs to be said about the recursive interference with understanding, or more exactly, about the tendency to perpetuate a given operator long after it has run its course. Why is repetition useful in some situations and detrimental in others?

The answer seems to lie in determining when the absence of a solution is worse than a bad solution. This question brings us back to the terror of the unknown, and why we are so reluctant to consider the post-Freudian metaphor. Just as self-analyses tend to spiral themselves into the ground, so to speak, so the psychoanalytic profession has tried to extract maximum mileage from the Freudian metaphor and to assume, without thinking, that surface is always deceptive and that everything must be explained. Meaning, in other words, is out there somewhere and is only waiting for just the right interpretation. Because this approach works a good part of the time, little consideration is given to the possibility that it may not work all the time and, to date, no serious consideration has been given to the difference between the two situations.

We now see why recursion is both a significant advantage and a misleading complication. Serial discoveries of a given theme in the patient's life are extraordinarily exciting, and as the presumed operator acquires credibility with the appearance of multiple examples, it becomes all the more difficult to set it aside when its promise begins to fade. Both the very strength that stems from repetition and the enormous importance of replicated persuasion in our clinical work make it that much more difficult either to look for a new recursive pattern when the time has come or to accept the fact that perhaps this material, at this moment, carries no more meaning than what we can see on the surface. But this option has no place in the received theory and, as a result, the search for variations continues. We find ourselves confronted by what might be called the recursive paradox. Repetition helps enormously to convince us that we are on the right track and have uncovered a significant theme which can be validated by an unfolding string of variations, but this very context of confirmation makes it hard to search for new operators and blinds us to new avenues of investigation.

References

Brookes, Peter (1984) *Reading for the Plot*, New York, Knopf.

Colby, Benjamin N. (1966) 'Cultural patterns in narrative', *Science*, 151, 793–8.

Erikson, Erik H. (1954) 'The dream specimen of psychoanalysis', *Journal of the American Psychoanalytic Association*, 2, 5–56.

Felman, Shoshana (1977) 'Turning the screw of interpretation', *Yale French Studies: Literature and Psychoanalysis: The Question of Reading: Otherwise*, 55/6, 94–207.

Freud, S. (1953) [1900] *Die Traumdeutung (The Interpretation of Dreams)*, in Standard Edition IV, V, London, Hogarth Press.

—(1955) [1919] 'The uncanny', in Standard Edition XVII, London, Hogarth Press, pp. 217–52.

Gadamer, H.-G. (1975) *Truth and Method*, London, Sheed and Ward.

Grünbaum, Adolf (1984) *The Foundations of Psychoanalysis*, Berkeley, University of California Press.

Hofstadter, Douglas R. (1979) *Gödel, Escher, Bach: An Eternal Golden Braid*, New York, Basic Books.

Johnson, Barbara (1977) 'The frame of reference: Poe, Lacan, Derrida', *Yale French Studies: Literature and Psychoanalysis: The Question of Reading: Otherwise*, 55/6, 457–505.

McCarley, Robert W. and Hobson, J. Allan (1977) 'The neurobiological origins of psychoanalytic dream theory', *American Journal of Psychiatry*, 134, 1211–21.

Schafer, Roy (1983) *The Analytic Attitude*, New York, Basic Books.

Spence, Donald P. (1981) 'Toward a theory of dream interpretation', *Psychoanalysis and Contemporary Thought*, 4 (3), 383–405.

—(1982) *Narrative Truth and Historical Truth*, New York, Norton.

—(1984) 'Perils and pitfalls of free floating attention', *Contemporary Psychoanalysis*, 20 (1), 37–59.

—(1986) 'When interpretation masquerades as explanation', *Journal of the American Psychoanalytic Association*, 34 (1), 3–22.

Vickers, Brian (ed.) (1984) *Occult and Scientific Mentalities in the Renaissance*, New York, Cambridge University Press.

Wasserman, Marvin D. (1984) 'Psychoanalytic dream theory and recent neurobiological findings about REM sleep', *Journal of the American Psychoanalytic Association*, 32, 831–46.

11

'Transference' as
trope and persuasion

CYNTHIA CHASE

What theory of rhetoric is implicit in the several related meanings
of the term 'transference'? And what relations can be established
between psychoanalytic and rhetorical theory? These questions
designate not only a barely broached theoretical issue but also a
field of inquiry – the rhetorical theory of psychoanalysis – that
already has an extensive history. Of its intricate and persisting
debates I'll evoke only some deployments of the term 'transference' that seem particularly compelling for our thinking about
the rhetoric of literary and interpretive texts.

That thinking has been powerfully conditioned by a rhetorical
theory emergent from the rereading of certain philosophical texts –
readings of Nietzsche, Rousseau, Kant, Hegel, and Heidegger, by
de Man (1979, 1983a and b), Derrida (1976, 1979, 1983), Kofman
(1972, 1979), Nancy (1973, 1976), Lacoue-Labarthe (1978, 1979)
and others, which in the last twenty years have deeply influenced
literary theory (at least in the United States). Those readings
explore the impact in both philosophical and literary texts of the
confrontation with rhetoric as the 'other' of philosophy; they
explore how an exclusion and at the same time exploitation of
literary strategies and rhetorical modes have been vital to the self-
construction of philosophical discourse in ways at odds with the
truth claims of philosophy. If rhetoric has been in some sense the
'other' of philosophy, what are the relations among rhetoric,
philosophy and psychoanalysis? This paper will suggest that
psychoanalysis is not only a rhetoric and a range of implicit
rhetorical theories, but also a 'philosophy' in the sense of a refusal

to read itself as a rhetoric – a refusal made visible by the rhetorical reading of certain literary texts. I shall end by confronting Lacan's Freud with de Man's Baudelaire.

I begin with Freud's two usages of the word 'transference': for the patient's 'transference' onto the analyst, and for the transference of affect from an unconscious idea onto a preconscious one. The same word designates a relationship to a person, a kind of *action* and a mode of expression, the condition of an idea's entering consciousness, a condition of knowledge. In *The Language of Psycho-Analysis* (Laplanche and Pontalis 1973) 'transference' onto the analyst is described as originating by what Laplanche would elsewhere call 'metonymical derivation' from the concept of transference in the first sense (Laplanche 1976). The former is:

> a particular *instance* of displacement of affect from one idea to another. If the idea of the analyst enjoys a special status, this is, first, because it constitutes a type of 'day's residue' that is always available to the subject; and secondly, because this kind of transference *aids resistance* in that it is particularly hard [Freud suggests] to admit the repressed wish ... to the very person the wish concerns.
>
> (Laplanche and Pontalis 1973, p. 457)

With this second reason why the specially favoured preconscious idea should be that of the analyst, Laplanche touches on the way the metonymically derived meaning swerves from the original. 'Transference' in the second sense is a resistance to the disclosure of 'transference' in the first sense: the patient's transference onto the analyst comes into play to thwart the effort to illuminate the fundamental transferential process revealed in free association. Transference, then, is an action destined to defeat a knowledge of transference, and to refuse the knowledge that *transference* is the condition of knowledge. Not only the patient but also the reader is destined by Freud to carry out this action. In introducing the first, 'specimen dream', his dream of Irma's injection, Freud writes, 'And now I must ask the reader to make my interests his own for quite a while, and to plunge, along with me, into the minutest details of my life; for a transference of this kind is peremptorily demanded by our interest in the hidden meaning of dreams' (Freud 1965, p. 138). To 'plunge into the minutest details' of a text and context, in quest of the 'hidden meaning', is indeed to *transfer* onto the text in such a way that its modes of expression and condition of knowledge – its transferences or tropes, and its status *as* trope – may never come to be known. Instead, the text will be experienced as a message in which we have an interest; not read as a set of mechanisms and process of displacement, but seen or heard like a dream or a voice. The transference 'peremptorily demanded' by the *hermeneutic* enterprise of interpretation, in short, conflicts with the *poetics* of the enterprise of textual analysis, which would have to trace, by means of displacements or transferences, not the meaning but the *devices* of meaning, the transferential process, of the text.

This conflict between poetics and hermeneutics is made plain in the closing passage of the seminar on the Irma dream, where Lacan speaks in Freud's voice, before concluding, 'That is the meaning of this dream' (Lacan 1978, p. 203). Lacan's formal analysis of the dream-text has led to the interpretation of the Unconscious as a signifying process rather than a meaning, and to the conception of knowledge, such as the knowledge of the Unconscious achieved with the creation of psychoanalysis, as an effect of the Unconscious. In the closing passage of the seminar, the hermeneutic imperative impinges on the reading, and Lacan responds to that demand for transference that we heard from the dreamer of the Irma dream as we set out to read his text. Lacan intones what he has inferred to be Freud's message to the 'future community' of analysts:

> I am he who wants to be pardoned for having dared to begin to heal the ill whom until now no one wanted to understand. . . . I am he who wants to be pardoned for that . . . I am no longer anything. . . . And just insofar as I have wanted to be, myself, the creator, I am not the creator. The creator is someone greater than me. It is my unconscious, it's that which speaks in me, beyond me.
> (p. 203)

Here the judgement that psychoanalysis is the creation of radically *impersonal* forces gets uttered in intensely *personal* form. At the moment of asserting that what creates is an unconscious signifying process remote from the conscious utterance of meaning, Lacan makes the text an utterance. The judgement that follows from Lacan's exercise in poetics or the textual analysis of the dream – the judgement that knowledge is an effect of automatic unconscious mechanisms or tropes – gets propounded in a mode that rejects that judgement in favour of the suggestion that knowledge is a

hidden meaning that can be discovered and voiced. The hermeneutic imperative requiring transference in the second sense
gives the interpretive text a performative dimension in conflict
with its constative and cognitive one, in conflict with the statement
responsive to the exigencies of poetics, to the mechanisms of
transference in the first sense. Or to put it another way, the
function of transference as persuasion – the text's rhetorical
designs upon the reader – obscures the status of the text as a pattern
of signs, its status as transference as *trope*.

What sort of trope is a transference, though: the displacement of
affect from an unconscious to a preconscious idea? Can it be right
to assimilate transference in this sense to the cognitive and
constative dimension of language, and see it in tension with the
performative dimension or speech-act to which we assimilate
transference in the second sense? To align transference in the
first sense with trope and cognition is odd in so far as that total
displacement of affect, a primary-process mechanism, *prevents*
cognition or re-cognition as much as it enables it. And transference
in the second sense, the refusal of re-cognition in favour of reproduction of pathogenic complexes during analysis, is not the
introduction of a non-cognitive dimension of language but strictly
the perpetuation of the non-knowledge that characterizes the
primary process and the defence mechanism that operates according to it, repression.

Yet just this non-knowledge, Lacan's texts posit, is the nature of
tropes and of signification. Lacan's uncompromising equation of
'condensation' and 'displacement' with metaphor and metonymy,
his reading of *trans-fer* as *meta-phorein, and* as a language *act*, gets at
the radically primary status of trope or figure, and the *dis*figurative character precisely of the figural dimension of language.
This Lyotard's rival account of 'condensation' (Lyotard 1971)
helps us to see, unlike the orderly but unrevealing view of
Silverman (1983) or Metz (1982), who carefully discriminate
primary process mechanisms such as condensation and displacement and transference both from the secondary-process operations
of the paradigmatic and syntagmatic axes and intermediate
operations constituting 'an almost perfect equilibrium between the
unconscious and the preconscious', metaphor and metonymy, the
tropes (Silverman 1983, p. 86). To take the view that rhetorical
figures, like verbal language in general, should be classed as an
effect of the secondary process, the *inhibition* of free displacement of

energy that permits the emergence of stable correspondences between affects and ideas, is to miss both the rhetorical status of Freud's key concepts and the radically primary status of rhetoric or trope. What Silverman calls Lacan's conflation of the Unconscious with the preconscious and Lyotard's 'tendency to pit the unconscious against the preconscious in ways which admit of no communication between them', make up, together, a more authentic rhetoric than an account that aims, like Silverman's, to 'maintain the semiotic integrity of the two psychic regimes while indicating their constant interaction' (p. 88). Freud's rhetoric brings us up against a difference *within* either the unconscious or the preconscious realm, instead of sustaining a difference, and an interaction, *between* them. Thus Lyotard's account of the primary-process violence of the dream-work, in his paper 'The dream-work does not think' (1983), deserves to be read into Lacan's evocation of metonymy and metaphor – tropes which have all the distortative power of the dream-work, while condensation and displacement, as Lacan maintains, have all the significative power of poetic language (Lacan 1966).

Lyotard disputes Lacan's equation of the operations of the dream-work with verbal tropes, and associates those operations instead with figurative, three-dimensional representation, imagining the distorting effect of 'condensation' on the properly verbal material of the dream-thoughts quite literally as their condensing or crumpling, like that of a banner with an inscription rippled by the wind in such a way that its letters are concealed or distorted. Such treatment of words as things, however, is distinctive of language itself, if not of the hypothetical transparent 'discourse' Lyotard invokes for the purpose of contrasting it with the 'depth' of non-verbal pictorial or figural representation. Not only in the dream-work but in speech and writing, 'one ambiguous word is used instead of two unambiguous ones', or 'our everyday sober method of expression is replaced by a pictorial one', to quote Freud explaining how dreams do not introduce, but 'make unashamed *use* of the advantages thus offered by *words* for purposes of condensation and disguise' [my emphasis]. 'Words, since they are the nodal points of various ideas, may be regarded as predestined to ambiguity' (Freud 1965, p. 376). Not the three-dimensionality of spatial forms but the rhetorical depth of the word as trope and figure is Freud's model for the effect of 'condensation'. There are obvious reasons to balk at what can be seen as Lacan's assimilation of language to the primary process, and to argue that the total evacuation of affect – such that *no* affect, no intensity, remains invested in the idea from which it was transferred – cannot properly be identified with tropes, which maintain the implicit presence of their displaced term so that it's possible, say, to distinguish between a metaphor and a metonymy according to whether the displacing terms are related by contiguity or comparability to the terms they displace. Just such a complete displacement, however, would constitute the fundamental tropological character of language, the import of the arbitrary nature of the sign. Lacan's classifications should be taken up as the insight that not only dreams and not only *Dichtung*, poetry, but language as such involves *Verdichtung*, condensation, because of 'considerations of representability', *Rücksicht auf Darstellbarkeit* – and that these conditions entail *non*-utterance, muteness, or disfiguration. 'Rücksicht auf Darstellbarkeit' (the phrase is the title for Section D of Chapter 6, 'The dream-work', in *The Interpretation of Dreams*, 1965): 'Watch out for the figure!', translates Lyotard (1983, p. 11) – a brilliant reading, only we must retranslate Lyotard's account of the violence involved in condensing discourse into images, into an account, instead, of the disfigurative impact of the figural dimension of language itself. *Darstellen*, to present, as image or figure, in the way that an idea can appear in a dream, becomes, as Freud's key verbs insist, *entstellen*, to distort: to disfigure, in the precise sense that an idea's figuration, its presentation as an image or picture (of a thing), deprives it of its figurative meaning.

The ambiguity of the word 'figuration' or 'figure', under these circumstances, is only one instance of a more general dilemma one could call disfiguration: that constitutive ambiguity of all words given their possibly figurative status, which has the result that, as Freud puts it, 'our understanding is brought to a halt' (Freud 1965, p. 376), we lose the capacity for figuring anything out. *Darstellen* is *entstellen*, figuration destroys the non-figural status of what exists in language – not only, I would suggest, in the phenomenon of dreaming, but in the dream-imaging which is language or the Apollinian guise of thought itself. Disfiguration would refer, ultimately, to the impossible mediation between language as music and language as figure, or the destruction, with the giving of face or figure, of the *non*-figural status of the sign.[1] By the non-figural status of the sign, I mean the *positing* of entities, not their presentation, and the *arbitrary* position not the expressive one, which is the only way in which such a thing as signification could originate, if not a mode in which it could persist.

How signification could originate, and the implications of that for the ways in which it *will* persist, is a problem for which the term 'transference' could provide the crux. By usage and etymology 'transference' is identified with metaphor (as transferal), metonymy (as 'displacement') and repetition (as resistance to recognition). To term the primary process in the dream-work 'transference', or the *displacement* of affect from an unconscious idea to a preconscious one, as Freud does in *The Interpretation of Dreams*, is to grant implicit primacy to metonymy or sheer displacement by contiguity as the basic condition of signification, but also to suggest the inevitability and necessity of metaphor as the displacement from one idea *to another of a different order*, essentially a displacement between signifier and signified: the condition of existence of the sign. In conceiving of the tropes as shifts along the paradigmatic or syntagmatic axes of discourse, by similarities or contiguities at the level of the signifier, rather than of the referent, Lacan grants an implicit primacy to metonymy. If it is a matter of *words* next to each other or comparable to each other rather than things (the proximity of *bateau* and *voile* in the word *bateau-à-voile*, not in a sailboat) (Lacan 1977, p. 156), then words *comparable* to each other, initially related along the paradigmatic axis, are ultimately contiguous; or as Laplanche puts it, 'if metonymy is based only on the word-by-word connections produced by discourse, might not every metaphor find at least a potential basis in a proposition that links its terms?' (Laplanche 1976, p. 147, n. 9). That we are basically engaged in an order of contiguous elements is implied by Laplanche's own point that the 'principle of neuronic inertia', Freud's first version of the principle of total displacement of affect, is not a condition of life, operating at the level of the 'vital order', but a principle operating at the level of 'ideational representatives'. That Lacan maintains the virtual homology of the two senses of transference follows from the primacy implicitly granted to metonymy by his conception of tropes. For the tropological nature of language then entails repetition – entails the utterance of words or the production of signs as an action rather than an act of representation. In so far as the system of tropes is fundamentally metonymic, a matter of *contiguity* between ideational representatives or signifiers rather than of contiguity or similarity between things in the world, speech then consists, as Wordsworth writes in 'The note to "The thorn"', not merely in words for things but in words *as* things, 'themselves part of the passion' (quoted in Owen 1974, p. 97) – which *will be repeated*, since what's involved is (here I borrow Ferguson's sharp reading) 'not the expression of an emotion, but an emotion about expressing' (Ferguson 1977, p. 13).

Seeing transference in these terms means seeing it not as a mere metaphor, a mere representation, not recognized as such, of a real conflict located prior to it and elsewhere, but instead as a continuation, as derived metonymically from the past conflict it plays out, and metonymically related too to the interpretive discourse that combats it. This view emerges at the close of the essay 'The dynamics of transference', where Freud writes:

> But it should not be forgotten that it is precisely they [the phenomena of transference] that do us the inestimable service of making the patient's hidden and forgotten erotic impulses immediate and manifest. For when all is said and done, it is impossible to destroy anyone *in absentia* or *in effigie*.
>
> (Freud 1958 [1912], p. 108)

The value of the transference, then, is that it is *not* a mere effigy of past real erotic impulses. But these sentences come at the end of a passage where the sense of the metonymical status of transference conflicts sharply with the sense of its metaphorical status, a passage which vividly describes it as phantasmagoria:

> Just as happens in dreams, the patient regards the products of the awakening of his unconscious impulses as contemporaneous and real; he seeks to put his passions into action without taking any account of the real situation. The doctor tries to compel him to fit these emotional impulses into the nexus of the treatment of his life-history, to submit them to intellectual consideration and to understand them in the light of their psychical value. This struggle between the doctor and the patient, between intellect and instinctual life, between understanding and seeking to act, is played out almost exclusively in the phenomena of the trans-ferences.
>
> (p. 108)

'It is on that field that the victory must be won', Freud goes on: the victory, this implies, of understanding over seeking-to-act, of remembering over reproducing. But that kind of victory is excluded by the final sentence of the passage: destroying can no longer mean, here, to force the *recognition* of the transference as mere reproduction, to expose it as mere effigy, which this passage says it is not. 'Destroying' takes on some less metaphorical meaning, the rhetorical movement of the passage would imply; the struggle Freud evokes would have to be played out not only over the phenomena but in the mode of the transference. Instead of the victory gained 'by declaiming the object to be dead', no longer real, and 'offering the ego the inducement of continuing to live', the struggle with transference would require loosening the fixation to an object as real as the self, to a past continuing into the future. 'Destroying' it, then, would entail not simply declaring it unreal, but – in the words of a bleak passage in 'Mourning and melancholia' – 'disparaging it, denigrating it, and even as it were killing it' (p. 257). Yet it is the metonymical status of transference presumed by the analytic aim to 'destroy', and not 'in effigie', a persisting persuasion, that ensures the possibility of cure or change evoked by Laplanche:

> If a transference takes on the dimensions of an event capable of changing something for someone, it is indeed because in one of its dimensions, it transcends the fantasmagoria to which it has occasionally been reduced. ... [Isn't it then] in that other dimension that we should be looking for its effectiveness, no longer in the carrying over (of past experiences) into another site, but in the *continuity* of its rhythm with a *vaster form of discourse*, that which we never stop holding with ourselves and which is held with us?
>
> (Lapalanche 1976, p. 138)

There is another sense, however, in which transference would mean a 'carrying over into another site', to borrow Laplanche's terms for distinguishing metaphorical from metonymical derivation of entities – the metonymical derivation being 'an extension through continuity, an imperceptible transition to an adjacent field' (p. 131). The term 'transference' can be called upon to describe the metaphorical derivation of the ego – the status of the ego, in Freud's thinking, not only as 'a prolongation of the living individual', a differentiated surface of the organism or the psyche, serving to adapt its impulses to reality (pp. 51–3), but also as a projection or an image of the individual, its carrying over into another site or another order, its status as an intrapsychical reality. It is the notion of *identification* that must 'account for the formation of the metaphorical agency of the ego', as Laplanche writes (p. 54), but at the point where there is as yet no identity and no separate individual, the hypothetical moment, for instance, at which the infant would differentiate a not-yet-self and a not-yet-object, the word 'transference' might serve to describe that primary projection or introjection, as Ferenczi's founding essay on 'Introjection and transference' (1910) was the first to suggest. In *The Interpretation of Dreams*, the term 'transference' appears instead of the term 'displacement' when Freud alludes to the displacement of intensity from an *unconscious* to a *preconscious* idea, or from an 'important' idea to a 'trivial' one. 'Transference' refers, that is, to the displacement from one 'idea' to another *of a different order*; and this usage implicitly raises the question of how such a difference of orders is instituted, or the nature of 'primal repression'.

More irreducible than the difference of orders between unconscious and preconscious ideas or processes is the distinction between affect and idea presumed by the primary process of displacement of affect from one idea to another. Freud's metapsychological writings do of course engage the question of the origin of ideas (by way of imagining the structure of the 'neurone' or the nature of an 'ideational representative', among other terms); it's the association of such an origin with the constitution of a gap, and that in turn with the emergence of the idea of the ego, that I want now to consider.

How is the gap constitutive of signification psychically established or maintained? One is asking here about the psychoanalytic meaning of the fundamental premise of linguistic theory, the constitutive status of the bar or gap between signifier and signified or sign and meaning, or what is known since Saussure as the 'arbitrary nature of the sign'. Lacan initiates thought about this issue in invoking the necessity of a specular moment, an original identification, a primary narcissism, implicit in the concept of the 'mirror stage' (Lacan 1966). Taking a different tack in a recent essay entitled 'L'abjet d'amour' (1982a) – 'The abject of love' – Kristeva interrogates in detail a key version of Freud's radical premise of 'primary narcissism'. The gap constitutive of signification would be established, she argues, precisely with 'primary narcissism', which is not an unanalysable concept referring to a monad-like state, but an initial ternary structure, consisting in a not-yet-ego (that of the infant), a not-yet-object or 'abject' (the mother, not yet an invested object of love) and a gap or placeholder between them: the 'not-me', or the Imaginary Father constituted by the mother's desire for something other than mother and child. Kristeva infers this composition of 'primary narcissism' from Freud's description of that earliest identification that founds the ego ideal, a point prior to any cathexis of objects. She draws her argument from a paragraph in the third chapter of *The Ego and the Id* that dates the founding of the ego ideal – a moment prior to and a condition for the emergence of the ego as such, by means of what Laplanche calls a *metaphorical* derivation from the living individual, the ego's emergence precisely as an *idea* of totality – from what Freud calls 'the individual's first and most important identification, his identification with the father in his own personal prehistory' (Freud 1961 [1923], p. 31). The emergence, by means of such an 'identification', of the *idea* of the ego would coincide with the emergence of the distinction between affect and idea, the distinction in effect between signified and signifier.

Kristeva places 'primary narcissism', as a first and immediate *identification*, at the origin of the establishment of the sign, its hierarchical distinction between signifier and signified. What is thus the fundamentally *motivated* character of the installment of an order that must be received as unmotivated – the unmotivated relation between signifier and signified, the 'arbitrary nature of the sign' – Kristeva further emphasizes by dwelling on a condition that would precede this decisive moment of identification, the condition she calls 'abjection'. In *Powers of Horror* (1982) Kristeva interprets the experience of the 'abject', of what evokes horror, loathing, revulsion; in the first instance bodily waste, foods, that which the body expels never completely; not certain objects, but what is less than an object: 'if the object, . . . through its opposition, settles me within the fragile texture of desire for meaning, . . . what is *abject*, on the contrary, the jettisoned object, is radically excluded and draws me to the place where meaning collapses' (Kristeva 1982b, p. 2). That place is originally the abjection of the mother, the condition of the primary identification with the 'Vater der persönlichen Vorzeit': 'the abject confronts us . . . within our personal archeology [or our 'prehistory,' echoing Freud] with our earliest attempts to release the hold of *maternal* entity even before ex-isting outside of her, thanks to the autonomy of language' (p. 13). This notion of 'abjection' lets us say something more about the nature of the performative in Lacan's interpretation of Freud's

Irma dream, and about the nature of his transference onto Freud. For Lacan stresses that there are two crucial moments or high points of the dream, and they consist in a moment of abjection and the moment of the emergence of the symbolic order or language. The first is the moment in the dream in which Freud peers into Irma's throat and beholds 'a big white patch' and 'extensive whitish grey scabs upon some remarkable curly structures ... visibly modelled on the turbinal bones of the nose' (Freud 1965, pp. 139–40). The second is the moment in which there emerges, 'as if printed in heavy type', the chemical formula for trimethylamin – the 'solution', according to Lacan's interpretation, not only to the dreamer's wish to determine a cause for Irma's illness discharging him of responsibility, but also to the far-reaching wish implicit in Freud's deeming this dream the 'specimen dream' of psychoanalysis and so destining it, as Lacan stresses, for the future community of analysts (Lacan 1978, p. 203) – the wish to grasp the nature of the Unconscious. The solution is that the Unconscious is structured like a language; this is the answer implicit in the dream's conclusion with a chemical formula, the form of which, its status as a written symbol, is the 'solution' to the problem of the dream and of dreams as such: in Lacan's words, 'Il n'y a d'autre mot, d'autre solution à votre problème, que le mot' (p. 190). And Lacan observes that this formulation is modelled on the formula of monotheism: 'There is no other God than God.'

What seems newly significant in the light of Kristeva's argument is the condition for this emergence of the absolute arbitrary authority of language: the earlier moment, when Freud, or Lacan, confronts 'la gorge d'Irma', Irma's throat, which appears in Lacan's reading as an appalling abyss. Lacan's interpretation much more than Freud's evokes the horror of this moment; the vision of the throat is 'a horrible discovery, that of the flesh one never sees, the bottom of things, the back side of the face, of the countenance ... the flesh from which everything comes out, ... the flesh inasmuch as it is in pain, formless, its form in itself something that provokes anguish' (p. 186). It is in Lacan's text rather than Freud's that the gorge rises. Abjection – *re*jection, of the condition of 'patient', of essentially female or maternal flesh; abjection of the dreamer, of Freud (who has Fliess operate, Lacan notes, on 'the turbinal bones' of *his* nose); this moment of abjection *in Lacan's reading* is the preparation and precondition for the final solution – the sovereign authority and sole creative power of the Unconscious or the '*word*'.² This is another way of discovering, no doubt, what was said earlier about the fundamental incoherence of Lacan's concluding utterance. A reading that consists in its cognitive dimension in the assertion of the radically autonomous power of language (or the Unconscious) is conditioned and contradicted by the primary role of a certain rejection and identification in the reading's performance. That contradiction, rather than the motivated nature of the sign's establishment as such, would be the essential intrinsic fragility of the structure of signification stressed (against Lacan) by Kristeva. But one should appreciate too that it is *in view of* the second moment that the moment of abjection becomes significant; the mother's abjection is in this sense the effect, rather than the condition, of the reign of the Word. (In the case of 'Irma', or Emma, Monique Schneider has pointed out, the internal trouble that evokes Lacan's horror was indeed not the revelation of primal formlessness but the fruit of highly civilized medical procedures – bungled operations by Fliess and Freud (Schneider 1980, p. 130).

Kristeva's reading in 'The abject of love', like Lacan's seminar on the Irma dream, concerns the composition and decomposition of the ego and the significance for the nature of language of the ego's sheerly composite status. The emergence of the *idea* of the ego, by means of the identification that Freud describes as the founding of the ego ideal, would coincide with the emergence of the distinction between affect and idea, the distinction between signified and signifier. Kristeva's reading of the passage on the formation of the ego ideal would in effect describe how trans-ference in the first sense – or the constitution of a gap such that there could be a transfer *across* it (a shift to a different order: 'metaphor') – depends on, is sustained by, a transference in the second sense, a narcissistic 'identification' with the gap, made possible through its identification with the father.

The condition of trope would be persuasion – a persuasion so immediate and total and so absolute, however, that it would be better named by terms describing something other than a figure or action of rhetoric: named either the performative power of language in its special sense as the power of positing (*setzen*) or sheer position, or else anthropomorphism, the imagination of a totality as human. To evoke the former alternative first, the condition of transference as trope or metaphor, *Übertragung*, the carrying over of something into another site, would be, at this

[handwritten marginal notes:] ego = idea coincides with distinction between Sgn / fied + Sgnfier. ↓ transferred across gap = metaphor identificat with this gap = id with fath

origin of the Imaginary where there is nothing to carry over, the *positing*, at a remove, 'above' (it's the origin of the ego ideal or the idea that we're evoking), of a site, a space, a figure, and with it, language: transference as translation, *Übersetzung*; not the transferal of an existing meaning, but the positing of an order over and above what simply functions, the inauguration of the possibility of signs. This *Übersetzung* would also be positing overmuch; the not-yet-ego's 'immediate identification' is not merely with a gap, with a not-me between or distinct from the infant-and-mother, but with a totality – not simply the actual father but 'the parents', in Freud's terms (Freud 1958, p. 31n), or in Kristeva's, the unity of the Phallus or the Imaginary Father, 'a coagulation of the mother and of her desire' (1982a, p. 22). And Kristeva traces to the existence of such a moment of 'identification' with such a Father the real possibility of *Agape*:

> an accord that comes to me from another, without mediation, which I submit to and to which I transfer myself without any investment of an object, without instinctual counterpart (without hate), and which remains, with these properties, incomprehensible. The 'God is love' of John, etc., would designate not a passivization of the subject or a successful Oedipal identification, but the mechanism of this *jubilatory* process.
>
> (p. 25)

Such a reading starts to seem tantamount to accepting the real existence of God with the absolute power of position or *setzen* in the creative Word, the monotheistic moment described and decomposed in Hegel's *Aesthestics*, with the analysis of 'The symbolism of the sublime'. 'The abject is edged with the sublime. It is not the same moment on the journey, but the same subject and speech bring them into being' (p. 11). The itinerary Kristeva evokes here is available in Hegel's account, which locates the sublime in monotheism and Hebrew poetry. In Hegel's description of the all-powerful Word (by way of quotations from Genesis and the Psalms) there emerges a fundamental incoherence which involves the 'complete collapse' (as this section of the *Aesthetics* concludes by saying) of 'the sublime relationship' and impels the abandonment of this conception of language. One suspects that the contradiction encountered in Hegel's text is also at work in the model of language both affirmed and exposed by Lacan and Kristeva. The incoherence in 'The symbolism of the sublime' is demonstrated in an analysis of this section of the *Aesthetics* by Paul de Man which is too difficult to recapitulate here (de Man 1983a, pp. 147–8). It turns on the conflict between the constative or cognitive and the performative dimension of language – the latter not only in the sense of a specific speech-act or of illocutionary force (such as the act carried out by Lacan when he speaks in Freud's voice), but in the sense of the capacity of language not only to recognize or represent attributes of things (its cognitive dimension) but also to posit or postulate entities. ('Posit', *setzen*, is the word in the passage from Nietzsche's *The Will to Power* from which the distinction between cognitive and performative functions of language, *erkennen* and *setzen*, is drawn by de Man 1979, pp. 121–2). The formulation in the seminar on the Irma dream – 'Il n'y a d'autre mot que le mot' – suggests that this performative or 'positing' power of language is implicit in the Lacanian conception of the Unconscious. Like Hegel's description of 'the sublime relationship', Lacan's and Kristeva's accounts of the conditions of signification entail the radical illogic of affirming simultaneously the absolute performative power of language and its status as the expression of meaning. In de Man's terms, 'Language posits and language means, but language cannot posit meaning' (1984, p. 117) – yet that contradictory notion would be what is implicitly asserted by claims for the founding of meaning in an act of transference, an identification with the father.

We are already, quite evidently, describing anthropomorphism, another possible term (in addition to the positing power of language) for the total and absolute persuasion evoked by Kristeva as the condition of trope, in her interpretation of primary repression as the 'immediate identification' with the father; another possible name, within a certain theory of rhetoric, for the condition of the possibility of tropes. Freud's 'anthropomorphism' is acknowledged and defended by Laplanche; those slightly ridiculous or pre-scientific-sounding personifying formulations 'should be taken literally', he writes, 'as truly constitutive of the human psyche' (Laplanche 1976, p. 36). The convergence of the metonymical with the metaphorical derivation of the ego means that 'the ego is an actualised metaphor of totality', and that not only metaphor but its complicity with anthropomorphism is impossible to transcend, that there is no non-rhetorical scientific language or other rhetoric by which we could account any better for the origin of ideas.

Rather than merely accepting that there is *no other rhetoric* which could account for the agency of the ego, we might again question the implications of the account of the conditions of signification we have just encountered in Kristeva. Her story differs from Laplanche's in one crucial respect, if only because he is attempting (in the middle chapters of *Life and Death in Psychoanalysis*, 1976) to summarize the full range of Freud's thinking about the ego, while she is focusing on the decisive moment of 'primary narcissism'. It is a moment incompatible with object-cathexis – prior to and by definition incompatible with the object-relations involved in the ego's function deploying the energies of the id and monitoring the reality of perceptions. This would mean, I take it, that at least this originary emergence of the metaphor of the ego does not occur in conjunction with the metonymical derivation by which the ego emerges as a specialized prolongation of the functional living organism. I am alluding again to Laplanche's distinction between the metaphorical and the metonymical derivation of entities – metonymical derivation being 'an extension through continuity, an imperceptible transition to an adjacent field' (p. 131), metaphorical derivation a 'carrying over into another site', a re-presentation in another order. No *continuity* between the mode of being of the organism and that of an emerging ego-function would come into play simultaneously with the originary emergence of the metaphor of the ego described by Kristeva. But the conjunction of the two modes of derivation is the condition to which Laplanche attributes the 'actualisation' of the metaphor of the ego, its 'precipitation in reality'. Kristeva's analysis of primary narcissism, then, would get at an underlying irreality of the ego and a concomitant fragility of the structure of the linguistic sign. Unaccompanied by a horizontal movement of displacement tending to establish the real efficacy of a discriminating function, the vertical movement of displacement founding the ego ideal and the hierarchical structure of the sign would tend always to collapse into the meaningless horizontal displacement that it is in fact – the patterning prior to signification that Kristeva calls the semiotic (as distinct from the symbolic) process (see Kristeva 1974; 1980, pp. 6–7).

This possibility of collapse plays itself out, I would suggest, in Baudelaire's poem 'Correspondances' – to shift here to a different kind of implicit theory of rhetoric. The last lines of the poem demonstrate how lyric voice, founded by anthropomorphism, cannot achieve a stable totalization. The poem begins:

> La nature est un temple où de vivants piliers
> Laissent parfois sortir de confuses paroles;
> L'homme y passe à travers des forêts de symboles,
> Qui l'observent avec des regards familiers.

Nature is a temple where living pillars sometimes let out confused words; Man there passes through forests of symbols that observe him with familiar looks.

The image here of symbols that gaze or look is an image of the text able to return a gaze or to speak that is the distinctive implicit premise of the lyric, the genre whose principle of intelligibility is the actualization of a speaking voice. The poem goes on to name some of the elements of this nature or multiplicity of symbols that look and that are said, finally, to sing; 'Les parfums, les couleurs, et les sons se répondent,' and the last six lines dwell on the perfumes:

> Il est des parfums frais comme des chairs d'enfants,
> Doux comme les hautbois, verts comme les prairies,
> – Et d'autres, corrompus, riches, et triomphants,
>
> Ayant l'expansion des choses infinies,
> Comme l'ambre, le musc, le benjoin et l'encens,
> Qui chantent les transports de l'esprit et des sens.

What I would call attention to, following de Man, is the collapse here of the metaphorical meaning of the word *comme*, which means 'like' in its first three occurrences in the tercets, but 'such as' in its final appearance in the penultimate line (see de Man 1984, p. 249). Lines 9–10 state the odours' resemblance to sensations of different orders, touch, sound and colour. We therefore tend to take the next lines too as affirming the odours' resemblance to things of a different order, 'infinite things', 'des choses infinies', with which they share the attribute of 'expansion'. What the lines actually say is that there are 'rich, corrupt, triumphant odours,/*Having* the expansion of infinite things,/*Such as* ambergris, musk, benjamin and incense.' The odours seem to be being said to be both a model or analogue of infinite things and a first exemplar of them, both their model or representation, and an instance of them. This double status would be the basis for the claim that seems to be made for them in the final line, that they *sing* 'les transports de l'esprit et des sens', 'the transports of the mind and the senses': as symbols in the sense of simultaneous synecdoches and analogies, the odours would evoke entirely adequately the totalizing movement that unites thoughts and sensations, the senses and the mind. The seeming double meaning or equivocation in the lines about the status of the odours is like the ambiguity remarked by Laplanche of Freud's term *Vorbild*: it gets translated according to the context as either 'model' or 'prototype', an ambiguity which reflects its double meaning as both theoretical model or analogue and 'first exemplar in a series of real phenomena' (Laplanche 1976, p. 133). Baudelaire's lines seek to evoke, it would seem, 'the *conjunction* of the process of derivation through contiguity and of the identificatory process' that alone ensures 'the precipitation of the metaphor of the ego' (p. 136) – or of the lyric voice – 'in reality'. That conjunction would generate an agency that could 'sing', achieve, celebrate, the movement from sensation to knowledge.

Instead, these lines do something else. They disrupt the continuity between contiguity and resemblance, between having and being (or libidinal investment and identification), between metonymical and metaphorical relationship. For what 'sings', doubly and ambiguously – 'chantent *les* transports de l'esprit *et* des sens' – are finite things, odours, which *have* the 'expansion' of infinite things but are *not* thereby capable of *being* infinite things, or being identified with them or 'like' them; for the signification 'like', just at this point, gives way to 'such as': the odours are said, not to be '*comme* des choses infinies', *like* infinite things, just as they were like sensation, colour and sound; they are said simply to be '*Comme* l'ambre, le musc, le benjoin et l'encens', '*such as* ambergris, musk', and so on. Instead of a movement through and beyond the senses, we meet with an enumeration of instances of a single kind of sense. The line that lists what are supposed to be singing, sounds less like singing than stammering. 'Correspondances' offers, though, far from a denial of the possibility of being or identity, an affirmation of it, but an affirmation that is unsustained by any solidarity between anthropomorphism and metaphor. Nature as a temple must be simply where one is; it is not reached by any movement or sustained by a tropological process of totalization. No correspondence reaches or returns from the condition of identity.

The difficulty of reading Baudelaire's 'Correspondances' demands another rhetoric than that which assumes the complicity of metaphor and anthropomorphism, of trope and an originary persuasion. It would begin with the critique of the *symbol* that we saw in the poem's decomposition of the symbolic instance called *Vorbild* in the text of Freud, whose narrative cannot relinquish such a category. The critical potential of Kristeva's account for the sign's origin comes through in the compulsion to repeat that her interpretation would account for and predict: the recurring effort to achieve a 'binding' or a lasting correspondence between instances linked only by displacement and an arbitrary equation (whether in the 'immediate identification' that forms the ego ideal, or in the metonymical link of a 'perceptual identity' to an 'experience of satisfaction' (see Weber 1982, pp. 36, 45). It would be possible though to conceive this 'compulsion to repeat' in other terms, as Laplanche does in imagining the promising implications of the metonymical dimension of transference, its status not simply as an unrecognized metaphor of a conflict located earlier and elsewhere, but as its continuation, metonymically related too to the interpretive discourse that combats it; for these reasons trans-ference operates as an event that effects change.

Repetition as the condition of *beginning* and of *change*: this we have been beginning to learn to think for quite some time now, since Derrida's 'Freud and the scene of writing' (1976) and Weber's *The Legend of Freud* (1982). It would imply as well another conception of the role of the ego: sheer enumeration, as the foreclosure precisely of that nostalgic movement of identification situated at a moment of origin or its recollection. Thus the stammering of the names of perfumes in 'Correspondances' might be reinterpreted as like the releasing enumeration in a *list* of the nostalgic exiles listed in the second half of Baudelaire's 'Le cygne'. Lyric might then achieve, in a prosaic mode, 'the forgetting, by inscription, of terror' (de Man 1982a, p. xxi), terror which one would have to see as the import of that positing of the hierarchical structure of signification. But the theory implicit in Baudelaire's rhetoric, as distinct from Freud's or his readers', would have to be the subject of a different paper. I end this one here as my own transference and compulsion to repeat asserts its hold.[3]

Notes

1 The distinction between language as music and language as figure is Nietzsche's in *The Birth of Tragedy*. See Warminski (1985). On the giving of face or figure, see Chase (1986); de Man (1981, pp. 30–4; 1984).

2 For this interpretation of Lacan's reading of Freud's Irma dream I am indebted to Neil Hertz (1985, pp. 230–9) on abjection as a constitutive moment in the structuring of signification.

3 On the rhetoric of Baudelaire, see Chase (1986, Chs 5, 9); de Man (1982a, 1983b, 1984); Frey (1979), and Johnson (1979). On 'enumeration' see de Man (1984, pp. 250, 254).

References

Baudelaire, Charles (1961) *Les Fleurs du mal*, Paris, Garnier.

Chase, Cynthia (1981) 'Paragon, parergon: Baudelaire translates Rousseau', *Diacritics*, 11 (2), 42–51.

—(1983) 'Getting versed: reading Hegel with Baudelaire', *Studies in Romanticism*, 22, 241–66.

—(1986) Chapters 5 and 8, in Chase, Cynthia *Decomposing Figures: Rhetorical Readings in the Romantic Tradition*, Baltimore, Johns Hopkins University Press.

de Man, Paul (1978) 'The epistemology of metaphor', *Critical Inquiry*, 5, 13–30.

—(1979) *Allegories of Reading: Figural Language in Rousseau, Nietzsche, Rilke, and Proust*, New Haven, Conn., Yale University Press.

—(1981) 'Hypogram and inscription: Michael Riffaterre's poetics of reading', *Diacritics*, 11 (4), 17–35.

—(1982a) 'Introduction', in Jauss, Hans Robert, *Toward an Aesthetic of Reception*, Minneapolis, University of Minnesota Press.

—(1982b) 'Sign and symbol in Hegel's *Aesthetics*', *Critical Inquiry*, 8, 761–75.

—(1983a) 'Hegel on the sublime', in Krupnick, Mark (ed.) *Displacement: Derrida and After*, Bloomington, University of Indiana Press.

—(1983b) *Blindness and Insight: Essays in the Rhetoric of Contemporary Criticism*, 2nd edn, Minneapolis, University of Minnesota Press.

—(1984) *The Rhetoric of Romanticism*, New York, Columbia University Press.

Derrida, Jacques (1976a) 'Freud and the scene of writing', in *Writing and Difference*, Chicago, University of Chicago Press.

—(1976b) *Of Grammatology*, Baltimore, Johns Hopkins University Press.

—(1978) *La Verité en peinture*, Paris, Flammarion.

—(1979) *Spurs*, Chicago, University of Chicago Press.

—(1981) 'Economimesis', *Diacritics*, 11 (2), 3–25.

—(1983) *Margins of Philosophy*, Chicago, University of Chicago Press.

Ferguson, Frances (1977) *Wordsworth: Language as Counter-Spirit*, New Haven, Conn., Yale University Press.

Ferenczi, Sandor (1910) *Introjektion und Uebertragung: eine Psychoanalytische Studie*, Leipzig, F. Deuticke.

Freud, Sigmund (1957) [1917] 'Mourning and melancholia', in *The Standard Edition of the Complete Psychological Works*, London, Hogarth Press, 14, pp. 237–60.

—(1958) [1912] 'The dynamics of transference', in *The Standard Edition of the Complete Psychological Works*, London, Hogarth Press, 12, pp. 97–108.

—(1961) [1923] 'The ego and the id', in *The Standard Edition of the Complete Psychological Works*, London, Hogarth Press, 19, pp. 1–66.

—(1965) *The Interpretation of Dreams*, New York, Avon.

Frey, Hans-Jost (1979) 'Über die Erinnerung bei Baudelaire', *Symposium*, 33 (4), 312–30.

Hegel, G. W. F. (1975) *Lectures on Aesthetics*, Oxford, Clarendon Press.

Hertz, Neil (1985) *The End of the Line: Essays on Psychoanalysis and the Sublime*, New York, Columbia University Press.

Johnson, Barbara (1979) *Défigurations du langage poétique: la seconde révolution baudelairienne*, Paris, Flammarion.

Kofman, Sarah (1972) *Nietzsche et la métaphore*, Paris, Payot; Paris, Galilée, 1983.

—(1979) *Nietzsche et la scène philosophique*, Paris, Union générale d'éditions.

Kristeva, Julia (1974) *La révolution du langage poétique: l'avant garde à la fin du dix-neuvième siècle: Lautréamont, Mallarmé*, Paris, Seuil.

—(1980) *Desire in Language: A Semiotic Approach to Literature and Art*, New York, Columbia University Press.

—(1982a) 'L'abjet d'amour', *Tel Quel*, 91, 17–32.

—(1982b) *Powers of Horror: An Essay on Abjection*, New York, Columbia University Press.

Lacan, Jacques (1966) *Écrits*, Paris, Seuil.

—(1977) *Écrits: A Selection*, London, Tavistock.

—(1978) 'Le moi dans la théorie de Freud et dans la technique de la psychanalyse', in *Le Séminaire II*, ed. Miller, Jacques-Alain, Paris, Seuil.

Lacoue-Labarthe, Philippe (1978) 'Mimesis and truth', *Diacritics*, 8 (1), 10–23.

—(1979) *Le Sujet de la philosophie*, Paris, Flammarion.

Laplanche, Jean (1976) *Life and Death in Psychoanalysis*, Baltimore, Johns Hopkins University Press.

Laplanche, Jean and Pontalis, J. B. (1973) *The Language of Psycho-Analysis*, London, Hogarth Press.

Lyotard, Jean-François (1971) *Discours/figure*, Paris, Kilncksieck.
—(1983) 'The dream-work does not think', *Oxford Literary Review*, 6 (1), 3–34.
Metz, Christian (1982) *The Imaginary Signifier*, Bloomington, Indiana University Press.
Nancy, Jean-Luc (1973) *La Remarque spéculative*, Paris, Galilée.
—(1976) *Le Discours de la syncope*, Paris, Flammarion.
Owen, W. J. B. (ed.) (1974) *Wordsworth's Literary Criticism*, London, Routledge & Kegan Paul.
Schneider, Monique (1980) *La Parole et l'inceste: de l'enclos linguistique à la liturgie psychanalytique*, Paris, Aubier Montaigne.
Silverman, Kaja (1983) *The Subject of Semiotics*, New York, Oxford University Press.
Warminski, Andrzej (1985) *Readings in Interpretation: Hegel, Heidegger, Hölderlin*, Minneapolis, University of Minnesota Press.
Weber, Samuel (1982) *The Legend of Freud*, Minneapolis, University of Minnesota Press.

Index